SUBSTANCE,
BODY,
AND SOUL

Edwin Hartman

Substance, Body, and Soul

Aristotelian Investigations

PRINCETON
UNIVERSITY
PRESS

Published by Princeton University Press, Princeton, New Jersey
In the United Kingdom: Princeton University Press,
Guildford, Surrey

Library of Congress Cataloging in Publication Data will
be found on the last printed page of this book

Publication of this book has been aided by
the Paul Mellon Fund of Princeton University Press

Printed in the United States of America
by Princeton University Press,
Princeton, New Jersey

FOR

M. S. H.

Table of Contents

Acknowledgments

A number of people have read parts of earlier versions of
the book and have made good suggestions. First among
them is David Furley, who went patiently through all of
an early, rough, lengthy draft and made a great many useful
criticisms. Others who read parts and made suggestions
were David Balme, Robert Bolton, Abraham Edel, David
Glidden, Barrington Jones, Jaegwon Kim, Edwin McCann,
Michael Slote, and an anonymous reader for the *Philosophical Review*. A number of graduate students were pretty
much forced to read bits of it, and most of them had intelligent remarks to make; I am especially grateful to Simon
Kirby, Deborah Mayo, Audrey McKinney, Carson Strong,
and Duane Williams. I am fortunate to have had two careful
readings and thorough critiques from Alexander Mourelatos,
the first reader for the Press; and Father Joseph Owens, the
second reader, rescued me from a number of mistakes and
infelicities. I profited from many conversations with Amélie
Rorty and Barrington Jones, and from the latter's seminar
on *De Anima* in Princeton in the spring of 1974. James
Cornman read several of my early attempts on the mind-
body problem and talked me out of some mistaken views.

For some years before I started writing this book, I had
the good fortune to learn about ancient philosophy and
related matters from some superb teachers, including David
Furley, Anthony Kenny, Gwilym Owen, Terry Penner,
Richard Rorty, Gregory Vlastos, and Michael Woods.
Penner supervised my dissertation on Aristotle's psychology;
and while I now think that it was largely wrong, except
for a few pages of which echoes may be discerned in some
passages in Chapters Three and Four of the present work,
I am grateful to Penner for not letting it be worse than it

was and for teaching me some lessons whose importance became apparent only later.

Some apologies are in order as well. The relative paucity of references to previous scholarship on Aristotle in some discussions may look like ingratitude; it is not. At many points I have profited from the scholarship of others but have not thought a summary of their arguments to be worth the space it would take; though if an interpretation is particularly novel, or widely accepted, or attractive but wrong, the temptation to take it on in the open has not always been resisted. Great names, such as Ross, Hicks, Jaeger, Brentano, Owens, and Themistius, get less mention than they deserve. The reader may infer that I think I have some reason for rejecting some contrary opinion I do not mention, but my refusal to debate does not betoken anything like certainty that I am consistently right.

Still more I regret having to be so brief in discussing contemporary treatments of the pertinent systematic issues and in setting forth my own views about them. Some of the best philosophers working on materialism, for example, do not lend themselves to easy comparison with Aristotle; so, much as I admire them, I do not discuss them. Happily, they can be read without any introduction from me.

I thank the National Endowment for the Humanities, which gave me a grant to spend the academic year 1973-74 in research and writing. Most of the work was done in the libraries of the British Museum, Princeton University, and the University of Pennsylvania.

A version of part of Chapter Two appeared in the October 1976 issue of *The Philosophical Review*, whose editors I thank for permission to use it here.

The manuscript was prepared for publication by Janet Wolf, Harry Jackendoff, Miriam Mann, Delinda Robbins, and Inez Elkins. I thank them for their diligence and for some editorial assistance as well.

Sanford Thatcher has been a patient, encouraging, and altogether professional editor.

Finally, thanks go to my wife for moral support and unflagging good cheer, and for being an inexhaustible mine of reasonable intuitions on questions philosophical and otherwise.

SUBSTANCE,
BODY,
AND SOUL

Introduction

> It follows that the soul is substance in the sense
> that it is the form of a natural body potentially
> having life. The substance is the actuality.
>
> *De Anima* II 1 412a18-20

ARISTOTLE holds that a person is a substance, a material object complete with form, matter, location, and some accidental properties. Accordingly, his doctrine that the soul is the form of the body is an application of his ontological views to some problems in what is now called the philosophy of mind. His position entails solutions for the problem of personal identity and the mind-body problem; for personal identity is a special case of the spatio-temporal continuity of a material object, and the relation of the soul to the body is a special case of the relation of form to the substance of which it is the form. My intention is to interpret Aristotle's ontological theory and then to show how it applies to the person. Along the way I shall frequently argue that what Aristotle says is true, or at any rate not absurd.

Those who are familiar with certain well-argued contemporary theories about ontological primacy, about spatio-temporal continuity, about personal identity, and about the mind-body problem ought to be struck on reading Aristotle by the similarities between positions he takes or implies and those that some philosophers hold today. Similarities must be investigated as we go along, but it is worth saying at the outset that one cannot adequately account for the similarity between Aristotle's views about persons and those of some philosophers writing now by saying simply that Aristotle precedes Descartes while contemporary philosophers have overcome him; for Plato, whose views on the soul do not resemble current ones, precedes Descartes too.

At the center of Aristotle's ontology stands the individual material substance. Throughout his philosophical career, despite uncertainties and changes of mind on other topics, Aristotle holds to the notion that the world really is populated by material bodies, that a rational science explains (and thus does not ignore or analyze away) those bodies, and that in a rational language one can define them, refer to them, and identify them. In his earliest works he seems just to insist, principally against Plato, that it is particular material objects rather than universals that are the primary sort of being and thus deserve to be called substances. Gradually he comes to see that his position is vulnerable on two flanks. Platonists can argue that material objects are short-lived and therefore unknowable; materialist reductionists can argue that matter, of which all else is predicated, is the logically original inhabitant of the world. Aristotle's reply is that individual objects are indeed knowable, because they are the objects of actual knowledge. Moreover, they are the things of which all else is predicated, because a subject of predication must be identifiable; and mere matter, lacking form, is not identifiable and therefore is not anything in particular.

There is room for doubt about whether Aristotle comes close to proving that material objects are primary—indeed, one may wonder whether he has a wholly coherent notion of what primacy is and on what basis one ought to attribute it. It is clear that he has not considered the ways in which advances in natural science might render his common-sense view of the world obsolete: even an Aristotle cannot be expected to have so much prophetic imagination. But I do not believe that the considerations that have since led some philosophers to regard categories of common sense as parochial and impermanent need to be taken as evidence that the concept of a material object is worthless. The least Aristotle has done is to show that it is always possible and sometimes necessary to carry on coherent discourse about a world of things in time and space. If, as some of his critics have argued, it is not the only way to talk about the world, it is one way—significantly, the way we usually talk about it.

A philosopher who commits himself to a particular kind of entity as primary ought to be prepared to state the criteria of identity for things of that kind. Aristotle does recognize the importance of identity from early on; in fact, he disqualifies matter as substance in part because one cannot generally state the conditions under which piece of matter A is identical with piece of matter B. More importantly, he recognizes the difficulties in finding criteria for identity of material objects. As Heraclitus has noted, material objects change over time; and there is a problem about holding that entities that have some different properties, or are made of different matter, are identical. Less obviously but more importantly for Aristotle's work on the nature of psychological events, there is a problem about identifying items that have different descriptions. Aristotle moves to solve the problems by identifying the material object with its essence. The relation between a thing and its matter, like that between the thing considered under one description and the thing considered under another, is mere accidental identity. But accidental identity is identity enough for practical purposes. Coherence does not require that the river not change at all, or that the road up and the road down be necessarily identical.

Since persons are substances, the criteria for substantial identity and continuity ought to apply to them, and to the events that involve them as well. And so they do: the problem of personal identity is a special case of the problem of spatio-temporal continuity, and the relation between mental and physical events is a special case of accidental identity. Thus the philosophy of mind is a branch of metaphysics. It is not surprising, then, that some familiar weaknesses infect Aristotle's account of the nature of mental entities and states. In the case of ontological primacy, the weakness is that Aristotle does not see how the categories of common sense might be upset, for example, by the progress of natural science. As he discusses mental events, he betrays an insensitivity to the epistemological features thought to be characteristic of mental events—that is, to the sort of privileged access to them that their owners have been thought (at least since Descartes wrote) to have. But once again Aristotle's problems do not render his account useless; for it now appears that the epistemological status of mental entities does not itself present either a barrier to materialism or a reason for supposing that the soul is the sort of thing that might coherently be said to migrate from one body to another. In holding that bodily identity is personal identity and that pains and sense impressions are accidentally identical with certain physical events, Aristotle achieves what many contemporary philosophers would consider respectability and some would consider truth.

The heart of the message is that Aristotle is a materialist in the most important sense of the word. Now it is utterly obvious that in so claiming I am making some presuppositions about what counts as materialism in the important sense. Aristotle himself denies that a mental event is strictly identical with its physical basis, but on just the grounds on which a substance is not identical with its matter (except in the case of events involving *nous*). I regard the sort of identity that does hold between events of these sorts as adequate for materialism, since it almost entirely overlaps with what is now called contingent identity. Insistence on a standard of identity that makes materialism false even for most inanimate objects is surely futile. Insistence that a materialism of Aristotle's sort is compatible with descriptions and explanations characteristic of psychology and common sense is surely correct.

On one point Aristotle is no materialist even by the loosest of contemporary standards. He denies that a characteristically human state of thought is accidentally identical with any bodily state. Aristotle's reasons for this position seem to be connected with the abstract nature of thought, intention, and belief. There are representational states of the body that are necessary conditions for thoughts; but since there can be no abstract representational states, while thoughts are abstract, there are no sufficient bodily conditions of thoughts. Although there are problems with Aristotle's views about both the nature and the genesis of thoughts, some of those views have had close counterparts in recent discussions. My own opinion is that Aristotle's doctrine of *nous* is a weak spot in an otherwise plausible and well-argued theory of mental entities and events. Significantly, he himself expresses some doubt about whether *nous* really requires modification of his materialism.

At some points I shall mention the views of such contemporary philosophers as P. F. Strawson, David Wiggins, and Thomas Nagel. The point of view of contemporary analytical philosophy is not the only one from which to see Aristotle, but I can think of two reasons why it may be one of the best. First, no philosopher before Kant has had on analytical philosophy an influence, in both style and substance, to match Aristotle's, in part through the prominence of his works in at least two curricula at Oxford, where all the philosophers mentioned above have worked—as have Anscombe, Geach, Parfit, Sellars, Owen, Penner, and many others to whom I am in debt for their views about philosophy as well as their views about Aristotle. Second, my inclination in favor of certain techniques and conclusions of analytical philosophy—though of an American more than an English sort—takes the form of a belief that the techniques are valuable and the conclusions true; and it is appropriate to measure Aristotle against what one thinks is true.

The reader will note, and may resent, that on a number of points I accuse Aristotle of confusion, incoherence, or inconsistency. Now it is perfectly true that this sort of attitude can be a cheap substitute for an effort to work out Aristotle's true position on some matter or other, but it is an appropriate attitude if Aristotle really is confused, as he sometimes is. It ought to be, though it is not, needless to add that I am aware that Aristotle was a very great philosopher indeed: I pay him the courtesy of taking his arguments so seriously that when I come upon what looks like a bad one I protest rather than condescend by saying something like "What Aristotle obviously *means* to say. . . ." This attitude presupposes that Aristotle speaks roughly the same sort of conceptual language we do, though he spoke over two millennia ago. The evidence for this presupposition will, I hope, emerge from this study, part of whose purpose is precisely to show that much of what Aristotle said can today be judged true, or at least promising. Surely a part of the explanation of this astonishing fact is that Aristotle was just that good a philosopher.

I have probably not avoided all anachronism, but I hope that what remains will not cause confusion. On two typical points it might be well to deliver a warning now. First, I shall often talk about the distinction between the mental and the physical, and apply it to Aristotle. The reader must be aware that it is not clear at the outset whether Aristotle has anything like a contemporary philosopher's concept of the mental, and it is certain that his notion of the soul does not correspond perfectly to ours of the mind. Moreover, our concept of physical event does not precisely fit anything in Aristotle, whose natural science is in so many respects different from modern physics. Second, I shall occasionally attribute to Aristotle the view that some proposition or other is a necessary truth; but the analytic-synthetic distinction is not Aristotelian. Definition, however, is; and there are some propositions that follow from definitions and some that contradict one or more definitions. There is not much one can do about difficulties of this sort, beyond keeping them in mind in discussions of the affected problems. Where I suggest that some of Aristotle's distinctions are less clear or less useful than ours, the reader will have good evidence that I think we have made some progress since Aristotle, thanks in part to Aristotle.

One might still object that whether Aristotle and we can talk to each other has nothing to do with whether he is a good philosopher, that the differences between our views and his are due not to the progress we have made since his time but instead to his having a profoundly different conceptual scheme, which it is a waste of time for us to try to criticize. Proponents of that view might do well to reflect on the difficulties that attend facile talk about alternative conceptual schemes that we cannot grasp. In some cases in which there is doubt about interpretation I shall rule out certain possibilities in part because they are implausibly odd, but it does not follow that I shall be ruling out in advance the possibility that Aristotle could have any odd views. There is a difficulty in principle in distinguishing between a genuinely inept view and a view that cannot be understood because one does not know the meanings of the words that are supposed to convey it.

Chapter One

THE PRIMACY OF SUBSTANCE

FROM the beginning Aristotle views the individual material object as the primary sort of being. He holds to the primacy of the individual throughout his career, despite difficulties he discovers as he goes along, and despite modifications and clarifications these difficulties require him to make in his notion of substance. In the *Categories* the individual is considered primary because the universal depends on it for its being, and the individual property for its identity, if not its being (Section I below). According to both the *Categories* and the *Posterior Analytics*, the world is reflected in the language in which we talk about it; so the syntactical relation between "log" and "white" in the sentence "The log is white" faithfully represents the predication of whiteness of a log in reality—"The white is a log" is a sign of bad ontology as well as bad grammar.

Yet there are other candidates for the title of primary substance, and each has a claim that must be taken seriously. One is the universal, which has the advantage over the material object of being knowable rather than merely sensible. But Aristotle argues that actual as opposed to potential knowledge is of the individual material object (Section II). Another candidate is matter, which seems to be that of which everything else, including what Aristotle has been calling substance, is predicated. Aristotle's strategy is to show that a substance must be, as matter is not, a unified and identifiable entity; only then can it serve as a reliable subject of predication. By the time he writes the middle books of the *Metaphysics*, which constitute his most mature work on substance, Aristotle has considerably sharpened his concept of priority in support of his argument that substance is prior to other things, and he has shown how form or essence makes what would otherwise be mere matter a substance by providing it with what any entity with a claim to priority must have: criteria for individuation and continuity (Section III). It remains to be seen how and why Aristotle finally identifies substance and essence, without abandoning his view that the individual material object is the primary sort of being.

Establishing the priority of the material object over space and time involves still further wiry argument, which Aristotle provides in the *Physics* as well as the *Metaphysics*. In so arguing, Aristotle often sounds much like one of our distinguished contemporaries (Section IV); but it is important not to lose sight of the fundamental ways in which his views differ from those of his modern successors (Section V).

The order in which Aristotle wrote the works that have come down to us is a vexed question indeed, and I have nothing substantive to add to the discussion of it.[1] Instead, I shall assume a certain order and hope the assumption does no violence to the exposition. Of the works I shall be discussing, I think *De Sophisticis Elenchis*, *Peri Ideōn*, the *Categories*, and the *Topics* precede the *Posterior Analytics*, which precedes all or most of the *Metaphysics*. The *Metaphysics* was clearly not written within a short period of time, nor in the order in which we have it. For present purposes it will suffice to assume that the part of Book M that I shall be discussing—namely, the second half of chapter 9 and all of chapter 10—is earlier than Books Z, H, and Θ, which I consider Aristotle's last word on substance, and certainly his best. Book Δ also precedes Z, H, and Θ. I think that Book Iota was written at about the same time as the "central books" of the *Metaphysics*, and that the pertinent

---

[1] There is an excellent summary of the most important contributions to the topic in the first two chapters of Joseph Owens's *Doctrine of Being*. The view I have found most persuasive is that of G.E.L. Owen in "The Platonism of Aristotle" and "Logic and Metaphysics."

passages of the *Physics* and *De Anima* were written after Aristotle last changed his mind on any important topic; but on this point, which is not crucial, I am far from certain. If this chronology be wrong, then I shall have succeeded only in arranging statements of Aristotle's position in order of increasing adequacy and sophistication. For his basic position does not change, though some details do; the enterprise is always a defense of the material object as the primary sort of being. It is conceivable that Aristotle had more sophisticated arguments for, and elaborations of, his position in early years than later; but it matters little to my argument, and it is in any case not likely.

I. ARISTOTLE'S EARLY NOMINALISM

From his earliest works onwards, Aristotle undertakes to establish that material objects, rather than Platonic Ideas or anything resembling them, are the primary substances. That much is clear even before it is clear what is involved in being a primary substance. As he progresses, Aristotle finds new arguments for the priority of material objects over other sorts of entity, and the new arguments sometimes incorporate new criteria for substancehood and therefore (since to be a substance is to be prior virtually by definition) for priority. These new criteria occasionally force substantive changes that look like partial concessions to the claims of Aristotle's philosophical opponents; and so, sometimes, they are. But the concessions are gambits; their result is a more defensible conception of the middle-sized material object as substance.

The most extreme form of nominalism would be the position that Ideas and even ordinary universals have no status at all, that there are no such things; and Aristotle is capable at least of taking that position seriously. In *De Sophisticis Elenchis*, an early and sometimes not very sophisticated tract, Aristotle states (in chapter 22) that there are no particulars over and above ordinary substances, not even individuals whose status is so attenuated that they should be called "such" rather than "this."[2] It is not clear how much Aristotle means to exclude by this statement, but he does continue to believe that a predicate need not signify anything other than the subject in order to be meaningful, though in some cases it may. At any rate, he is not always a nominalist of the most extreme possible sort. In *Peri Ideōn* he is willing to commit himself to universals so long as it is quite clear that they are not Platonic Ideas. For example, he admits what he calls *koina* (common entities), which seem to be extra-linguistic items (79. 19), and he allows that in predicating something of a number of things one is predicating some one entity of them (81. 12ff.—the point is incidental to what he wants to say in the passage, but there can be little doubt he believes it).

What is uppermost in Aristotle's mind is the primacy of the individual material object, rather than the utter non-existence of all other possible beings. What is not at first so pressing is the need to say precisely what counts as an individual material object. In the *Categories*, then, as he presents a plausible if not always closely argued account of the priority of individual substances, Aristotle relies on simple examples and the reader's intuition to communicate what an individual material object is, and what makes it individual.

Aristotle states in the *Categories* that individual substances are prior to their properties, both those which are "said of" those substances (roughly, species and genera) and those which are "in" them (roughly, what will later be called accidental properties). As Aristotle says in the *Categories*[3] (14a6-10): ". . . if all were healthy, sickness would not be. Similarly, if all things were white, whiteness would be, but

[2] *Soph. El.* 22 178b36ff. In truth, the passage is a difficult one, for Aristotle also says that the real problem comes of making the predicated item a "this."

[3] The last six chapters of the *Categories* are probably a later addition, sometimes called the *Postpraedicamenta*. See J. L. Ackrill, *Categories*, pp. 68f.

blackness would not." This view would not be acceptable to a Platonist, who would hold that there would be whiteness even if no object in space and time were white. Here, then, is a point of clear disagreement between Aristotle and the Platonist over priority. There can be sickness only if there are sick people, whiteness only if there are white things. Aristotle is concerned to make individual substances prior to universals, both to the universals that are in things and to those that are said of them.

Individual substances are prior to their properties, and their individual properties are prior to the corresponding universals. "A certain white" and "a certain grammatical"[4] are unit-properties; so, when Aristotle says of entities of this sort that they cannot exist apart from what they are in, he is in effect excluding the possibility that they are universals, like a particular shade of white. A shade of white might appear on more than one object; for example, two people might have the same complexion. But Aristotle is talking about properties that are individuated by their owners, so that you and I necessarily cannot have numerically the same complexion. This is a controversial interpretation, for there are some who deny that Aristotle countenances spatio-temporally locatable individuals in categories other than substance.[5] I shall not review the whole argument, but two points deserve special mention. First, it is true that there is very little to recommend unit-properties from a philosophical point of view.[6] But the fact is that Aristotle is elsewhere clearly committed to them;[7] so, if the position is a mistake, it is one that Aristotle is demonstrably capable of making. Second, it is difficult to see what sense could be made of

[4] The Greek terms are *to ti leukon* and *hē tis grammatikē*.

[5] Chief among them is G.E.L. Owen in "Inherence." For the view that they are unit-properties, see J. L. Ackrill, *Aristotle's Categories*, pp. 74-76; R. E. Allen, "Individual Properties"; Gareth B. Matthews and S. Marc Cohen, "The One and the Many"; Barrington Jones, "Individuals in Aristotle's Categories."

[6] Owen, "Inherence," pp. 101f.   [7] E.g., in *Physics* V 4.

unit-properties in the category of time, for example, as opposed to quality, which most commentators seem to take as typical of the secondary categories.[8] Here too the difficulty is probably in Aristotle's position rather than in the interpretation. One can understand intuitively how a particular color could be dependent on a substance by virtue of being predicated of it as a subject, but it is difficult to see how that picture applies to the relation between time or location and substance. Nothing Aristotle says in the *Categories* persuades the reader that substance is prior to place and time, very probably because those are not the secondary categories Aristotle has in mind when he gives his introductory exposition. In due course this weakness must be remedied (see Section IV below).

Even in the case of qualities there is a problem about priority. From the fact that there can be no whiteness unless there are white substances it does not follow that substances are prior to colors. For it is equally true that there can be no white substances if there is no whiteness and, generally, that there can be no substances if there are no properties. What accounts for our intuitive acceptance of the priority of substance over quality? I think Aristotle's point is this: a particular white—say, Socrates's complexion —endures just as long as Socrates is white, and no longer. There are no imaginable circumstances under which it could qualify any other substance, for then it would no longer be Socrates's white; it depends for its identity on Socrates. Socrates, on the other hand, can survive the disappearance of any of his qualities (on the understanding that it will normally be replaced by another in the same category).[9]

[8] Owen, "Inherence," p. 102.

[9] I must admit that Aristotle is not always careful on this point. Consider this passage from *On Generation and Corruption*: "But if in such cases any property (one of a pair of contraries) persists in the thing that has come to be just as it was in the thing that has passed away—if, for example, when air changes into water, both are transparent or cold—the second thing, into which the first changes,

So the substance is durable relative to what is predicated of it. If this interpretation is correct, then it provides support for the notion that it is spatio-temporally locatable unit-properties rather than universals that are the primary items in the secondary categories. That the interpretation is in fact correct is strongly suggested by the most famous passage in the *Categories*:

> What seems most characteristic of substance is that, while being one and the same, it can receive contraries. One could not produce anything else numerically one which could receive contraries. For instance, a color that is numerically one and the same will not be black and white, nor will numerically one and the same action be bad and good; and so it is in the case of everything else that is not substance. A substance, on the other hand, numerically one and the same, can receive contraries. For instance, a man, one and the same, becomes now pale, now dark, and hot and cold, and bad and good. In the other cases, nothing of this sort happens. (5 4a10-22)

I am not sure the matter is entirely clear in Aristotle's mind, for he does return to this notion of priority as simple existence-dependency often again. Thus in the definition of the term in Book Δ priority in substance and nature belongs to what can exist without something which cannot, in turn, exist without it. The passage echoes *Cat.* 12 14b5ff. Sometimes, as at *Met.* M 2 1077b1ff., he speaks of separability instead of priority: what is prior is what can exist

---

must not be a property of this persistent identical thing." (319b15-25) That Aristotle is willing to say that there is an item persisting through such a change indicates that he is ignoring the doctrine that such a property cannot remain the same through this process because its identity depends on that of the substance it qualifies. I can only say that Aristotle was being careless. (The passage is found and the point made by Nicholas White in "Origins of Aristotle's Essentialism," p. 73.)

separate from that to which it is prior, and not vice versa.[10]

Primary substances are prior to secondary substances, universals in the category of substance, in a way different from that in which they are prior to individuals in the secondary categories. Aristotle has said in *Soph. El.* 22 that the word "man" in "Callias is a man" does not refer to any sort of entity over and above particulars; perhaps the point is that it refers to nothing but Callias. That it does refer only to Callias seems more probable when one sees how Aristotle reduces secondary substances to primary ones in the *Categories*. He claims (*Cat.* 5 3a33-b9) that man can be predicated of Socrates, and animal of both man and Socrates, synonymously;[11] differentiae too are synonymously predicated of both species and individuals. So one can say without fear of ambiguity that Socrates is man, man is animal, and (therefore) Socrates is animal.[12] What one cannot say is that Socrates is a man, man a species, and so Socrates a species. In the absence of explicit quantifiers, "man is animal" must be read as "all men are animals." It follows that when one talks of species and genera, in a first-order way, what one says can be translated into talk of their members, according to Aristotle. Therefore nothing he says in the *Categories* commits him to species or genera as distinct from their members. By parity of reasoning, the universal white is exhausted by the various particular whites, in whose absence it does not exist.

Aristotle leaves the reader with the strong impression that there is more to be said about the relation between species and primary substance than he is taking the trouble to say

[10] Terry Penner first convinced me of the importance of this passage.

[11] *Ibid.*

[12] Aristotle gives one reason to wonder how clear all this is in his mind. Cf. *Cat.* 5 2b34-3a6 for a statement that man is literate if one man is. Does it follow that to be a man is to be literate? Cf. Russell Dancy, "On Some of Aristotle's First Thoughts About Substances," p. 357, n. 30.

explicitly in the *Categories*. In particular, there is a suggestion that species has something to do with the individuation
of substance. He says at *Cat.* 5 2b29ff. that to state the
species or genus of something is to reveal the primary substance, that this is particularly true of the species, and that
it is not true of any sort of predicate but those two. In
other words, the species says most clearly of a man what he
is. But having said this, Aristotle softens it by saying
(3b10ff.) that secondary substance terms signify a "such"
rather than a "this" because they apply to a plurality of
things. Still, they signify a "such" concerning substance;
that is, they indicate what sort of substance a substance is.
Aristotle is working towards this position: the species is
determinate of substance in the sense that a substance can
remain self-identical while undergoing changes as long as it
remains in the same species. Just as long as Socrates remains
a man, he continues to exist, whatever other changes may
come upon him. The view is not well articulated in the
Categories, but it is spelled out clearly in the *Metaphysics*.
When it does get spelled out, in *Met.* Z and H, some altera-
tions are called for. At *Cat.* 5 3a29ff. Aristotle has implied
that the parts of a substance are themselves substances, at
least in some cases; but in *Met.* Z 16 he must deny that
implication, as parts are not themselves members of species
and so must borrow what substantiality they have from the
things of which they are parts.

In the *Categories* certain dubious cases of substance are
tolerated because Aristotle is operating with a sort of implicit
grammatical criterion of substance: it is what is denominated
by the subject-term in an ordinary Greek sentence. Non-
substances attach to substances rather in the way in which
predicates attach to subjects, for predicates denominate
those non-substances that have dependent existence. Substances are those things of which other entities are predicated. That is the predicability test; and in time it is to be
subjected to criticisms that will force elaborations on it.
The first criticism appears in the *Posterior Analytics*, where

Aristotle imagines someone saying to him (and quite rightly too), "We can say, 'This white was once a branch; then it was a log; then it was a chair; now it is kindling.' Such a locution passes your test of durability and predicability. Are whites then substances?" Aristotle answers in *An. Post.* I 22 83a4ff.: "When I say 'The white is a log,' I mean that something which happens to be white is a log—not that which is the substratum in which log inheres, for it was not *qua* white or *qua* a species of white that the white came to be a log; so the white is only accidentally a log." The further test effectively introduced here is reminiscent of *Cat.* 5 4a10 (cf. 2a11): if one can say "X came to be a Y," then "X" is a substance-term. The test is of dubious value, for it will not be effective against anyone perverse enough to make the challenge in the first place and thereby to question the linguistic intuitions Aristotle invokes. The use of coming-to-be as a test for substance does, however, suggest that nature countenances certain patterns of genesis and growth, namely those that happen according to species, and not others. This too will be developed further in the *Metaphysics*.

In this same chapter of the *Posterior Analytics* Aristotle says a predicate signifying substance signifies that the subject is identical to the predicate or to a species of it. The statement is reminiscent of the *Categories* doctrine that in stating the species of something one reveals the primary substance. Moreover, to those who are aware that Aristotle later says that a thing is identical to its essence or form, this passage signals the beginning of a recognition that to say what the species of something is is to say *what it is* rather than to say (as lines 31f. state is the case for accidental predication) something other than what it is. The suggestion that a thing is somehow directly signified by its species-name in the predicate position is not defended, but the intuition is a sensible one worth further elaboration, which Aristotle provides in due course.

To this point, then, Aristotle's ontological theory is fairly straightforward and untroubled. There are primarily material objects. They are prior to their properties in the sense that the properties cannot persist without the substances they inhere in, while the substances can outlast the properties, as our ordinary language would seem to indicate. All this is what is involved in saying that items that are not material objects exist[13] by virtue of being predicated of material objects, which are substances. Aristotle has dealt rather quickly with an objection to his implicit grammatical test for predicability, and he has suggested that species has a special role to play in the delineation of substance. Beyond that he has neither stated nor defended his views carefully. As far as one can tell, he has not seriously considered the possibility that his criteria of substancehood are deficient, nor the possibility that items other than material objects are better candidates for substancehood even under the criteria he is using, nor that it might be difficult to show that substance is prior to place and time. But the time comes when Aristotle has to face all three of these problems. As to the first: he must deal with the objection that substance as so far defined is not, as it surely ought to be, knowable. As to the second: Aristotle must consider the possibility that it is matter which underlies change and can exist independent even of any material object, and which therefore deserves to be called substance. In the best and most important parts of the *Metaphysics* Aristotle faces these problems and some related ones and makes progress towards solving them. Finally, as to the third problem: in the *Physics* he outlines the way in which substance is prior not only to quality but also to place and time. The next three sections deal with Aristotle's successive assaults on the problem raised by the requirement of knowability, the problem of the predicability of matter, and the problem of the relation of substance to space and time. Though these assaults are not uniformly

13 Whether or not Aristotle fully understands the existential use of the verb "to be," he sometimes makes what are clearly statements about existence.

successful, the result as a whole is a sophisticated conception of substance and its priority over other things that there are.

II. KNOWABILITY

If Aristotle's conception of substance is to meet any but the most parochial criteria for substancehood, he must take account of the Platonic but still plausible notion that what is real is knowable. In the *Posterior Analytics* the topic of knowledge has not been far from his mind. While holding out in that work for an anti-Platonic view of substance, he has been putting forward some views about the conditions of knowledge that show the imprint of the hand of Plato, and in particular of the doctrines of the *Meno*. This is not the place to explore Aristotle's suggestive but not entirely convincing view of concept formation (see further Chapter Six); it is enough to note that he regards each instance of the proper sort of knowledge as the conclusion of a sound deductive syllogism. Aristotle does not say at first, as one might wish him to say, that even true belief presupposes a facility with concepts and therefore universals; but he does not shrink from the conclusion that knowledge of a particular (or, as he sometimes seems to mean, of a matter of fact concerning a particular) involves universals.

Yet the actual criteria of substance put forward in the *Categories* and in the *Posterior Analytics* have included nothing about knowledge, and from that point of view the individual substance is vulnerable. Critics of Aristotle are fond of saying that he is faced with this inconsistent triad: (1) the individual primarily is; (2) what primarily is is knowable; (3) the universal and not the individual is knowable.[14] Aristotle sets himself this problem in *Met.* M 10; in trying to solve it, he makes some elaborations and improvements in the theory of substance.

[14] For a review of the criticism and the evidence, see Walter Leszl, "Knowledge of the Universal."

At the beginning of the discussion Aristotle explicitly assumes that both he and Plato want substances to be separable. There are grounds for taking Plato to believe that Ideas, his substances, are particulars; but it is clear by now that that is not all Aristotle means by separability. Plato's Ideas do not depend for their existence on their participants, whereas Aristotle's universals do depend on their instances; so there is a genuine disagreement between them about what is prior. But Aristotle has noticed that if one pushes for this sort of separability, there will be a premium on particularity; for if universals are constructs out of individuals, one might suppose that individuals are constructs (in a slightly different sense) out of their elements. What, then, is so attractive about making middle-sized objects, temporary combinations of material bits, the primary existents? Here Aristotle is aware of the attractions of a sort of atomistic reductionism. The view he presents takes each bit of something—he does not say how small the bits have to be, but perhaps they will be indivisible—as unique: it is not considered to be of a certain sort. There is one kind of thing per thing. The analogy Aristotle uses is the syllables and their parts (*syllabē* meaning either syllable or composite, *stoicheion* either element or letter); so the position he is criticizing is one whose logical conclusion is that a syllable (the token, but considered just in itself) is the basic unit of discourse. The reasoning leading to this position, which Aristotle chooses for its implausibility, can be extended to show that it is the letter-tokens—in fact, the individual spoken or written inscriptions—which are really the substances. If syllable-types are only convenient fictions, then by parity of reasoning syllable-types are only convenient fictions, too. There may be some confusion here between the type-token distinction and the universal-particular one, but the analogy has force: it is absurd to insist in the context of a language that nothing counts but letter-tokens, and Aristotle finds some of the same absurdity in the view that nothing in the world counts but individual entities, whether substances or bits of matter.

Aristotle quickly dismisses the claims of the universal to substancehood (and in so doing gratuitously adds to his difficulties by claiming, what he will deny in *Met.* Z 13, that the element or principle is prior to that of which it is an element or principle); his discussions of Platonism are supposed to suffice on this point.

Now the analogy Aristotle has used to state the problem helps solve it. We can carry on discourse without supposing that there are Ideas of letters and syllables over and above their possibly many instances. Potential knowledge is of the universal, actual knowledge of the particular. Accordingly, the reader or grammarian is able to understand a particular letter or syllable (that is, an inscription) because he has universal knowledge, which is actualized not by his cognition of some universal object but by each instance of his recognizing a particular letter or syllable—or, for that matter, a particular instance of a color or any other sort of thing—as being of a certain sort. This account would not satisfy a Platonist; in fact, one might infer from what Aristotle himself says in the *Posterior Analytics* that the only possible form of knowledge, given universal premises as a starting point, is the universal conclusion. But Aristotle tells us here that all universal knowledge can be analyzed into a plurality of instances of knowledge of like particulars.

In all this discussion it appears that one clear case of knowing, for Aristotle as for Plato, is that of knowing some item, which for Aristotle is a matter of knowing what the item is—that is, knowing its essence. As Aristotle says in the first chapter of *Met.* Z, we know a thing most fully when we know what it is; and he means this, I think, as a point in favor of identifying substance with essence. Some confusion might be avoided if Aristotle always thought of propositions rather than items as knowable, though the problems I shall be raising would still not be solved.

Thus far Aristotle's views about knowledge owe something to the nominalism of his earliest anti-Platonic works, cited in Section I above. Just as the meanings of predicates said of subjects depend not on their designating entities that are universals or suches, but instead on their designating particulars in a certain way, so here in actual knowledge one knows particulars in a certain way. Still, Aristotle is now aware that the tendency away from Platonism can take him only so far: universals do play a part in knowledge and cannot be reduced entirely away, even though they are posterior to their instances. There is that much right about the Platonic account, and there is accordingly that much revision to be done on the facile ontology of the *Categories*.

But Aristotle's position still raises some difficulties, not least about his consistency.[15] To begin with, it is standard Aristotelian doctrine that particulars are supposed to be sensible but not knowable.[16] What, then, precisely is the cognitive relationship between the person and the contemplated particular when the person is familiar with some of the universals of which the particular is an instance? He senses it—and what else? The answer:

> That all knowledge is universal, so that the principles of things are necessarily universal and not separate substances, creates more problems than any other statement thus far made; but it is true in one way and false in another. For knowledge, like the term "to know," has two meanings: potential and actual. The potency is like matter, universal and indefinite, and it deals with what is universal and indefinite. The actuality, on the other hand, being definite, deals with what is definite; being itself a "this," it deals with a "this." But sight sees universal color accidentally, because this particular color which it sees is a color; and this particular A which the grammarian examines is an A. For if the principles are necessarily uni-

[15] See particularly Harold Cherniss, *Aristotle's Criticism of Plato*, pp. 340ff.

[16] Examples can be cited from all over the corpus. See, e.g., *An. Post.* I 18 81b5-7, 31 87b28ff., *Met.* Z 15 1039b27ff., *De An.* II 5 417b23f., *Rhet.* I 2 1356b31f.

versal, then necessarily what derives from them will be universal, as with demonstrations; but if so, then there will be nothing separable, no substance. But it is clear that knowledge is universal in one sense, but not in another. (*Met.* M 10 1087a10-25)

Now it is all very well to say that one has potential knowledge concerning each triangle in that one knows the universal truth that every triangle has interior angles equal to two right angles. But it does not follow from my knowing that every triangle has interior angles equal to two right angles that I know that this triangle does, for I may not know that there is a triangle here. Nor does my having the concept of blue or having philological expertise about the letter A imply anything about what I know about this blue thing or this A, though it is a necessary condition of some of my knowledge about it.

It is reasonable to suppose that an example of knowledge is a proposition about a particular inferred from known propositions of which some are universal, rather like the application of a general rule to a particular situation. One must also recognize the particular as being of a certain sort; if it is entirely unique, nothing can be known about it. So Aristotle says in *An. Post.* I 1 71a20ff. But then the problem is this: how is one to know precisely that this very thing is a triangle, or blue, or an A? For however true it may be that knowledge of a particular is the actualization of a potential for knowing particulars, or the explication of universal knowledge, the fact remains that such knowledge is worthy of the name only if it is possible to know propositions about the particulars to be true. And it is primarily because particulars are transitory and indefinable that Aristotle says we cannot have knowledge of them.

Understanding Aristotle's position thoroughly requires working out what he says about two topics I cannot fully discuss here. The first is the relation between a substance and its essence. I shall argue in Chapter Two that Aristotle identifies substance and essence as a response to problems about the transitoriness and indefinability of particulars: if one understands that a substance is a persistent form that is at any time associated with some matter or other but not identical with it and not a compound of some form and some particular parcel of matter, then one can see how and to what extent a substance abides through change and so can be known. The second topic is the nature of perception and in particular what one knows or believes in virtue of perceiving something. When Aristotle says at *An. Post.* I 31 87b28ff. that perception is of the such and not just of the this, he is showing us the tip of a deep iceberg. What does knowledge of a universal confer on our cognitive experience of a particular, and vice versa? Does perception of a particular bring belief with it, or does that too depend on having universals? A related question: do universals function for Aristotle as we think concepts do, or as propositions? These questions come to the fore in Chapters Five and Six, but the promissory note will not be fully redeemed in clear answers to them all, as I do not think clear answers can be found in Aristotle.

Aristotle's confusions on matters of this sort provide good reason not to insist that he be taken consistently to hold any particular view about what sort of thing one knows. His willingness to admit candidly, as at the outset of *Met.* M 10, that a particular view of his has its difficulties gives the exegete grounds for admiration, but not for confidence. My discussions of substance and essence and of perception and universals will reflect this same view of the totality of Aristotle's writings and of their value: first, Aristotle is not perfectly consistent on all points throughout his works but instead changes his mind as he thinks he is making progress; second, he takes certain positions for dialectical or experimental purposes and for that reason alone is not to be held to them in the face of evidence that he elsewhere clearly believes otherwise; third, some of the best or most important views found in Aristotle are those that Aristotle is working towards but is not able to state very clearly. I grant that there is something odd about imputing such views to Aristotle and that one should not do so without indicating how much one is adding to what the text says.

Another promissory note: Aristotle's views about knowledge bear directly on what Aristotle says about the relation between mind and body—not surprisingly, since in that case epistemological questions are crucial to the ontological ones. So I shall hold off discussion of Aristotle's epistemology for the time being. What I intend to show in Chapters Five and Six is that there is evidence that Aristotle regards the particular as epistemologically as well as ontologically basic in a significant way.

Aristotle's interest in knowability as a criterion of substance stems, as he sees Plato's interest in it does, from consideration of problems about knowing anything about material objects in the world. In *Met.* M 9 and elsewhere Aristotle notes that Heraclitus convinced Plato that the sensible world was in flux and therefore would not stay to be known or correctly denominated. Ideas, on the other hand, do. That the problem of flux is on Aristotle's mind from the beginning is evident from the importance he places on persistence through change as a criterion of substance: *Cat.* 5 4a10 shows the importance to him of being able to say that something keeps existing for a period of time despite certain changes in it during that time—changes of a sort Heraclitus can be interpreted as having used as evidence that nothing remains self-identical through time. In response, Aristotle lowers the standards of self-identity to a reasonable level, then sets about specifying them at that level as best he can.

Aristotle wants to show that durability and knowability are complementary criteria for substancehood and that both of these criteria permit individual material objects to be primary substances. By themselves they might seem to favor universals, but universals are ruled out as substances because they are (depending on whether there are unit-properties in the system) either predicates of substances or reducible to predicates; in either case they are posterior to material objects. Up to this point, then, there has been no good reason to object to the view that what is most durable is also that of which everything else is predicated, and that that is the material object.

a. Identifiability and the Posteriority of Matter

But now there is another problem, in the form of another strong candidate for substance, one indeed which seems to meet the criteria so far used. The discussion of knowability touched on this candidate but did not take it seriously. The candidate is matter, and it promises superior performance with respect to both durability and predicability, which for it too are coextensive.

Though predicability may be a controversial test for substance—it is not one that Plato would use—durability is one on which philosophers of various persuasions can agree. Not only Aristotle, not only Plato, but also many of the Presocratic philosophers can be read as having regarded something or some sort of thing as real in proportion as it is long-lived. Aristotle seems to have believed that some Presocratics took that which underlies change—that is, that which does not change qualitatively but only constitutes those things which do, or at least seem to by virtue of the changing arrangements of the components—as the primary reality. If so, then atoms and the void, or water, or what Anaxagoras calls *homoiomeriai* (microcosmic bodies) alone would be real, and middle-sized objects only convenient fictions. Persistence as a criterion of ontological privilege may cause one to believe that there is some incompatibility between the view that all is in flux and the view that what is most real is what abides, or that it follows that there is nothing that is real; but if, as even Heraclitus seems to Aristotle to believe, there is some sort of stuff that abides through all change, then it has a claim to be what is really real.

Moreover, matter, unlike the Platonic Idea, seems to fare well on the predicability test too, since it appears to be what everything else, including Aristotle's substance, can be predicate to. "That stuff is a man" looks like a perfectly respectable statement. So does "My arm is strong." For if a man is a substance, then why not an arm? In the *Categories* an arm is indeed a substance. But then why not a piece of bone, or an atom? So Aristotle puts himself in the way of a temptation towards atomistic reductionism. At the same time, he cannot but sense that there is something wrong with reducing everything to bits. Meditation upon knowability has convinced him of something he showed signs even in the *Categories* of having noticed: there is a role for universals in the account of substances, though not exactly the role Plato had in mind for the Ideas.

One gets some sense of Aristotle's hesitation between these two directions from reading the entry under substance in *Met.* Δ, his philosophical lexicon, the eighth chapter. Simple bodies and things composed of them are called substances because things are predicated of them but they are not predicated of anything. But then what makes a substance what it is, as essence does, is also called substance, as we suggest when we speak of the substance of something and mean its essence (cf. *Met.* Z 7 1032b1-2; recall that the importance of species was hinted at in the *Categories*). Aristotle concludes that substance has two main senses: (1) the ultimate substratum and (2) that which is a "this" and separable, meaning the form. If this were the last Aristotle had to say about substance, the reader might justly conclude that Aristotle could not decide whether matter or form is the best candidate because the criteria for substance just conflict. (And the reader might wonder why form is a "this" and separable.) Matter is the subject of predication; form is what makes a substance what it is, and is therefore at least a necessary condition of the substance.

Aristotle faces two overlapping tasks in the last of his works on metaphysics. He must show why the material object, rather than matter, ought to be considered substance; and he must show how it is form that makes something a material object. On the whole, in *Met.* Z and H he does not argue as though against an opponent who refuses to admit that Aristotle's kind of substance deserves to be called substance, but concentrates instead on the second task; and for that reason some of his readers have found those two books unsatisfying.[17] But Aristotle does score some points against his skeptical opponents, both those who would make matter substance and those who are Platonists. So, for example, in the course of explaining how it is form that makes a material object what it is, Aristotle will argue that even on the predicability test matter does not do so well as expected. Still, one cannot claim that Aristotle gives a full hearing to every candidate for the role of substance. He is predisposed to favor the material object, and the greater part of his effort is devoted to showing how it is possible and even convenient to take material objects as substances, and less to eliminating every other possible candidate. It is his job to save common sense, refined as necessary but not undermined by the knowledge of the expert.[18] To demonstrate that a world largely in accord with common sense is populated by substances that are reasonably permanent, that are not reducible to other entities, that can be known, referred to, and defined is to make it unnecessary to resort to esoteric entities in explanation of the phenomena.

At the beginning of *Met.* Z, in which Aristotle explicitly considers what most deserves to be called substance, it is stipulated that substance is a "what it is" and a "this." The point, which Aristotle puts in a mode halfway between formal and material, is that one can call a substance "this"—

[17] Especially Harold Cherniss in *Aristotle's Criticism of Plato.*

[18] See, e.g., *Nic. Eth.* VII 1 1145b2ff. and *Met.* Γ 5 1010b1ff. Robert Bolton's review of Henry Veatch's *Aristotle* is an economical summary of Aristotle's attitude towards common sense and expertise.

that is, successfully refer to it—and say what it is. The formulation suggests that Aristotle is interested in both the individual substance as a whole and that of the individual which, as its essence, makes it what it is. The latter is by definition the form or essence.[19] For the moment, the important points are that a substance must be some sort of thing—there must be some privileged answer to the question, "What is it?"—and that it must be something that can be referred to. The structure of the sentence suggests a close connection, not a contrast, between these two marks of substance.

Aristotle's emphasis on the predicability criterion makes matter a prime candidate for substance. In Z 3 Aristotle accordingly considers matter, but decides it cannot be substance: "That is out of the question, because separability and being a 'this' are supposed to belong to substance. . . ." (*Met.* Z 3 1029a27-29) What does this objection, which also reminds one of Δ 8, amount to? Begin with matter not being a "this." Earlier in Z 3 Aristotle has said that matter is itself nothing in particular. At Z 16 1040b5ff. he elaborates: many of the things previous philosophers have thought to be substances are only potencies, mere heaps, which cannot qualify as substance until they are worked up into a unity. At Iota 1 1052a21ff. he says a thing is more properly one if it has form than if it is simply continuous in space. The point in these passages is that a substance must be *something*—not just a quantity of material, but something that qualifies as a real thing because it has a form and is thereby a member of a species (the word *eidos* meaning both "form" and "species"); for only if it is such can it undergo certain changes and still remain what it is, as substances character-

---

[19] For the identification of form and essence, see *Met.* Z 7 1032b1f. I shall have more to say in the next two chapters about the development of the concept of form. For the moment not much is lost by considering form and essence synonymous and taking either to be that by virtue of which something is of a certain species and is therefore a substance.

istically can do. How could one decide on the conditions under which a pile of material remains the same, or a piece of rock, particularly if it can be broken into two items each of which equally deserves to be called a piece of rock? How much could be chipped away without one's being left with a different rock? That under those conditions something has unity suggests that it is countable and so identifiable and reidentifiable through time and space; so it is a "this" in the sense that it can be picked out in that way, referred to, identified and reidentified. All that can be done because, unlike mere matter, a substance has some feature "by which," as Aristotle says at Z 3 1029a22, "being is bounded." That is, it has form, "by virtue of which something is called a 'this' " (*De Anima* II 1 412a8f.).[20] And it is separable in the sense that it is not logically dependent for its existence or its identity upon any other entity. A substance is a self-subsistent, independent entity that can be directly and securely referred to by one who knows its form or essence.[21]

Even on the predicability test matter does not do well. If a blob of bare space-occupying matter cannot be exactly

[20] Cf. along the same lines *Met.* N 1 1087b33ff. Aristotle says form is a "this" at *Met.* H 1 1042a29, Θ 7 1049a35, and Λ 3 1070a11. That is compatible with form being what makes something what it is, but I shall argue in Chapter Two that there is more to it than that.

[21] P. T. Geach has often defended a view of this sort: see, e.g., *Reference and Generality*, pp. 39-44, and *Three Philosophers*, pp. 86-88. (G.E.M. Anscombe discusses the view as found in Aristotle in the latter, p. 10.) I am indebted to Edwin McCann, whose Ph.D. dissertation on Locke contains (pp. 107-111 and pp. 113-115) a lucid discussion of the current controversy over the necessity of sortals for naming. He concludes, quite rightly I think, that at least in some cases one can refer to something despite having a false belief about what sort of thing it essentially is. Aristotle would equally rightly insist that the clearest and most secure cases of reference are those in which the essence of the object referred to is known. See Gerald Vision, "Essentialism and the Senses of Proper Names," pp. 326ff. (cited by McCann, pp. 114f.) for a judicious compromise view.

or securely referred to, then, since Aristotle has no reason to think one's predicating something of A is any more secure than one's identification of A, it will be natural for him to choose as a paradigm some sort of predication in which the subject can be specifically and securely identified. "That stuff over there is white" would be a bad example of predication, since it might be hard to identify what stuff was meant, harder still to know under what circumstances it would remain the same stuff. Just uttering the word "this" and pointing in some direction is not referring. It is difficult to specify that way exactly what part of the universe one has in mind in pointing. More important, it is impossible to indicate that way whether one has in mind a thing or its matter or a temporal stage of it; relatedly, it is impossible to indicate by pointing what would count as future circumstances sufficiently similar to the present ones to warrant a reidentification of "this." The problem is especially pressing if the topic of conversation is changing in some way even as one is referring to it.

Aristotle concludes in *Met.* z (see especially chapter 17) that the form provides the what-it-is of the thing and thereby allows us to refer to it and talk about it. As *eidos* means both form and species, we have our substance concepts straight from nature. Unless a certain lump of material has the properties that qualify it for membership in a natural species, it is not a substance but only a piece of matter. If it does qualify for species membership, it is a substance and remains that substance for just so long as it remains in the same species.

As Aristotle suggests in *Met.* z 7-9, the species lines can be discovered by attention to the way in which natural things normally reproduce. (Artifacts are not substances in the fullest sense, as Aristotle says at *Met.* H 2 1043a4 and b21; so it is not to be expected that one can so easily decide between essence and accident in their case, particularly if something that is apparently one item is defined according to two or more distinct purposes people may use it for.) Thus we can use the organization nature provides to divide the world into substances and count as a single substance that which does meet the requirements for species membership and does not divide into a plurality of things each of which can also be a member of a species.

Aristotle has begun by asserting that individual material objects are substances and are prior to all other sorts of thing. Faced with the possibility that matter might be primary by virtue of being the subject *par excellence* of predication, he does not abandon the predicability test but refines it, in order to show that it does not after all clearly favor matter. In the process Aristotle has refined the notion of priority as well. At its crudest, priority is a matter of what sort of thing can exist without what other sort of thing. In the *Categories* priority is a matter of the ability to retain identity through change; so, though a substance cannot exist without properties, it can persist as the same entity while its properties (at least the accidental ones) do not all retain their identity. In the *Metaphysics* the position is that what maintains its identity must be an identifiable something; and that requirement disqualifies matter and promotes form to the position of prominence for which Aristotle has been grooming it as early as the *Categories*. Material objects remain prior, but priority has become a complicated issue. It is to become still more complicated.

b. Priority in Definition

In the first chapter of Book Z, Aristotle promises to produce something worthy of being called substance by virtue of its priority in three respects: definition, order of knowledge, and time. The third respect just amounts to the ability to exist independently, and so (as it turns out) to be identifiable; that is what the previous section was all about.[22] The

---

[22] Again, it may not be entirely clear to Aristotle that the ability to persist independently is the most that can be made of the ability to exist independently. Moreover, Aristotle is not consistent about

second sort of priority is familiar from the earlier parts of the *Metaphysics*, in which Aristotle argues that the material object is indeed knowable. (As I shall argue in the next chapter, this criterion leads Aristotle to identify a substance with its essence, since knowing a substance amounts to knowing its essence.) About priority in definition little has been said thus far. It is rather a new test for substance, and it occasions a new and subtle reason for taking Aristotle's kind of substance to be prior.

What does Aristotle mean by priority of definition? Different things, evidently, in different places. At *Met.* M 2 1077b1ff., for example, Aristotle says that priority in definition and priority in substance do not always go together: white is prior in definition to white man, because the color can be defined without reference to this or any man. He does not deny this in Book Z, where by priority in definition he means something else. The point must be that one cannot know what white or any color is unless one understands its relation to substance, because white is essentially a quality of a substance. In general, this talk of priority in definition is of a piece with Aristotle's belief that there is an isomorphism between the world and language, that therefore a condition of our understanding the world aright is that the structure of the world be grasped and conveyed by the utterances of our language, in particular by its definitions. There is some of the same motivation behind the *Categories*, and a recognition of the difficulties of that approach in the *Posterior Analytics*. At best, Aristotle can prove something about the priority of substance by examination of the structure of language. At worst, relations among linguistic items may serve as helpful analogues in the exposition of ontological relations.

---

identifying temporal priority with the ability to exist independently. In *Cat.* 12 temporal priority is just greater age, and what is later called temporal priority is there called what does not reciprocate with respect to implication of existence.

Accordingly, in *Met.* Z 4 Aristotle argues in some detail that the essence-accident organization of the world should be and is reflected in language. After having made a career of insisting in his arguments against Platonism that distinction between univocity and equivocity is exhaustive and that the latter applies to the word "is," Aristotle comes in Book Γ to realize that there is a third alternative: the senses of "is" may be systematically related in that the "is" appropriate to substance is the sort that gives the others their meaning.[23] Aristotle's inference from this is that non-substance items exist and have essences and therefore definitions in a secondary sense, parasitic on the way in which substances have essences and definitions. Aristotle thereby suggests—but as far as I can see does not say—that statements about non-substances can be translated straight into statements about substances; thus, for example, "There is a white in Coriscus" can be translated into "Coriscus is white," and so on. This is not a purely linguistic matter: such a translation is possible because the existence of the whiteness of Coriscus depends on Coriscus and is in fact the same thing as Coriscus's being white.

The senses and definitions of "is" and their dependencies reflect relations among sorts of real entity. Aristotle holds in Z 4 and elsewhere that the essence-accident organization of the world is catered to by the distinction between definition and mere description: a definition of something (insofar as it is possible to have a definition of a particular thing) must name the essence of the thing and must therefore be true of it throughout its existence, whereas a description of the thing may be true of it at one time but not at another, since any accident may change without the thing ceasing to exist.

[23] Thus G.E.L. Owen, "Logic and Metaphysics." The view that what Owen calls "focal meaning" is a distinct alternative is not universally shared. For a review of opinions and the evidence, see Barrington Jones's forthcoming "Introduction to Aristotle's *Metaphysics*."

Now just taking it for granted that ordinary language is isomorphic to the world and that therefore what is primarily definable is primarily real does not prove anything. Still, Aristotle's distinction between description and definition, particularly in *Met.* Z 12, can work as an analogy. He means to show how a definition is unitary, not just a group of words; and in that respect it is like that of which it is a definition, namely a substance, which is unitary rather than just a bundle of elements, or of properties, such as whiteness, animality, and so on. A substance is not just a bundle of properties because it has a certain essence by virtue of which it is a member of a species and can therefore be identified and reidentified through time; and it is not identical with humanity plus whiteness plus animality in part because the substance can abide even if the whiteness does not, in part because its humanity entails animality. The problem concerning definition is this: why is "two-footed animal" (a typical definition) unitary, as it must be in order to define substance, whereas "white man," evidently no more complex linguistically, is not? Since definition consists of genus and differentia, the question becomes, why is "white" not part of the differentia? (The parallel question for substance is, why is whiteness not part of the essence?) The question is a central one, since Aristotle regards the differentia as determinative of the definition because each species implies a genus—which, indeed, exists only insofar as there are species of it. Aristotle does not directly say white is not a differentia. He says only that there is not a differentia for every property and that therefore one cannot divide the differentia "footed" just any old way, as for example into "feathered" and "featherless" or "white" and "black." He believes the facts of biology indicate that there is no division of species between white men and black men and that therefore their differentiae and hence their definitions are not different.

Just as a thing is in a way a combination of form and matter, though the matter and the form are not two elements in it of equal standing, so a definition is in a way a combination of differentia and genus, though those two are not equally elements of it; in the case of the definition it is the differentia that makes it what it is, and in the case of the substance it is the form. As Aristotle says in *Met.* H 6, a definition is unitary in the same way and for the same reason a substance is unitary. A substance is unitary because the form and the matter are the same thing in that one is potentially what the other is actually, and a definition is unitary not only because it is a definition of one thing but primarily because its parts are related as matter and form.

The analogy is not an entirely happy one. The relation between a thing and its matter is more like the relation between a thing and one or more of its accidents than it is like the relation between genus and differentia. Aristotle is trying to draw significant inferences from the way in which being in a certain species (and so being a certain sort of thing) normally implies a certain sort of matter, as for example being a man, having that form, being in that species, requires organs that can perform certain functions characteristic of men (this point he discusses mainly in Z 10 and 11). Similarly, something's being in a certain species requires that it be in a certain genus. On the other hand, something's having a certain accidental property neither entails nor is entailed by its being in a certain species. But surely a property is accidental *or genuinely material* just in case it neither entails nor is entailed by a species. Thus in that respect accident and matter are on all fours, and equally analogous to genus.

Aristotle has set himself an impossible and probably unnecessary task. He wants to show how substances are definable; but as he says himself in *Met.* Z 13 and 15, respectively, universals are not substances and individuals are not definable. He is faced with the sort of inconsistent triad he discovered in attempting to show substances to be knowable. He concluded in that case that actual knowledge is of the particular and potential knowledge of the universal.

His example of actual knowledge was the grammarian recognizing a particular syllable. The suggestion was that knowledge does not require Ideas of syllables, but only a capacity to recognize an instance when it appears. This was not, however, a hard nominalism, for Aristotle rejected the view that letter-inscriptions are the only really real entities and syllables convenient fictions. So he steered a course between Platonism and atomistic reductionism more by just rejecting both than by giving a definitive defense of his own position. Where the topic is definability, he takes the same sort of line, though less explicitly. Universals rather than individuals are definable; *a fortiori* bits of matter are not the only entities that can claim respectability. In finding a middle way, Aristotle again (in Z 17) invokes the analogy between substances and syllables, though this time it is put to slightly different use. A syllable is not identical to the letters that compose it; their arrangement is what makes them constitute the syllable. Again the conclusion is that there are entities in addition to the smallest parts, and again there is no reason to suppose that those entities are in any way dependent upon universals.

But in this case as in the case of knowledge, the problem is not entirely solved. Since Aristotle does not abandon the view that it is universals and not individuals that are definable or the view that substances are not universals, he fails, perhaps inevitably, to achieve the objective he has set for himself. He does not clearly show how an individual substance can be definable, as he has not clearly shown how it can be knowable. In the next chapter I shall offer an interpretation that somewhat softens the apparent contradictions in Aristotle's words, but does not eliminate them.

IV. ARISTOTLE AND STRAWSON ON THE PRIORITY OF SUBSTANCE

One more sort of priority needs to be discussed. It is not yet clear how substance is prior to space and time. In the

logical and metaphysical works, Aristotle has mainly discussed qualities, matter, and universals in relation to substance; seldom has he said anything about other items in the
secondary categories. But he does have views about space
(or place, as he says) and time; he does think they are dependent on substance. In showing how Aristotle reaches
this conclusion, I shall compare his position with that of
P. F. Strawson in his *Individuals*, an influential contemporary work explicitly in the tradition of descriptive metaphysics, of which Aristotle is acknowledged to be the most
distinguished practitioner.[24] Strawson does not try to find in
Aristotle a notion of conceptual priority that meets all the
demands of modern analytical philosophy, but he is right in
believing that both he and Aristotle "describe the actual
structure of our thought about the world,"[25] though Aristotle thinks he is describing the actual structure of the
world.

Strawson wants to elucidate our conceptual scheme. He
sometimes suggests that no other conceptual scheme is available to us, and thereby he seeks to vindicate the one we do
use.[26] At the very least, he describes the broad foundations
of our world, and in so doing extends this challenge: this is
the way in which we view the world; and if there is any
other possible way for us to view it, nobody has yet successfully said what it might be.

One of Strawson's primary objectives is to prove that
material bodies are the basic particulars in our conceptual
scheme. He wants to do this not by showing that they are
separate in Aristotle's early sense, according to which substances (which are just what Strawson calls material bod-

[24] P. F. Strawson, *Individuals*, p. 9.   [25] *Ibid.*

[26] That is vindication enough for many philosophers, especially
post-Kantians. A world of which we could not conceive is surely
not a live alternative. Aristotle sometimes (e.g., *Met.* Z 4 and Z 12)
writes as though we need not trouble ourselves over the possibility
that the world might be radically out of phase with the structure of
the Greek language. I think Aristotle's position on this point is a
matter of facile if fortunate assumption rather than anything carefully worked out.

ies)[27] can exist independently of items in other categories but not vice versa; instead, Strawson argues, as Aristotle does in his later metaphysical writings, for priority in respect of identifiability. So it is Strawson's task to demonstrate that the identification and reidentification of material bodies do not depend on the identification of other sorts of item (such as sounds, events, and places), whereas the identification of the latter does depend on the identification of material bodies.

It does not follow that one could not identify a particular instance of color on a particular occasion if one could not also identify a particular material body on that occasion— one could, of course, identify such an item in at least a rough and approximate way by its space-time coordinates —but only that one could not in general identify items in other categories if one could not ever identify material bodies at all. Moreover, one could identify material bodies even if one could not identify places, times, events, and unit-properties. This is not to say that one could have the concept of an individual thing without having the concept of time, the concept of space, the concept of size, and several others.

The sort of priority Strawson claims for his basic particulars is similar to the sort of priority Aristotle claims for substance in the latest metaphysical works: material things are primarily identifiable. Does any other sort of priority follow from the superior "thisness" of material bodies? Strawson seems to believe it does: "That it should be possible to identify particulars of a given type seems a necessary condition of the inclusion of that type in our ontology."[28] But this is not to say, nor is there any reason to believe, that there could be material bodies if there were

[27] At least Aristotelian substances are good examples of what Strawson calls material bodies. Exactly what a material body is may be hard to specify exactly. Is a fire a material body? A rainbow? A cloud? Mona Lisa's smile? Aristotle pays careful attention to what counts as a substance; Strawson seems to be less careful.

[28] Strawson, *Individuals*, p. 16.

no space, no size, and none of a number of other such items. Generally, there could not be a thing without properties. I do not think Strawson denies this. Instead, he concentrates on what one can conceive of and what notions one cannot understand without first understanding what other notions. This is because Strawson holds that deciding what we can conceive of and must believe in is the most that philosophers can do towards deciding what there is. Strawson does seem also to be saying that our ability to identify something is a necessary condition of our having reason to believe it exists. But again, from the proposition that we can believe in only what we can identify and the proposition that the identification of things of sort A depends on the identification of things of sort B, it does not follow that the existence of B's is similarly dependent on that of A's.

Now to a brief summary of Strawson's argument. We do hold discourse with ourselves and others concerning individual things. Our ability to do so presupposes an ability to identify and reidentify those individuals we talk and think about. Such identification demands that we be able to discriminate one such particular from another—that, consequently, we know or truly believe some individuating fact about them, or some of them. The demand is not that each particular be subject to such individuation first-hand: some particulars can be identified by our being able to state the unique relation each has to a particular that can be identified first-hand. So our enterprise requires a system that uniquely relates those particulars which are not available for identification in our first-hand experience with those which are. Fortunately, we have just such a system ready to hand: it is the unitary space-time framework, and no other. We need this spatio-temporal system in order to have the general ability to identify particulars; but, the next question is bound to be, where do we get the system? There must be some particulars that can constitute the system; and they are those very particulars of whose identification we have been speaking, for they alone "can confer upon it its own fundamental characteristics"[29] because they have three dimensions and endure through time (the prime characteristics of the system). And, as is necessary if they are to be observable to such as ourselves, they "collectively have enough diversity, richness, and stability and endurance to make possible and natural just that conception of a single unitary framework which we possess."[30] And "they" are and must be just those material bodies.

Material bodies constitute the space-time framework by serving as reference points on which one can base space-time coordinates. If there were no stationary material bodies, there would be no way of measuring movement through space, since there would be nothing relative to which we could say that other things were moving; hence we could not have any reason for saying that anything was moving rather than at rest, or vice versa. And these particulars that constitute the framework will provide a reference point by which other particulars will be able to be identified; in that sense these framework-constituting particulars will be basic.[31]

[29] *Ibid.*, p. 39.   [30] *Ibid.*

[31] Note that Strawson thinks the particulars constitutive of the framework must themselves have the characteristics they confer on the framework. Hence they must be three-dimensional, they must last for a while, they must be publicly observable, and they must have diversity and richness (which I take it means at least that they must be distinguishable from each other; what else it means I do not know). But the passage quoted above stipulated that they be *collectively* three-dimensional and the rest. It does not follow from the demand Strawson puts forward here that each item of the sort that constitutes the framework must have each of the features the sort as a whole must have. It is of course not the case that each is of itself diverse; and though many must last for a substantial length of time and overlap to form a continuing stream of things through time, and though all must be in principle observable and locatable, I cannot see why they must be three-dimensional in order to confer three-dimensionality on the framework as a whole. Surely the framework of solid geometry is three-dimensional; but points, or lines, and planes, not themselves three-dimensional, combine to constitute solid figures.

This much at least seems true: material bodies are the only sort of item actually available, in practice, to constitute our conceptual framework. Given how we learn about the world, the use of (say) microscopic objects would be so awkward that we could not begin entification with them. Thus we should be ruling them out as basic on pragmatic grounds, whereas by contrast we should rule out such things as sense data on grounds that we could not conceivably know anything about our sense data without first knowing about objects in the public domain. This practical priority of material bodies is less than Strawson claims to have shown, but it seems worth showing, and it is akin to what Aristotle does.[32]

But now the question arises, why must we say that it is things rather than events that are basic in our conceptual scheme? It is true that one could not locate a battle without locating dying men and a field[33] (Aristotle's examples of dependency of event on thing include walking on the walker: *Met.* Z 1 1028a20-24); but it is not clear that one could always locate a thing with a characteristic activity without locating the characteristic activity.[34] Strawson does not prove that agents are more basic than actions; and occasionally, though not often, he writes as though he were concerned with mutual rather than one-way dependency of identifiability. Thus it is, he suggests, between things and

[32] In one important respect what Strawson does is very different indeed from what Aristotle does. Strawson presumably takes it for granted that there are discoverable scientific laws that describe and explain regularities among events involving microconstituents of ordinary material bodies. Aristotle does not believe this. For him there is no distinction between scientific investigation and the investigation of our ontological framework of substance, property, process, and actuality; for there is no science of matter, which is unknowable. (See Section V, *ad fin.*)

[33] Strawson, *Individuals*, p. 57.

[34] On this point see J.M.E. Moravcsik, "Strawson and Ontological Priority," esp. p. 118.

places.[35] Perhaps he would have done well to have continued in that direction.

In the interests of defining substance Strawson introduces the notion of a sortal concept as opposed to a characterizing concept:

> A sortal universal supplies a principle for distinguishing and counting individual particulars which it collects. It presupposes no antecedent principle, or method, of individuating the particulars it collects. Characterising universals, on the other hand, whilst they supply principles of grouping, even of counting, particulars supply such principles only for particulars already distinguished, or distinguishable, in accordance with some antecedent principle or method. Roughly, and with some reservations, certain common nouns for particulars introduce sortal universals, while verbs and adjectives applicable to particulars introduce characterising universals.[36]

Clearly a language adequate to a conceptual system based on material bodies requires the distinction Strawson makes here, namely an essence-accident distinction. And to use sortals—thus to talk about things—presupposes having a principle of dividing the world into individual things; and it presupposes, what Strawson does not mention here, having a principle by which one can decide whether a thing persists through time. In other words, the sortal should enable us to count at a time and through time. It should divide the world into subtances. Probably all sortals that permit one to count through time permit counting at a time as well, and vice versa. Surely a criterion of identity through time presupposes a principle of individuation at a time, since knowing how many items of a certain sort one saw, total, at t_1 and t_2 requires knowing how many one saw at t_1. Nor is it likely there could be a criterion of individuation at a time

---

[35] Strawson, *Individuals*, p. 37.   [36] *Ibid.*, p. 168.

too weak to provide a criterion of continued existence. Identifying something as being of a certain sort presupposes identifying it as a material object, which in turn presupposes that the object(s) counted could be observed from different points of view, though not necessarily from all at the same time. So the very notion of any sort of thing—as well as the very notion of a thing—would seem to come equipped with some criterion for continuity.[37] The very least this argument shows is that there is no likelihood that beings with anything like our conceptual system (that is, one of space and time) could have substance concepts that provide a principle of counting in space but not in both space and time. (As Chapter Two indicates, Aristotle treats these problems separately but uses the same device to solve each.)

On the ontological status of space and time there is a striking similarity between the positions of Aristotle and Strawson. Strawson does not discuss the question fully, but he makes it clear what his position is when he says that identifying places rests on identifying bodies.[38] No doubt he would say the same about time. Aristotle gives place a status different from that of matter, at least with respect to the thing that is in the place, since the place is separable from the thing in a clear sense in which matter is not, and other non-substance components of things are not; place is not a component of a thing. Place seems to be parasitic on substance just in the sense that it is definable only by reference to substance: it is the boundary of the containing body at which it is in contact with the contained body (*Phys.* IV 4 212a5ff.), a non-portable and motionless vessel (of substances, that is; a13ff.), the innermost motionless boundary of what contains (a20f.). Aristotle says in passing (211a11ff.) that place would not have been thought of if there had not been motion from place to place; so motion (of substances) has some sort of conceptual priority to place. In much the

---

[37] My arguments are borrowed from Michael Woods, "Identity and Individuation."

[38] Strawson, *Individuals*, p. 38.

same way motion and therefore substance are prior to time: though we perceive motion and time together (IV 11 219a4ff.), time is defined as the number of motion (220a24) and impossible without it—though no doubt motion is equally impossible without time, just as substances presumably could not exist without places to exist in. Aristotle seems to portray a complex interdependency, though his official view is that in respect of definition and existence substance is primary. So with Strawson, who, however, would probably not be able to say how we could have the notion we have of substance or identify what we call substance if we could not use the notions of space or time.[39]

Again, there is some reason to say that Strawson has shown only that material bodies and events exhibit a mutual dependency. It is certainly true that one would have a difficult time in identifying anything in our world if there were not persisting, identifiable, and reidentifiable material bodies and therefore also concepts that enable us to sort them. It is also true that we standardly locate non-substance items by reference to substances, particularly those the non-substances qualify; and though we can occasionally identify them otherwise, we could hardly do so all the time. But surely it is no less true that one cannot actually tell whether this substance is the same as some previously seen substance unless one can identify it by reference to certain properties it has. The way Moravcsik[40] puts the point is this: the evidence we have for many statements of reidentification brings events into play and depends on our ability to correlate certain objects, times, and places. Similarly, Aristotle

[39] I shall not be discussing Part II of Strawson's work, in which he argues that what we can say about the elements of predication, the object and the concept, stands in a mutually reinforcing relationship to what he has said about particulars and reference to them in Part I. Surely Aristotle would agree with Strawson about the necessity of treating these topics together, and his passages on the unity of definition indicate as much. Some passages in the *Categories* and *Posterior Analytics* are Aristotle's analogue of Strawson's Part II.

[40] In "Strawson on Ontological Priority," p. 116.

says in *Met.* Z 8 that it is matter that permits us to distinguish between two substances in the same species. We distinguish Socrates from Callias and identify this man as being Socrates rather than Callias on the basis of some features that are not essential.

One might object that it is not the retention of certain inessential features that actually makes Socrates Socrates, that that is only a practical requirement of identification in the individual case. But whereas Aristotle can consistently make this claim, Strawson cannot; for dependency in regard to identifiability is the only sort of priority that interests Strawson when he is talking ontology. And if Strawson tries to introduce some such notion as in-principle identifiability, he owes us an explanation of it worthy of the name and of the standard way in which we do identify things.[41]

There can be little doubt that Aristotle's discussion of substance is aimed in much the same direction as Strawson's argument for the priority of material bodies and Strawson's suggestions about what a substance concept is. Like Aristotle, Strawson is concerned to demonstrate the ontological priority of material bodies to items in other categories; like him, he thus suggests the beginnings of an account of what makes a substance a unitary and abiding thing rather than a succession of things, or a random lump of material, or some indefinite number of things.

Neither Aristotle nor Strawson has proved that the world can be seen only as a plurality of substances involved in events in space and time; indeed, I cannot imagine how anybody could prove such a thing once and for all. Aristotle gives some signs in *Met.* Γ of trying to argue that to obliterate the distinction between essence and accident is to

---

[41] Note that on Aristotle's account a thing could be the same thing as something sighted at some previous time even if it shared almost no accidental properties with it. The view can be defended, but it has its problems—particularly, as I shall argue in Chapter Three, in the case of personal identity.

obliterate the law of non-contradiction and with it the possibility of meaningful discourse an any subject, but he does not come close to succeeding in this proto-transcendental argument. On the other hand, it is worth arguing first that we *can* coherently view the world in this way, and second that there are difficulties involved in viewing the world in any other way anybody has seriously proposed.

The next task is to describe in more detail Aristotle's account of what makes substance unitary—that is, form. How form performs this function and how form is related to substance are the topics of the second chapter, which argues that Aristotle solves his problems by identifying form and substance. But before turning to that discussion, I want to deliver a warning.

V. ARISTOTLE'S WORLD OF SUBSTANCES: A CAUTIONARY NOTE

By this time the reader may have concluded that I am advertising an Aristotle who could converse easily with Strawson and other contemporaries of ours who acknowledge their debt to him. It is therefore in order to mention some fundamental differences between Aristotle's worldview and that of most contemporary analytical philosophers.

In Greek philosophy before Aristotle, there is evidence of a temptation towards a doctrine of two worlds, one perfect and knowable and entirely real, the other none of these. Plato's ontology could be crudely described that way; and to his credit Plato concerned himself with the mysterious relations between spatio-temporal objects and the Ideas. What precisely does it mean to say that the former participate in the latter? How can persons, examples of the former, act on the latter even cognitively, as the system demands? The possibility that the *Parmenides* and the *Sophist* may contain the beginnings of solutions to the problems they raise does not alter the fact that there are problems. The cliché about Aristotle is that he assimilates the two worlds by introducing forms into space and time rather than keeping them in a separate place of their own; and though the cliché is too crudely stated to be clearly significant, much less true, there is something to it. But there is also something to the view that Aristotle's ontological economy is less radical than he sometimes suggests; and this should not be surprising, since the rejection of some sort of dualism often leads to an acceptance of some other sort—for example, two sorts of entity become one sort that demands two sorts of explanation. And so it is with Aristotle.

The distinguished work of Father Owens,[42] among others, has made it difficult to maintain that Aristotle dispensed entirely with ontologically independent purely formal entities (though, as Professor de Vogel[43] has argued, not impossible). But Aristotle's significant contribution, at least from the point of view of contemporary analytical philosophy, is that he substitutes a dualism of description and explanation for a dualism of entities. The man, Coriscus, the musician, and the pile of flesh and bones are not four different items; but given the subtle relations among their descriptions and their identities, they are not in every respect identical either. The state of the heart and surrounding organs and the psychological state are not two different states, but they are distinguishable by the two quite different

---

[42] Joseph Owens, *The Doctrine of Being*. Even Father Owens does not claim that Aristotle showed "how separate Entity is expressed in every predication of Being, as the science outlined in E 1 would seem to require" (p. 454). I think one is clearly justified in considering Aristotle's views on sensible substance by themselves, without regard to divine substance. What I have to say about what is not sensible will appear as part of an account of the unembodied part of the soul, in Chapter Six.

[43] C. J. de Vogel, "La méthode d'Aristote en métaphysique d'après Métaphysique A 1-2." The paper is a criticism of Father Owens's attempt to find foreshadowings of theology in Aristotle's writings on substance.

sorts of explanation appropriate to them. Thus explanations multiply, but not entities, or at least not entities in the same category. What distinguishes Aristotle from the reductionist of the hard materialist stripe is that Aristotle thinks taxonomy is crucial. Quite aside from anything else Aristotle may be granting properties in the way of status, the classifying job done by the formal characterization really counts; it is not arbitrary. As we know, it follows the lines along which nature works, it lays down or at least implies conditions for being a substance, and it thereby enables one to understand the world as consisting of material objects rather than just lumps of matter or clouds of atoms or collections of properties. The correct taxonomy of the world is of the essence.

Aristotle's modified realism about essences seems to contrast pleasingly with Plato's inflationary view, in part no doubt because Aristotle's position seems in accord with common sense. I have read his metaphysical arguments as attempts to defend something like a common-sense view of the world, or at least to make such a view coherent and therefore not in need of any defense. Aristotle does not thoroughly explore possible alternative views for coherence because the common-sense framework seems somehow unarguably right; that is one reason why some of his arguments against Plato and the Presocratics meet with such severe criticism from Cherniss and others. Individuals are a given, and increased knowledge about how they operate and what they are made of should have no tendency to undermine their reality or importance. But the plain evidence of one's senses can lead to overconfidence. Aristotle is sanguine not only about the existence of substances but about their nature —for example, they must be three- and not four-dimensional—and he regards teleology as a given too.

At the beginning of the *Tractatus* Wittgenstein lays it down that the world is the totality of facts rather than of things. This suggests, what is true, that a list of the facts about the world, if such were possible, would more adequately describe it than a list of the things it contains. Now this is compatible with the notion that substances are ontologically prior to events, but I do not think Aristotle's overall view of the world would survive his careful consideration of what Wittgenstein says. For Aristotle thinks of the world as being essentially populated by substances that have certain determinate natures which explain what these substances do: in particular, they explain how the substances grow and develop and in some cases how they function, unless interfered with, when they are fully developed. To explain what happens in the world or some part of it, one must know what the respective natures of its inhabitants are. So what in Aristotle's system passes for a law of nature is not normally a law relating sorts of event but a statement about how a particular sort of thing tends to behave, particularly if not prevented from doing so by other things. In view of this outlook on the world, it is not surprising that Aristotle often thinks of *aitiai* (reasons or causes) as being of things rather than of events, nor is it surprising that he talks of knowing individuals or universals rather than propositions.

The notion of a power in a thing is not the same as the notion of a dispositional property.[44] The latter involves the nomic necessity that a thing be in a certain state in certain circumstances; the former seems to range between the conceivability that something will come to pass and the fact that it will provided nothing prevents it. The discussion of potency in *Met.* Θ, particularly the defense of potency against the skepticism of the Megarians, indicates that Aristotle is not a determinist, despite his remarks about rational versus non-rational potency. There seem to be some states about which one can say only that they might or might not

[44] On this point see Wilfrid Sellars, "Aristotelian Philosophies of Mind," esp. pp. 545f.

come to pass. This indeterminism comes through in some of Aristotle's biological works as well: for example, see *De Generatione Animalium* IV 10 778a4ff.,[45] according to which nature is irregular because matter is undetermined and may give rise to spontaneous action. The same suggestion is found in *Met.* E 3 1027a29-b17. Now though it would be impossible for Aristotle to find any conclusive evidence that nature does not work according to immutable laws, he is content to hold that it does not, or at any rate not entirely. Matterless things do: there is no uncertainty about mathematics comparable to what attends descriptions of and predictions about material objects. And as matter is the source of the indeterminacy of the world, that is to be expected.

To put the point another way, when we are talking just about form, all is neatly determined, regular, coherent, predictable, knowable; but when we are talking about matter, nothing is quite certain. The sort of necessity that resides in matter we call hypothetical necessity: in order for such and such to happen, such and such must necessarily be the case. Typically, something must be made of a certain sort of matter in order for that something to achieve a certain end (*Phys.* II 9 199b34ff.; *De Partibus Animalium* I 1 639b21ff.). In such cases, given the end, we know a significant amount about the nature of the matter; but the converse is not true. In these and other passages Aristotle sug-

---

[45] On this and some related points I am guided by D. M. Balme's *Aristotle's De Partibus Animalium I and De Generatione Animalium I.* See esp. p. 82.

I want to avoid possible misunderstanding on two points. First, I do not hold that Aristotle's doctrine of chance is primarily about indeterminism. On the contrary, chance is compatible with determinism, for it amounts to no more than the occurrence of a result that was not intended but might have been (see *Phys.* II 5). Second, on the other hand, Aristotle is not an indeterminist in the sense that he carefully considers determinism and rejects it. For him the important choice is between chance and teleology, not between a law-governed universe and a random one (see *Phys.* II 8).

gests that form somehow struggles to overcome refractory matter and its irrational necessity in a way reminiscent of Plato's *Timaeus*: even where matter is not irregular, we may infer, it can sometimes be counted upon to resist being turned to a particular good end. (This sort of interpretation should not be taken too far. The nature of a particular sort of matter does put certain limits on what one can do with it, but sometimes some sort of matter is highly appropriate for a particular purpose.)

Nevertheless, there is more than just a faint echo of an older two-worlds doctrine in Aristotle. Regularity is the province of forms, spontaneity of matter. Aristotle does not consider the possibility that the microstructures of objects might follow rules too complicated for us to discover. He seems to regard it as obvious from the fact that certain things regularly reach certain good ends that there are final *aitiai* in nature (normally connected with form rather than matter, particularly when the essence of something is in part determined by a state it is supposed to attain), but it is hard to see what he can mean by this other than that certain natural things do regularly achieve certain states that seem somehow desirable for them from our point of view. Aristotle does not think there would have to be some sort of conflict between some natural necessity on the level of matter and the workings of a final *aitia*, any more than something's having an efficient *aitia* would have to be incompatible with its having a final one (see, for example, *Part. An.* II 16 658b27ff.). He just thinks matter is in fact not dependable.

Aristotle's ideal of dependability is not something that changes regularly according to a law of nature, but rather something that does not change at all: for example, something that is purely formal, or a mathematical entity. As with Plato and other predecessors, Aristotle seems to think of simply being in time, rather than being outside it as mathematical entities are, as being somehow exposed to corruption and decay.[46] He does make time and change imply each other. How, Aristotle and others may have wondered, can knowledge and change be reconciled? How is one to explain a world in which things change by reference to things that do not change? One way would be to show that things change according to certain immutable laws, but Aristotle does not in general do that. He does not consider events as fulfilling laws in part because he does not think of events as being the ontological data that have to be accepted and explained. It is things that are prior, things that are to be explained, even things that are qualified by time; and the universals that explain things are species and genera rather than law-like propositions. Where there are law-like explanatory generalizations, they are in effect definitions of sorts of thing; and such a definition explains what happens in the world not by laying down laws that can predict the interactions of quantifiable entities but by describing what some entity ought to be like and thereby indicating how it ought to act and in the absence of interfering factors probably will. Aristotle's way of explaining what happens in the world makes it inevitable that he should reject determinism, that he should regard matter as disorderly and therefore resistant to understanding if not to the achievement of proper ends, that he should think form alone is knowable.

One of the most pressing problems of recent philosophy, indeed of much philosophy since the seventeenth century, is the relation between the immediately available world of middle-sized material objects, persons, and minds on the one hand and the world described by natural science on the other. The latter threatens to consign the former to illusion. The hope of many analytical philosophers in the past twenty-five years has been to show that these two ways of viewing the world are compatible. Thus free will, it has

---

[46] On this and some related topics see G.E.L. Owen, "Plato and Parmenides on the Timeless Present."

been argued, can coexist with determinism, thoughts and intentions with materialism, physiological psychology with morality. There are many ways to explain events, as there are to describe them. Aristotle most heartily agrees. But we give Aristotle too much credit if we do not acknowledge that the problem of possible conflict between the world of common sense and the world of natural science did not press very hard upon him. To be sure, some of his predecessors believed microexplanations were available for all phenomena. But it is one thing for a Democritus to say that everything reduces to atoms and the void, quite another for a Newton to demonstrate the laws by which the atoms operate, yet again another thing for a psychologist to predict and even control apparently voluntary behavior. These battles Aristotle does not have to fight. Therefore one's amazement at Aristotle's astuteness ought to be tempered by the recollection that he was oblivious to certain difficulties his successors had to overcome. This has been true of his views about substance; the case will be clearer yet for his views about the nature and individuation of the person and about the relation between the person's soul and his body.

Chapter Two

THE IDENTITY OF SUBSTANCE AND ESSENCE

ARISTOTLE'S conception of substance eventually requires not only defense but also refinement. He does not abandon the position that a substance is a material object, but it becomes clear that not just any piece of matter qualifies as a substance. A substance is the sort of thing it is by virtue of its form or essence, which is therefore a necessary condition of it. This chapter explores a further advance, at least in exposition; for it turns out that an essence is a sufficient as well as necessary condition of a substance, and even that the relation between each substance and its essence is identity. A substance is a material object, but not a combination of form and matter. Aristotle takes this position in response to two important philosophical problems, both presented strikingly by Heraclitus. The first is that over a period of time an ordinary substance must change in certain ways and yet retain its self-identity. This is not a problem to which Aristotle first addresses himself late in his career: it is there as early as the *Categories*. But it is only later that he says clearly that a substance must be identical to its essence if one is to be able to step into the same river twice (Section I; Section II deals with some possible objections). The second problem is that even at a particular time what occupies a certain space can be described from many different points of view and may therefore be thought to be a plurality of things, or even an indeterminate number. The relation between matter and form is not identity; but what is it? And what is the relation between essence and accident? Are there then two or more things where it seemed there was one? Properly understood, the doctrine that form is substance permits one to answer that question, or at least to avoid its force: the road up and the road down are not precisely one and the same, but they are not precisely distinct (Section III). The identification of substance and essence is a step towards solving some problems of identity through time and identity at a time. But it is not the whole solution: Aristotle does not say enough about continuity through time. There are no criteria for sameness in number, as opposed to mere sameness in species, for an entity (or entities) persisting but changing through time (Section IV). One of the most important outcomes of the discussion, from the point of view of Aristotle's psychology, is that the form-matter relation can usefully be considered a special case of accidental identity.

Taken by themselves, some passages in *Metaphysics* z would look like decisive evidence in favor of identifying substance and form or essence. Aristotle has asked at the beginning of the book what qualifies as substance; and in the last chapter, having explored all the alternatives he can think of, Aristotle concludes: "So what we are looking for is the reason why the matter is some particular thing; and that is the form" (1041b7ff.; cf. 1041a28)[1] He has eliminated matter, the combination of form and matter, and the universal as candidates for substance. What remains is the form, which, as Aristotle says elsewhere, is truly an individual—thus *Met.* H 1 1042a29, ☉ 7 1049a35, Λ 3 1070a11ff., where he calls form a "this." The sixth chapter of *Met.* z is devoted to proving that a primary substance is identical to its essence. The case appears to be closed: form is substance.

But it is not so easy. To begin with, that conclusion appears to be a definite change from the doctrine of earlier works, in which a substance is a material object, not just a

---

[1] Christ and Jaeger delete "that is, the form" from this passage in their editions of the *Metaphysics*. There is no reason to do so, and in any case the deletion is not enough to alter the point of the chapter.

form. One would like to find an interpretation of the late *Metaphysics* that is not so disruptive. This can be done, I believe. Notice that the passage from Z 17 says that matter is some particular thing, by virtue of the form. So perhaps the question Aristotle answers here is: what is it about the substance that makes it what it is? And the almost trivial answer is: the form or essence. In that case the form of something would be identically the substance in the sense of being the *substance of* something, rather than being the thing itself as a whole. On this account, "substance" is ambiguous, whether Aristotle knows it or not: it may mean "thing" or "essence."² Form is a "this," not in itself, but because it is that by virtue of which something is a "this," as Aristotle says at *De Anima* I 1 403b1ff.

For several reasons this interpretation will not do. It is true that the essence of something makes it the substance that it is; but it can be shown that the essence is identical to that substance. Moreover, the proffered interpretation has nothing to say about *Met.* Z 6, in which Aristotle argues that a substance is its essence, or about Z 3, in which Aristotle states that a substance is not a combination of form and matter. Finally, it saddles Aristotle with a readily avoidable confusion. The correct interpretation is this: a substance is its essence.

I. ON STEPPING INTO A RIVER TWICE: IDENTITY OVER TIME

Because a substance is its essence, one can step into the same river twice; if Heraclitus says one cannot, he is wrong. Aristotle answers him in this way: "For we must think of the tissue after the image of flowing water that is measured by one and the same measure; particle after particle comes to be, and each successive particle is different" (*De Gen.*

---

² This is a widespread opinion. See, e.g., Ross's commentary on the *Metaphysics*, II, 159f.

et Corr. I 5 321b24f.; Joachim's translation). The point, correctly interpreted by Miss Anscombe,[3] is that different lots of stuff successively come to be—that is, constitute— this particular measure of water, or whatever the substance is. The interpretation is supported by *Met.* N 1 1087b33-88a14: "One signifies measure. . . . [Things to be measured] must always have as the measure some identical property: e.g., if horse is the measure, they are horses, if man, men . . . ."[4] The measure in the case of rivers is river. If there were no measure, there could be no way of saying of a certain lot of water or any matter whether it is one or many. Mass terms by themselves do not easily accept consistent enumerative qualification: they are much or little and not many or few or one, at least not dependably. Talk about one river presupposes that river is the operative measure or individuating concept.

What, then, does it mean to say that this river before you is the same as the one you swam in last week? Not that the water is the same; indeed, in this case, it certainly is not. All that need have remained from time t_1 to time t_2 is the form or essence. I mean this particular form, not a universal; for the claim is not just that there is some river or other here now, just as there was last week, but rather that this particular river is still here. It is here because the essence that was here last week is here, not because the particular water is still here, or because the fishy smell is still here, for neither is. In this familiar sort of context, then, it makes sense to say that what the thing is is a particular form rather than a particular parcel of matter.

The position that it is form or essence that persists through change of matter is a corollary of what Aristotle asserts in the famous *Cat.* 5 4a10ff.: substance survives acci-

---

[3] In "The Principle of Individuation," pp. 83ff.

[4] The translation is from A. C. Lloyd, "Aristotle's Principle of Individuation," p. 520. He refers also to *Met.* B 4 1001a25-27 and *Phys.* III 7 207b7f.

dental change.[5] And what counts as substance surviving accidental change? When the question is put that way, the answer is not hard to find: what counts is the persistence of the essence. Once Aristotle has developed a notion of form that is virtually indistinguishable from essence,[6] it stands to reason that matter will be in the same position as accident with respect to change. It will not therefore be a proper substrate for accidental change, as one would expect it not to be if it is true, as I have argued in the first chapter, that matter does not perform well on the predictability test. Aristotle says at *Met.* Z 3 1029a3 that it may turn out to be form that is substrate as substance is supposed to be substrate, and so it does. The term usually translated "essence"— *to ti ēn einai*, literally, "the what was to be"—suggests the importance for substance of persistence through time. The verb *ēn* is in the imperfect tense, which in this sort of use probably conveys omnitemporality or even timelessness, and thus freedom from contingency. It is what the substance always is as long as it exists, and so what it necessarily is.[7] What more could one ask of a substrate? (See note 20 below.)

Again, it is clearly only the individual form, not the universal, that is what is most permanent about the individual substance; and there is abundant evidence in the *Metaphysics* that Aristotle is indeed committed to the individual

[5] As I said in Chapter One, Section II, there are some early hints that Aristotle will end by identifying substance and essence. See, e.g., *An. Post.* I 22 83a31f.

[6] I shall say more in Chapter Three about how Aristotle does this.

[7] The relation between omnitemporality and necessity in Aristotle is explored in a number of papers by Jaakko Hintikka; see especially his "Necessity, Universality, and Time" and "Time, Truth, and Knowledge." He presses hard on passages like *Met.* E 2 1026b31ff., in which Aristotle says that what is accidental is what is neither always nor for the most part. See also Joseph Owens, *Doctrine of Being*, pp. 182-185.

form.[8] When he says that substance is form, he cannot very well mean that the object of his search is the universal. That he has never believed,[9] and he firmly rules it out again in chapter 13 of Book Z, in which he states that things whose substance and essence are one are themselves one (1038b-14f.). His doctrine that the soul is the form of the living body is alluded to often in the middle books of the *Metaphysics*, usually in a way that makes it clear that each person has his own soul—thus Z 10 1035b25ff., for example.[10] It is true that Aristotle does not often say that the forms that are identical to substances are particulars, but there are a number of passages in which he countenances individual essences.

There is one such passage in *Met.* Z 4. "To be you," Aristotle writes at 1029b14f., "is not to be musical, for you are not musical in virtue of yourself." The locution "to-be-something or other" is frequently used for an essence. In this case it is clear that the essence is primarily attached to an individual person rather than to a species, for *you* is singular. Each person has his own essence, as he has his own musical talent.[11] According to Z 6, every self-subsistent sub-

[8] But see Rogers Albritton's pessimistic review of that evidence, "Forms of Particular Substances in Aristotle's Metaphysics." I am in debt to Albritton and his fellow symposiast, Wilfrid Sellars, whose "Aristotle's Metaphysics: An Interpretation" is, among other things, an attempt to clarify and defend Aristotle's notion of individual form.

[9] In the *Categories* he does call species and genera secondary substances, but thereafter he drops the term.

[10] I shall not argue directly for the particularity of the soul; but what goes on in later chapters, particularly the fifth, will prove that each person has his own soul, according to Aristotle.

[11] Recall the controversy, mentioned in Section II of the previous chapter, about whether Aristotle has individuals in categories other than substance. He does.

What I have translated "to be you" might more literally have been translated "being for you." The dative of the personal pronoun indicates possession, and its singular number indicates that your essence is nobody else's. It does not follow that your essence is different in kind from anybody else's, but only that it is different in number. See further Joseph Owens, *Doctrine of Being*, p. 187, esp. n. 88.

stance not only has its own essence but is the same as its essence, and not accidentally so.[12] Towards the end of that chapter he writes: "The sophistical objections to the view [that a self-subsistent thing is the same as its essence] and the question whether Socrates is the same as to be Socrates clearly have the same answer . . ." (1032a6-8). This passage makes it hard to deny that Socrates has—or rather is—an individual essence.

In Z 13, the main point of which is that a universal cannot be a substance, Aristotle says that the substance of each thing is what is peculiar to it (1038b9f.) and that those things whose substance and essence are one are themselves one (b14f.). If essences were always universals rather than particulars, then Z 13 would force us to the very odd conclusion, which Aristotle gives no sign of believing, that there can be only one instance of each such universal. In chapter 16 he makes the same point again, when he says that things whose substance is one are themselves one (1040b16f.). In these passages *substance* is being used synonymously with *essence*, without confusion.[13] The substance of a thing is identical to it, because the essence is; there is no distinction between a substance and the substance of it.

Nor are individual essences confined to the latest metaphysical writings. Thus in Λ 5: ". . . your matter and form and efficient cause [are different from] mine, but the same in universal definition" (1071a28f.).

To say that your essence is different from mine is not to say that you and I have different essential properties (for example, different personalities) that distinguish us each from all others. That would be a traduction of the notion

---

[12] This chapter alone might be thought to show that a substance is identical to its essence, but it does not. Aristotle says in Z 6 that it is self-subsistent things like Platonic Ideas that are the same as their essences, whereas a white man is not. At Z 11 1037b1ff. Aristotle refers back to Z 6 and restricts the identity to such items as curvature and other things that do not include matter. I shall return to this chapter and to Z 11.

[13] *Pace* Ross and others. See note 2 above.

of essence, in particular of its connection with form and species. Thus at Z 7 1032b1f. Aristotle states that by form he means the essence of each thing and the first substance; moreover, *eidos*, the word usually translated "form," can mean "species" as well (and must at Z 12 1038a5ff.). And when he says at Z 4 1030a11 that only species of genus have essences, he clearly means that it is the species (as opposed to musical talent, for example) that determines what the essence of something is.

Your essence is to be distinguished from mine in just the way in which you are to be distinguished from me, since each person is identical to his essence: we are to be distinguished in that we have different matter (Z 8 1034a6f.). To say that two substances in the same species are distinguishable in virtue of their matter is to say that they are at the same moment made up of numerically different lots of matter. Perhaps two contemporaneous lots of the same sort of matter are different if and only if they differ solely with respect to the accidental attribute of place. (Conceivably that is what their having different prime matter amounts to, if the only attribute of prime matter is that it occupies some space; but I would not insist on that interpretation.) Then difference in location will be necessary and sufficient for distinguishing contemporaries in the same category, and a sufficient condition of difference for any two or more items. The very existence of a particular essence requires that there be some matter constituting it; but that is not to say that the essence, or the substance, is identical to its matter.

Thus far an essence is a necessary condition of a substance, and the essence in question is a particular essence. What remains is to show at least that the existence of a particular form or essence is a sufficient condition of the existence of a particular substance, that is, the whole material object. *Metaphysics* Z 10 and 11 seem to be occupied with that task. Aristotle says in Z 11 that something's having a certain essence may put certain requirements on its matter as well:

for example, a man cannot be made of just any old sort of material, but must be made of the sort of stuff that enables him to do what men characteristically do. Thus Z 11 1036b21: some things are essentially this form in this matter. Snubness is like that, though it is not a substance: where there is snubness, there is flesh as substratum; for only noses can be snub (Z 10 1035a4f.; cf. Z 5 *passim*). More importantly, man and soul are like that.

Why, then, does Aristotle hesitate at the end of chapter 11 to say that the material of which something is made is really part of the essence?[14] In part because the sort of essence in question requires at all times a sort of matter but not a particular lump of that sort of matter, in part because that sort of matter is only a necessary condition of the essence. Still, Aristotle could safely and accurately say that certain apparently material properties are essential properties in the sense that they are entailed by something's having a certain essence. Thus weighing 150 pounds is an accidental or material property of a man, but having some weight is not.[15] The very terms "form" and "matter" suggest—what is true for Aristotle's simple textbook cases of substance, as for example the statue—that a substance is the sort of thing it is by virtue of having a certain shape, and that the stuff of which it is made is of no importance.[16] But with living

[14] In Chapter One, Section IIIb, I said Aristotle's analogy between the substance-matter relation and the species-genus relation was weak, because substance does not imply matter in the way in which species implies genus, for matter is what can be otherwise. Perhaps the analogue Aristotle wants in *Met.* H 6 is the relation between substance and a certain sort of matter that is implied by the form; and that just shows that certain stuff-predicates—e.g., "has weight"— are not purely material predicates.

[15] There are some problems here; not the least of them is that the structure and all the stuff are presumably jointly sufficient conditions of the thing. I shall discuss some of the difficulties in Chapter Three.

[16] As Alexander Mourelatos has reminded me, even in the case of a statue the shape is not a necessary and sufficient condition for its being the sort of thing it is, whether a statue of someone in particular or just a statue.

beings, which alone are genuine substances, the situation is different. It is usually not structure but certain patterns of activity that make a living substance what it is; structure takes its place with stuff as necessary but not sufficient for the existence of the organism. In some cases the matter of something primarily determines what it is: so with honey-water (H 2 1042b17). In other cases a certain quite specific sort of matter is necessary: for example, for a book (1042-b17f.). In others presumably almost any sort of matter that will serve a certain purpose will do: for example, a threshold or a lintel, which is primarily defined by its position with respect to a door or a window and could be made of stone or wood but not of water. Nearly every sub-stance of the sort Aristotle discusses in *Met.* z and H makes certain demands on the matter of which it is made; there must, at the very least, be some matter or other of which it is made. Moreover, the substance must have some color or other, some location, and some other accidental proper-ties. But one would not say that an ordinary substance is a compound of its essence and (for example) its place, for that would mean—if it means anything—that it must have a particular location and retain that location in order to remain what it is.

And now it is clear why Aristotle would want to deny that a substance is a compound of form and matter, as he does in z 3 1029a30-32, peremptorily. Even if the substance in question must have a certain sort of matter, the particular matter of which the substance is made could disappear while the substance itself remains. To say that a substance still exists is to say that its form still exists; to say it is no more is to say that its form is no more, though its matter may abide. So Aristotle says: ". . . those things which are as matter or are combined with matter are not the same [as their essences] . . ." (z 11 1037b4f.). Thus substance is not this form plus this matter. If it were, one could not step into the same river twice. On the other hand, the essence is a sufficient condition of some matter or other of a certain sort, in virtually every case. So if there is the essence of a river on your land, it follows that there is some water for you to step into.

II. PROBLEMS IN THE IDENTITY OF FORM AND SUBSTANCE

Unfortunately, there is some evidence that Aristotle is not perfectly consistent in saying that a particular material object is identical to its essence. In Z 11, the chapter in which he denies that a thing combined with matter is identical with its essence, Aristotle gives curvature as an example of a primary substance identical with its essence; in Z 6 the Platonic Idea is Aristotle's example. So it would seem to be not Socrates but his form that is the sort of substance that is identically its essence.

> It is clear that the soul is the primary substance and the body is matter, and man or animal is the compound of the two, taken universally; for "Socrates" and "Coriscus"—if the soul too is Socrates—are ambiguous, for some mean the words to refer to the soul, some mean them to refer to the compound; but if each name means simply this particular soul plus this particular body, then it is with the particular as it is with the universal. (Z 11 1037a5-10)

The evident conclusion would be that Socrates's soul is identical to its essence but that the whole bodily ensouled person is not. If when I say "Socrates" I mean the whole bodily ensouled person, then I am referring to a compound, just as when I use the term "man" universally I am referring to a universal compounded of (presumably the intersection of) body and soul of the appropriate sorts.[17]

Much the same seems to be true of a passage in Z 8 in which Aristotle denies that a form can be produced and

[17] For an argument along these lines, see Chung-Hwan Chen, "Universal Concrete."

states that only the compound of form and matter can be (1033b5ff.).[18] It is the latter, a certain sort of form in matter, that is the individual substance (1034a5f.). It would follow that if a substance is a material object, it is not a form but a combination of form and matter.

Now these passages do not show that Aristotle makes substance a combination of form and matter; they do not contradict his flat statements that a substance is form rather than the compound.[19] When Aristotle does say a substance is form and matter, he can only mean that (for example) Callias is associated with some matter of the appropriate sort at all times. It does not follow that he is identical with something more than his essence, for his identity with his essence does not excuse him from necessarily having matter. Callias also necessarily has some color or other, and a weight greater than zero, and location; but Callias is not a combination of his form and his color. It is in just that sense that Aristotle denies (at Z 11 1037b4-7) that things that are combined with matter are the same as their essences, because the particular matter of which the thing is made is neither a necessary nor a sufficient condition of its existence. One might wish Aristotle had not used such items as curvature and the Platonic Idea as examples of primary substances identical with their essences; but *Met.* Z 11 is, after all, a tentative and dialectical chapter, so full of reversals, rhetorical questions, and vague promissory notes that it might be well not to take any of its contents as final.

[18] This passage may profitably be compared to Z 15 1039b20-26, where Aristotle says that to be this house—a particular essence, surely—admits of generation and destruction, though to be a house—a universal—does not.

[19] There are similarly troublesome passages in *Met.* H 3, *De An.* II 1, and elsewhere; but these serve primarily as brief and simple introductions to or summaries of Aristotle's ontology, and so cannot be taken as authoritative on the details. It may well be that Aristotle is not so clear on the distinction between an essence with matter and a combination of form and matter as to be able to put it into a short sentence or two for a beginner.

But in this chapter, particularly at 1036b21ff., Aristotle clearly makes the crucial point that the correct sort of definition of a substance has implications for the sort of matter the substance will always have and the sort of state it will be in. Recognition of the demands form makes on matter, along with the conclusion that the existence of a particular form involves the existence of some matter of the appropriate sort, can be detected in z 12, where Aristotle's explicit subject is the unity of definition. What is two-legged, Aristotle argues, is already an animal; there are no two-legged plants. It would therefore be a mistake to regard the genus as a part of the definition independent of the species, which entails it. For similar reasons it would be a mistake to regard the matter of the defined things as utterly independent of the essence, which implies that there is that sort of matter, though not that there is that particular matter. Aristotle does not say in *Met.* z 12 that the solution to the problem of the unity of definition is also in effect the solution to the problem of the unity of substance, but he says it in *Met.* H 6: the relation between species and genus is analogous to that between form and matter.

One passage in chapter 11 deserves special mention. At 1037a5-10 (see quote on page 67 and also note 17) Aristotle seems to state that Socrates considered as a material object is an instance not of the universal man but of a universal somehow compounded of soul and body, as though, if the thing is composed of form and matter, then so must be the universal of which it is an instance. But the lesson of the passage is surely the opposite of the apparent one: it is to show precisely that—and how—the individual substance is just the instance of the form-universal. If, as Aristotle believes both in *Met.* z and in *De Anima* II, the soul is the form of the body, then the universal soul is just the universal man; in this one case, the essence happens to have its own name independently of the substance, because the Greek language is geared to psychophysical dualism rather than hylomorphism. Now Aristotle has written, "if each name means simply this particular soul plus this particular body," then the material object is an instance of the compound universal (1037a8-10). But if there is any view Aristotle firmly rejects, it is precisely that a man is a soul plus a body, which is a corollary of the view that a substance is some matter combined with some form.

To the compound universal Aristotle does not remain committed, as one can infer from what he says in Z 12. The universal man is not a combination of soul and body for the same reason it is not a combination of biped and animal: biped implies animal, and soul implies a body of a certain sort. For the same sort of reason, the individual man is not a combination of form and matter. One of the most important lessons to be drawn from Z 10-12 is that the relation between form and matter is not a relation or combination of logically independent entities of equal standing. They are not elements of a particular thing, nor are they both properties of a particular thing, nor is either a property of the other. Nor is the relation between matter and form just another instance of the sort of predication discussed in the *Categories*.[20] To affirm that a substance is a combination of form and matter is, as Aristotle evidently comes to see, to invite all these mistaken notions back in. On the other hand, to deny that a substance is a combination of form and matter is to suggest that it is pure form, and so to encourage the Platonists (cf. Z 11 1036b22f.).

One may still feel that, despite all I have said, it is at least

---

[20] Aristotle does not abandon the view that form is predicated of matter, presumably in statements of the form "This stuff is a man." At *Met.* Z 3 1029a21ff. he says that predicates other than substance are predicated of substance, while substance is predicated of matter; cf. H 2 1043a5f. But he also says that, in one sense, form is the subject of predication—thus Z 3 1029a2f. and H 1 1042a27ff., which also permit matter and the combination of form and matter as possible subjects of predication. Form may seem a less good substrate than matter, since matter is substrate to form; but Aristotle might have said, consistently with the rest of his view, that form is substrate to matter since it persists, unitary and identifiable, through material change.

conceivable that Aristotle ends by giving up the view that material objects are substances and replacing it with the view that individual essences are substances. I hope I have shown that there is a problem about distinguishing the alleged new view from the old one. On the alleged new view, a substance is not, after all, identical with a material object, which is a combination of form and matter. So the thing's form is not the same as the thing, because the thing is matter plus form. But what is the force of the "plus"? It surely cannot mean that this particular matter—for example, the water in the river just now—is itself either necessary or sufficient for the particular substance. It cannot mean that the matter is an equal partner to the form in determining what —or that—the thing is; for form is necessary and sufficient for the thing, and matter is at most necessary in a way. Perhaps a defender of the distinction would say that the "plus" just indicates that substances require some sort of matter, that the individual form cannot exist alone; but that is, as I have argued, quite compatible with the view that the form is the thing in a clear and pertinent way in which the matter is not. Perhaps the resistance to identifying a material object with its form comes of a mistaken impression that the identity of substance and form makes substances matterless; but it does not, nor does it make them accidentless. A substance *is* an essence (a form); it *has* accidents (matter).

III. THE ROAD UP AND THE ROAD DOWN: IDENTITY AT A TIME

In Chapter One I argued that Aristotle uses form as a device to individuate substances both at a time and through time. It should now be clear how the identification of substance and form permits the substance to persist through time and changes; individuation at a time is a slightly more difficult case. The problem is not that the substance changes from time to time, or even that it has many parts, but that at each moment there are many logically independent descriptions true of it. It is not immediately clear why that should be a problem, but Aristotle takes it as a serious one. At *Topics* V 4 133b21ff., for example, he worries about someone fallaciously arguing that a man is one thing and a white man another, on the grounds that being a man is one thing and being a white man is another. The problem is not merely of historical interest, since some of the reasons Aristotle gives for worrying about the identity of substances are still regarded by some as grounds for denying the identity of certain events described differently.

Aristotle's views on the status and nature of properties are far from clear and may not be entirely consistent. But there is evidence that at least sometimes when Aristotle talks about a quality or some other property, he means some substance as introduced under a description that incorporates that property. If so, then it is reasonable to suppose that an essence is just a substance as introduced under a definition or an essential term. Some passages and examples will make the point clearer and will show how the road up and the road down are and are not the same.

> Each thing should be said to be the form and insofar as it has form; the material element in its own right should never be [identified with the thing]. (Z 10 1035a7-9)

The second clause of this crucial sentence is clear, and compatible with what I have said so far about matter. The first clause is a puzzling one—Aristotle uses a difficult term, which I have translated "insofar as," which some translators render with "*qua*."

The word in question, in Greek ᾗ, is in origin the dative singular feminine of the relative pronoun; the ordinary meanings closest to the philosophical one are "where" (as a conjunction), "as," and "insofar as." Happily, Aristotle gives an explicit account of his use of the term in *Met.* K 9:

> So the actuality of what potentially is, when it is complete and actual, not *qua* itself but *qua* movable, is movement.

By *qua* I mean the following: bronze is potentially a statue, but it is not the actuality of bronze *qua* bronze that is movement. For being bronze and being a certain potency are not the same. (1065b21ff.)

It is not in virtue of being bronze that some lump of bronze changes from not being a statue to being a statue; rather, it is in virtue of its capacity to change. The "because" here is something like a logical relation, and being bronze is not a logically sufficient condition of being potentially a statue.

This passage seems to say that each thing's having a certain form is a logically sufficient condition of its being what it is. So much is suggested by the first half of the first clause, which identifies the substance with its form. But beyond that, the passage provides evidence that Aristotle countenances what might be called *qua*-entities in response to certain problems of identity.

As his use of *qua* suggests, Aristotle distinguishes entities according to their descriptions; thus an entity under a certain description is not fully identical to what would normally be considered the same entity under a different description. In effect, Aristotle makes mutual logical dependency a requirement for true identity; and the logical equivalence is the relation between the descriptions under which the putatively identical entities are individuated. If this interpretation is correct, it helps to show why Aristotle identifies a substance with its form or essence (*Met.* Z 17 1041-b4ff.) and not with its matter (Z 3 1029a26ff.), why he says a musical man is not identical with his essence, though a substance is, and men are substances (Z 6 1031a20f.), and why he says a white man is not a substance (Z 4 1030a4ff.).

The last denial is particularly good evidence for this interpretation, as it is a puzzle for nearly any other:

. . . a white man is not what a "this" is, since being a "this" is a property only of substances. So there is an essence only of those things whose description is a definition. (1030a4-7)

On its face the passage appears to say that if Socrates is white, then he is not a substance. Worse, one is left in the dark about what sort of thing could possibly have an essence; for it is not clear that there is anything of which *the* description is a definition. Surely everything has an infinite number of true descriptions, most of which are not definitions. One might say there is an essence only of that which has a definition among its descriptions, but Aristotle does not say that. Anyway, a white man would not obviously be such a thing.

Now consider the possibility that when Aristotle is talking in this passage about a white man, he means something individuated by the description "white man." For such an entity one can construct a term suggested by what Aristotle says at Z 10 1035a7-9: call the entity Callias-insofar-as-he-is-white, or Callias *qua* white. It is not by virtue of being white that Callias is a "this" and a substance, and there is no definition of Callias insofar as he is white. So when Aristotle says "white man" in this context, he means some man *qua* white. An entity called man *qua* white has only one proper description—"white man"—and that description is not a definition, at least not of the primary sort. Callias *qua* man does have a description that is a definition.

When Aristotle says a substance is identical with its essence, he means that the real Socrates is Socrates *qua* man, not Socrates *qua* white or Socrates *qua* musical. When he denies that a substance is a compound of form and matter, he means at least that Socrates *qua* man-composed-of-this-particular-matter does not have a definition, whereas Socrates *qua* man is a definable substance because the definition of "man" defines Socrates. He is not saying that Socrates is non-identical to his essence if he is white or has matter, as Z 11 1037b4-7 and some other passages might easily be taken to mean.

This interpretation shows why Aristotle denies in *Met.* Z 4 and Iota 9 that a thing is identical with any of its accidental properties. Under the usual interpretation one would not expect Aristotle to bother to deny that a substance is identical with any accidental property it has, since substances and accidents are not the same sort of thing. But that denial is not absolute: Aristotle says in *Met.* Δ 6 that (supposing Coriscus is musical) Coriscus and the musical are *accidentally one* and that (supposing he is both musical and just) the musical and the just are accidentally one while Coriscus is one in his own right. The point is that there is a weak sort of identity between Coriscus *qua* musical and Coriscus *qua* just.

It would be wrong to infer that accidentally identical items are numerically distinct, for Aristotle explicitly holds that they are not. At *Topics* I 7 103a29ff. he illustrates identity in number by saying that I may ask you to call a particular person to me by telling you the person's name or by referring to the man who is sitting down, for they are numerically identical. But elsewhere in the same work (*Top.* V 4 133b31ff.) he allows that a man and a pale man are somehow different—not simply, but in that their being is different. They are not two different items. (Cf. *Soph. El.* 22 178b39ff.)[21]

To Aristotle this distinction between full and accidental identity is more than a casual one. It has the same basis as the distinction between form and matter. In fact, I think Aristotle considers the form-matter distinction a special case of accidental identity. As is normal in accidental iden-

[21] These passages and some others are cited by Russell Dancy in "Aristotle on Substances," pp. 366ff. Dancy's diagnosis of Aristotle on identity is like my own on several points, but he is interested primarily in paronymy in the *Categories*. He cites Nicholas White's "Aristotle on Sameness and Oneness" and Fred Miller's "Did Aristotle have the Concept of Identity?" as having made some important points about the substitutivity of identity and referential opacity, and so they have; but his analysis goes beyond theirs, and so does the present one. Roughly, White holds that when Aristotle identifies A and B, he means that "A" and "B" are terms for the same thing; Miller holds that they are terms for different components of one thing. My interpretation, like Dancy's, is between those of White and Miller.

tity, at most one of the descriptions is sufficient for the other, though there are a few cases in which the matter-description is sufficient for the form-description. Most contemporary philosophers would divide the cases and deny that the form-matter relation is a case of contingent identity. As I shall argue in Chapter Four, it is important to Aristotle to assimilate accidental identity to the form-matter relation in aid of making bodily events the matter of corresponding mental events. His evidence is that they occur together but their descriptions are different and at least logically independent.

For most accidentally identical items, a significant barrier to their full identity is that they are not, or may not be, always identical. Aristotle says at *Met.* E 2 1026b31ff. that what is accidentally the case is so neither always nor for the most part. The color of the substance, like the particular matter of which it is at any given moment made, does not always attach to it; or if Coriscus is in fact always white, Coriscus *qua* man is still only accidentally identical to Coriscus *qua* white because men are not always white. And it is probable that the reason Aristotle has for denying that entities that have different definitions or are introduced by different descriptions are strongly identical is that entities thus related are not always identical. Coriscus could get a tan, and then the statement that Coriscus is white would turn false. In effect, all contexts are intentional contexts with respect to full identity; so "the white man" cannot be substituted for "Coriscus," *salva veritate*.

I do not myself approve of all this. It is incorrect to infer from the non-identity of being musical and being Coriscus that this musical item and Coriscus are less than perfectly identical. Contemporary essentialists might be more sympathetic to Aristotle's position, but they carefully restrict the view that all identity is full-time and necessary identity. Since "the white man" is presumably not a rigid designator, the transient and contingent nature of Coriscus's pallor does not disqualify the statement "Coriscus is the white man" as an identity.

To be sure, items that are identical must be always identical; that is good reason for distinguishing between a substance and its matter. But it is not good reason for distinguishing between Coriscus and the man who is white, even though Coriscus may not be white forever. Aristotle does not realize that a description can contain an implicit reference to a time because he fails to see that a statement may remain true despite time and change because it refers implicitly or explicitly to a particular time.[22]

Aristotle's position as applied to events looks more plausible: some philosophers would agree that my crooking my finger is not identical to my shooting the archduke. But there is something strange about that position too, for any reasonable defense of it is also a defense of the view that my crooking my finger is not identical to my crooking my left index finger, as on this occasion it surely is. The fact that I am crooking my left index finger is not identical to the fact that I am crooking my finger; but that just shows how facts differ from events and states. And even if that difference could not be made out, there would still be the difference between the individuation of states and that of things. Aristotle has probably done more than any other single philosopher to distinguish between states and substances, but on this point he has left some work for his successors.[23]

The device of individuating items through their descriptions solves the mystery, discussed by Aristotle in *Physics*

[22] See further Hintikka, "Time, Truth, and Knowledge." For a defense of a better version of the "life-histories principle," see David Wiggins, "Identity-Statements."

[23] Questions of event identity will come to the fore again in the discussion of psychological events and physical events, some of which Aristotle thinks are related as form and matter. His direct descendants among philosophers of mind would agree that mental events are not identically physical events, but I shall argue in Chapter Five that their criteria of event identity are unduly stiff.

III 3, of the road up and the road down, which according to Heraclitus are one and the same. The puzzle about the road is, roughly, this: the road from A to B is surely the same as the road from B to A; but how is that possible, since the road from A to B goes uphill and the road from B to A goes downhill? There are two sorts of solution: (1) If the road is considered a strip of concrete, then its going uphill from A to B, far from being incompatible with its going downhill from B to A, entails that it does. (2) If, on the other hand, the road is directionally defined, considered a sort of possible route made of but not identical with a strip of concrete, then indeed the road from A to B is not the same as the road from B to A. Aristotle seems to choose the first alternative: he says (202a20f.) the roads are one and the same, though they can be described differently. But then he goes on to do something rather different: he compares the ascent and descent (or the Thebes-Athens road and the Athens-Thebes road) to teaching and learning, which are events he now says are the same only in a way, and in another way different. Each is a necessary and sufficient condition of the other, they are not obviously separated in either time or place, but they differ in direction.

Aristotle is consciously setting high standards for identity of events, and equally stringent standards for the identity of substances, or at least roads, which would seem to be respectable artifacts. He has denied that a substance is identical with its matter on the grounds that it can persist without the matter of which it is now made; but the Thebes-Athens road cannot persist without the Athens-Thebes road. So it is not only the possibility of eventual divergence that distinguishes a substance from its matter; they are already non-identical in virtue of having different definitions. In general, Aristotle's view is that A and B are only in a limited sense identical if "A" and "B" have different definitions— or, to put it in the material mode in which Aristotle's talk about definitions is couched, if A and B have different definitions. Now "from Athens to Thebes" and "from

Thebes to Athens" are not definitions but only descriptions, as Aristotle says at the beginning of *Phys.* III 3. Aristotle will hold that the road up is not strictly identical to the road down just because the descriptions under which they are introduced are different. The road *qua* going from Athens to Thebes is only accidentally the same as the road *qua* going from Thebes to Athens.[24]

But to say that the roads are not strictly identical, or that in general a substance is not identical to any of its accidents or to its matter, may be misleading. Having said in *Topics* V 4 and *De Sophisticis Elenchis* 22 that the man and the white man are not two different things, he makes the same sort of point in the late *Metaphysics* in order to avoid the same sort of misunderstanding: the form and the matter of a particular substance are not two different things.

> . . . the proximate matter and the form are one and the same thing, one potentially and the other actually. So it is like asking what, generally, is the cause of unity and of a thing's being one; because each thing is a unity, and the potential and the actual are somehow one. (H 6 1045b17-21)

Now, although Aristotle does not hold that the form and the matter of a substance are strictly identical, in H 6 his attention is fixed on the importance of the coincidence of form and matter, and not on their non-identity. The

[24] The example shows that there may be mere accidental identity between items that, under their respective descriptions, are necessary and sufficient for each other. As one might expect if the form-matter relation is a special case of the relation of something *qua* A to itself *qua* B, the matter of some things is sufficient for the form. This would presumably be true of anything whose form is its capacity to perform certain acts, its matter being its physical structure—for example, an axe or a man. This difficulty, if that is what it is, will come up again in Chapter Three, in which I shall discuss a claim made by J. L. Ackrill in "Aristotle's Definitions of *Psuche*" that Aristotle's account of the soul is damaged by his inability to disentangle form and matter in the case of living beings.

passage attempts a final resolution of difficulties felt in Z 11, where Aristotle considers the possibility that the material object is properly an instance of the combination-universal and denies that things combined with matter and things that are one accidentally are the same as their essences. What Aristotle says in H 6 comes as an important announcement only because there may by that time be a presumption against it; he wants to make sure his readers have not concluded that Socrates and the matter of which he is just now made do not coincide at all, or that they are related as two parts of one item. They are accidentally identical. When Aristotle says that the proximate matter and the form are the same, one potentially and the other actually, or that what is potential and what is actual are in this case somehow one, he means the following: the form of the tree is what occupies this space *qua* actual tree; the matter of the tree is what occupies this space *qua* able to be a tree under certain minimal further conditions. The matter of a thing is just the thing insofar as it is made of a certain stuff, in the simplest cases; but in more complicated cases, where matter is not just stuff, the matter of a thing is the thing insofar as it has all but some property necessary and sufficient for membership in a species. (But see note 24.)

This use of *qua* has its problems, but they are problems of the sort one might well expect Aristotle to have. When Aristotle says a white man is not what a this is because a white man is not a substance, though he does believe a man is a substance, one can only take him to be saying in the material mode what would be rendered in the formal mode as: "white man" is not an essence-term because it is not a term that has a proper definition; "man" is definable in the proper way. Aristotle's statement about the white man is an instance of his habitual use of the material mode; another instance is his way of defining things rather than terms. When Aristotle says a man has a definition, there is a way to rewrite what he says into the formal mode. How can he say in the material mode that "white man" has no definition?

If two and a half millennia of Aristotelian scholarship are any indication, it is misleading to express that thought by saying that a white man cannot be defined. What I think he means can be put in the material mode least misleadingly this way: a man *qua* white has no definition. As long as it is terms and not things that are being defined, the predicate "has a definition" is applicable without problems—for example, to "man" but not properly to "white man." But if things—individuals, universals—are definable, then "has a definition" will be intentional, and so applicable to some items under certain descriptions but not under others. Thus Socrates *qua* man will be properly definable, but not Socrates *qua* white.

This interpretation suggests a way of handling a well-known Aristotelian dilemma. Aristotle says in *Met.* Z 15 and elsewhere that there is no definition of the individual. But substance is definable (Z 1 1028a31-b3, Z 5 1031a1f., and elsewhere), and the universal is not substance (Z 13 and *passim*). Socrates *qua* man is perhaps the least unsatisfactory candidate for definition under these strict conditions. "There is," Aristotle writes, "an essence only of those things whose description is a definition" (Z 4 1030a6f.). Socrates has many descriptions; Socrates *qua* man has only one, and that is a definition. To put it another (and better) way, Socrates has a definition *qua* man; so he does not have a definition of his own, which distinguishes him from other men. There is some justification for this way of dealing with the problem: the definition states what is true of Socrates for as long as he exists, no matter what happens to him, no matter how he may change. That is what one might expect a definition to do, if one is willing to allow that definitions apply not primarily to linguistic items but to non-linguistic items—substances or universals, for example—and that in consequence such an item will typically be definable under some descriptions but not under others. Thus Socrates is after all definable because he is definable *qua* man; and it is Socrates *qua* man (rather than, say, Socrates *qua* white or *qua* this lump of flesh) that is permanently and therefore properly identical to Socrates and to the essence of Socrates.

The definability of substance gives rise to the sort of inconsistent triad that turned up in the case of knowability; in both cases there must be some compromise of the principle that only what is universal and permanent can be known or defined. Socrates *qua* man is the best—but clearly imperfect—solution to both problems. Socrates can be known just in the sense that his essence can be known. "To know a thing is to know its essence" (Z 6 1031b20f.—this is part of Aristotle's evidence for saying that a thing is identical to its essence).

In his early metaphysical writings (*Met.* M 9-10, for example) Aristotle allows that knowledge is actualized in sensible apprehension of particulars, which are perceived to be of some sort (thus *Posterior Analytics* I 31 and II 19). Therefore the individual is primarily knowable in that actuality is standardly prior to potency. But there is no science of the individual (see *Met.* A 1); that is, medicine investigates not what is healthy for Socrates or Callias but what is healthy for a certain sort of person, or a certain condition. This is not to suggest that Socrates cannot be cured by the science of medicine; instead, the doctor considers him apart from the properties he has that are irrelevant to the treatment of his ailment. In knowing what is wrong with a particular patient and knowing what to do about it, the doctor does not wholly know the patient; he knows that patient only under some medically pertinent description.

All knowing of individuals must be knowing them under one or more descriptions, and such knowing is the actualization of knowledge of general truths about individuals of that description. Accidental and material predicates of individuals are or can be transitory with respect to the substance of which they are true (see Z 15 1040a3; cf. *Rhet.* I 2 1356b31f.). So to know Socrates as being white or as being fat is to know him unreliably, for he may continue to exist without being white or fat; but to know him as a man is to know him as what he must always be. Of all the universals of which he is an instance, which provide opportunities for knowledge because he is an instance of them, there is only one that he instantiates reliably, in the sense that his being an instance of it is a necessary and sufficient condition of his existence. Thus it is Socrates *qua* man that is primarily knowable. Primarily knowable, but not perfectly: Socrates *qua* man is not eternal, as the object of genuine knowledge ought to be.

One may wish Aristotle had thought of propositions rather than things and universals as knowables. Then, on his terms, the proposition "Socrates is a man" would be more knowable than "Socrates is white" because it is true for as long as there is Socrates to predicate anything of. But even in that case there will be problems. It is not clear how one can know that this is Socrates, rather than Callias, or how our actualized knowledge about the perceived individual Socrates can be any more reliable than our identification of him. Given that we know a thing only when we know its essence, how can we know whose essence this essence is? One cannot knowingly individuate particular essences, if what individuates them is precisely what is not knowable. One cannot know *this* essence, as opposed to *that* one in the same species.

IV. A DIFFICULTY

If a substance is a form, then we might expect that one-ness in form is coextensive with oneness in number; but this clearly cannot always be the case. Normally Aristotle regards two items in the same species as the same in form but different in number because their matter is different (*Met.* Z 8 1035a5-8). But Aristotle does not have adequate criteria for the identity of things considered at widely different times in what may or may not be their common career. These items, which do not always have the same matter all their lives, are identical if they have numerically the same form; but Aristotle gives no independent way of deciding under what circumstances items with different matter have numerically the same form. How can one identify an essence without first identifying the thing whose essence it is?

Aristotle does not satisfactorily answer this question. He ought to say that unity over time requires some sort of continuity of form through time just as the unity of a thing at a particular time requires continuity of matter in space— the latter being a point of which he makes much in *Met.* Δ 6 1016b31 ff. What that requires is a way of tracing through time, one which guarantees that from each moment of time to the next the thing can be seen to persist because (among other things) any change in it, particularly any change in space, comes about gradually. Form helps us perform this task: a necessary condition of persistence is that the gradually changing matter have or constitute a particular form at each moment, with no gaps. But Aristotle does not say that form has this function, even though it is a position that fits well with his statements about rivers and other things. He is left with the necessity of saying what sort of sameness or oneness connects A at time t_1 with A at time t_2 so that they are the same thing, or the same in number. What sort of similarity between these entities counts as identity? The only answer he gives is sameness in form, and that does not tell you which of these mighty oaks is identical to the sapling you planted many years ago. Each is identical in form to the sapling; neither, probably, is identical in matter to it. For an oak to survive from seed through sapling to maturity requires the persistence of a particular form. But how are we to know which of these oaks has or is the right particular form? The most natural way might be to seek some connection through time that holds in one case but not the other.[25]

---

[25] A clever, but in my opinion mistaken, interpretation of Aristotle on continuity through time is Nicholas White's (in "Aristotle on Sameness and Oneness," 194f.): "He is claiming a connection between a thing's having a form and its having a career which is in some

In dealing with the identity of movements in *Physics* V 4, Aristotle stipulates that for a movement to be one it must keep going continuously through a stretch of time and not stop and then start again, for that would make it two movements; and certain other requirements suggest that spatial as well as temporal discontinuity is excluded. Here he has the beginning of a useful principle of the continuity and therefore identity of substance through time: he can require that the particular form and hence the particular substance trace an unbroken path through space and time, with no gaps or interruptions. One might then think of each thing as a four-dimensional object, a river of matter flowing through time and space. But Aristotle does not relate substances and time in this way; in particular, he does not use tenseless verbs to solve apparent difficulties about how something can have different and even incompatible properties at different times.[26] If he were willing to countenance logically tenseless verbs and four-dimensional objects, then he could rationally say that there is just no contradiction in Coriscus being thin at time t_1 and fat at time t_2 while remaining the same person from one time to the next. Instead, Aristotle permits Coriscus$_1$ and Coriscus$_2$ to be numerically

---

sense unitary, which cannot be divided up into any natural parts. . . . Aristotle is often ready to think of the form of a thing, especially a living thing, as its characteristic way of behaving, of going on, *in time*, and not just its 'shape' at a given instant." At *Met.* Iota 1 1052a22ff., which White cites in support of his interpretation, Aristotle says that for a thing to be a proper substance it must have motion. Aristotle means by that what he says at *Met.* Δ 6 1016a5f.: for a thing to be continuous its movement must be one and indivisible. This just means that a thing literally holds together just in case when part of it moves we may say the thing itself is moving. In the first chapter of Book I, Aristotle is seeking criteria of physical continuity at a time, not through a stretch of time, and chooses identity of motion as a way to make his point. In any case, when a sort of behavior is essential to a thing, it is the behavior characteristic of a species, not of a particular member of it.

[26] See again Hintikka, "Time, Truth, and Knowledge."

identical even though they do not weigh the same, as though imperfect identity were identity enough. This is, I think, unduly fastidious, as though one were to deny perfect identity to Coriscus because his nose is not the same color as his feet.[27]

For all its difficulties, Aristotle's view of a world populated by substances that are identical with their essences provides the basis of a subtle and plausible theory of the mind; and it is to the application of the ontological theory to psychology that I now turn. Persons are substances; the soul is the form of the living body; living bodies are therefore souls. It follows that personal identity through time is a special case of bodily continuity. But it is only the body *qua* living that deserves to be called the body; the continuity of what remains after death is only temporarily accidentally

[27] Peter Geach, who for various reasons rejects four-dimensional entities, attacks the issue by relativizing identity (in *Reference and Generality* and elsewhere). For this case he might say that Coriscus₁ is the same man as Coriscus₂ but not the same lump of flesh. I gather this is not the same as saying that Coriscus₁ and Coriscus₂ are the same in species but different in weight. The latter is the sort of thing Aristotle says about non-identical things, and in this context it raises the problem I think Aristotle really has: namely, that in treating continuity he is wrong in making sameness of species suffice for numerical sameness without further explanation. At one point Aristotle does seem, like Geach, to relativize identity in a context having nothing to do with time. He says at *Met.* Δ 6 1016a14ff. that a bent line is both one and not one; this could only mean that the lines are the same *qua* line but different *qua* straight line. On the whole, Aristotle's strategy is rather to get clear first on just what it is—the line, or the straight line, or the substance, or the matter—that is being identified with what, rather than to import unclarity into the identity sign. When one says that *this* is identical to *that*, one must first be clear on what *this* is; and in the primary sort of case, it is the form that is *this*. See further the first few pages of David Wiggins's *Identity*, from which I have profited on this and other topics. I cannot discuss the controversy in detail, but it is worth noting that Geach's position is extensively defended, and not just a crude mistake. In fact, it rests finally on a view of substance and time that has much in common with Aristotle's.

identical with the soul, and therefore with the person. The body *qua* lifeless flesh and bones is mere matter.

Clearly the soul is not related to the body as an independent substance, as the Platonists and the Cartesians have supposed; instead, the relation is identity. How the engine of the organism can be its essence is a long and difficult story, but a rewarding one. The heart of it lies in Aristotle's account of the accidental identity of psychological events with their accompanying physical events, which are related as the road up and the road down, or as form and matter. The theory is economical enough to be a kind of materialism, but far richer than anything dreamt of in Democritus's philosophy.

Chapter Three

CONTINUITY AND PERSONAL IDENTITY

THE form-matter relation may seem ill suited to encompass the relation between the mind and the body; but if it is correctly understood, it works rather well. This chapter will concentrate on how it works as a basis for solution of what is now called the problem of personal identity. Form is, after all, a subtle notion: the form of something is just its shape only in those few simple cases in which it is the shape of a substance that makes it what it is. Aristotle's discussion of the cases, more common but less well suited to introductory philosophical exposition, in which the notion of form or essence is more complicated and more adequate prepares one for his exposition of the way in which the soul is the essence of the human being (Section I). His discussion does raise a problem, in that he stretches the form-matter relation to a point at which form and matter are logically inextricable; but that will appear an inconvenience rather than a catastrophe to one who understands Aristotle's views about identity, and in particular about the accidental identity with itself of an item as introduced under multiple logically independent descriptions (Section II). Once the role of the soul as form of the body is understood —that is, once it is understood that the body is not mere matter but a substance—it becomes clear that Aristotle is offering a reasonable solution to the problem of personal identity, namely, a version of the body criterion. Aristotle's view of what counts as bodily continuity is (at any rate, implicitly) subtle and detailed enough to get around at least one plausible standard objection to the criterion (Section III), and his view is shared and supported in some good recent work on the nature and the identity-conditions of the person (Section IV). In the end, however, Aristotle's inattention to some special features of mental states makes it impossible for him to deal with certain problems about his altogether too neat way of individuating persons both through time and at a time (Section V). But it is encouraging to see that Aristotle is aware of some vexed questions about the unity of the self, which may be a substance but certainly is a uniquely complex one (Section VI).

In discussions about persons in this chapter and elsewhere, I shall normally treat the words "soul" and "mind" as synonyms. *Psyche* (soul) is the more general term, because it can be extended to animals and plants; moreover, some events that on Aristotle's terms are events of a human soul are not mental events. But the relative breadth of Aristotle's concept of the soul is not a problem so long as the discussion is confined to the faculties and events that Aristotle attributes to the human soul and that we consider mental. Perhaps this is one of those points at which one can hardly decide whether philosophers are defining different things or giving different accounts of the same thing. If the distinction makes any sense at all, then many contemporary philosophers and Aristotle are doing the latter. Indeed, it will turn out that their respective accounts of the soul or mind are after all not radically different.

I. THE SOUL AS A DIFFERENTIA

Aristotle's doctrine that the soul is to the body as form is to substance does require considerable stretching of the concept of form, until it is only distantly related to the simple formulas and examples by which it is introduced. But this stretching is a gradual process, for the most part not done in order to shoehorn the soul into Aristotle's picture of the world. On the contrary, within the boundaries of the *Metaphysics* Aristotle gradually develops a notion of form— or essence, which, as part of the process, he comes to regard as the same as form (see, for example, *Met.* Z 10 1035b14-16, which is about the soul)—that is quite ready for the demands to be made on it by Aristotle's analysis of the substance called man. This section, which is in part a review of the first two chapters, briefly traces that development to an account of essence not only useful to Aristotle's psychology but good enough to be admired for its own sake.

In the simplest cases the form of a substance is its shape: the near-synonymy of the Greek words *eidos* and *morphē* on their most ordinary interpretations is not ignored in Aristotle's most rudimentary discussions of *ousia*, whose definition in *Met.* Δ 8 and mention in many other places include the words "form and shape" (*eidos kai morphē*). There are some clear cases in which the shape of something makes it what it is: the bronze statue is the most familiar example.[1] A shape-predicate may make it possible to divide the world or some part of it into individual, countable objects, in somewhat the way in which a cookie-cutter divides a quantity of dough into a certain number of cookies. This is the sort of dividing that a color-predicate, for example, does not do. Less clearly a simple object can often be said to remain what it is so long as it retains its shape. If it is reduced irretrievably to pieces, one is inclined to say that it no longer exists, though the material of which the object is formed remains. Of course shape can take on all importance if one believes (as Democritus does: see *Met.* H 2 *ad init.*) that everything there is is made up of the same sort of matter.

But despite the recurrence of simple-minded examples like the bronze statue, Aristotle recognizes that an essential predicate, a genuine sortal universal and a guarantor of continuity, is not always a shape. There are some things whose criteria for continued existence through time involve more than just retaining a certain shape, and there are some things that cannot be individuated by their shape alone.

[1] But see Chapter Two, note 16.

Aristotle, whose criteria for continued existence are sometimes very rigid, thinks thresholds and ice are examples of
the former sort of thing; and he thinks persons are examples
of both sorts.

In *Met.* H 2 Aristotle is interested in the variety of sorts of
predicate that could be essential predicates. Part of what
makes Aristotle's presentation in H 2 a bit odd is that he
explicitly states that he is talking about artificial rather
than genuine substances (1043a4); but since what he says
is supposed to apply by analogy to ordinary substances,
the reader can ignore the warning at least for the time being.
There are, Aristotle claims (1042b15), many differentiae;
that is, there are many ways in which something can be
said of matter in such a way as to mark out a substance
through the appropriate species. For instance, you can say
that a certain kind (or kinds) of matter is (constitutes)
honey-water because it is mixed in a certain way; or a
bundle because it is bound together in a certain way; or a
threshold or lintel because it is placed in a certain position;
or dinner because it is eaten at a certain time. Aristotle draws
the dubious conclusion that the word "is" has as many
paraphrases as there are different sorts of differentia and
therefore things; for example, the being of a threshold is
that it is situated in a certain way, and the being of ice is
that it is solidified. So when ice melts, it ceases to exist, as
does a threshold removed from its place before the door.

It sounds reasonable to say that a dead man or melted
ice is no more, but that a threshold taken out of position
is no more is less clear. Without denying that this piece of
wood is a threshold, one might still not regard such an identification of it as essential. On the other hand, if someone were
to chop the threshold into hundreds of tiny pieces, it would
clearly be true that it no longer existed, even if the pieces
lay before the door.

There are not many things whose spatial or temporal
position is clearly essential to them. That is why it might
seem odd to have to deny that the form and the matter of

something like a threshold are different: surely, some people would be tempted to say, the threshold is identically this piece of wood. But Aristotle has on his side the possibility that the two have different life-histories and so are related as Roosevelt Boulevard and U.S. Route 1. (The Boulevard coincides for its entire length with Route 1, but not vice versa.) Aristotle does just that with thresholds, and he does something like it with roads, as the previous chapter indicates.[2]

Aristotle continues with a suggestion for yet another sort of differentia, a complex one: some things, like the human hand or foot, are defined by all the differentiae just mentioned, in that some parts of them are mixed, others blended, others bound, others solidified, etc.

What other sorts of differentia are there? Aristotle mentions quantity-differentiae, shape again (but using the word *schēma* rather than *morphē*, which he uses in the general sense near the end of the chapter; it seems clear that in 1042b35 he is talking about the *schēma* of the sort characteristic of geometrical figures), and mixture again. Most importantly, Aristotle suggests that some differentiae and therefore definitions make reference to purpose (1043a9). Then he again defines a house, this time making the differentia "a receptacle to shelter chattels and living beings" and thereby bringing purpose explicitly into the differentia—or actuality (*energeia*), as he now calls it—of an artifact.

At the beginning of chapter 3 Aristotle forges the link between metaphysics and the philosophy of mind by using

[2] He does not do it with heavenly bodies. In *Met.* Z 15 he considers and rejects the possibility of defining the sun by its orbit. In addition to the indefinability of the individual, the orbit is neither a necessary nor sufficient condition of the sun's being the sun. "Sun" is a proper name, not like "Mayor." This probably fits most people's intuitions; and on questions of this sort intuitions are often the best guides we have available. What would Aristotle say about the Morning Star and the Evening Star? I speculate—nothing more definite is possible—that he would have said they are accidentally identical, like the musical Coriscus and the just Coriscus.

the soul as an example of such an *energeia*. How is it supposed to fit the classifications of chapter 2? Aristotle means that the soul makes a body a human being in the way in which (to take two examples from H 2) blending makes certain ingredients honey-water or position makes a piece of wood a threshold. Now the soul is not blending or position, nor is it any obvious combination of any of the common sorts of differentia, as hand and foot are said to be. Aristotle does not say here precisely what sort of differentia soul is. In *De Anima* he makes himself clearer.

In *De An.* II 1 Aristotle states that soul is substance as form or actuality is.[3] But in cases in which the essence of a thing involves what it does, one must distinguish between its first and second actualities: the second is its actually doing it; the first, properly identified with the essence, is its ability to do it. The soul is a first actuality, since it does not disappear when one is asleep or otherwise inactive. In that chapter Aristotle compares a person to an axe, whose second actuality is cutting, as seeing is the second actuality of the eye and being awake (that is, conscious) is of the person. Each first actuality is a potency with respect to the activity characteristic of that sort of thing. A house, one of Aristotle's examples in *Met.* H, is defined by its use but remains a house even when nobody is living in it. The soul is what makes the person act in a way characteristic of persons.[4]

A part of the body is to be defined by reference to its function, or the set of actions by which it characteristically contributes to the person (see *Met.* Z 10 1035b16-18). The soul too is to be defined by its function; but that function

---

[3] Chapter Four will treat in more detail the first two chapters of *De Anima* and the definition of soul they contain.

[4] The word "makes" in this sentence is ambiguous, for it could refer to a formal "cause" or an efficient one. Both sorts of "cause" are involved, since the relation between the soul and human activity is both causal and logical, the soul being by definition what causes human activity. I shall discuss this topic in Chapter Four.

will be the function of the whole person, not of a contributing part of the person: "The function (*ergon*) of man is the activity of the soul in accordance with *logos*, or anyway not without it" (*Nicomachean Ethics* I 7 1098a7f.). So there is a function of man, just as there is a function of each part of the human body, somewhat as there is a function of the house and the axe. The function of the man is the characteristically reasonable activity (*energeia* is often used in this sense) of his soul; so his capacity for such activities is his soul.

A number of details must be noted.

First, *energeia* usually means actuality rather than activity in *Met.* H. In that sense of the word, which in the context is interchangeable with *diaphora* (differentia), the soul is an *energeia*. In the stronger sense of *energeia* in the passage from the *Ethics*, the soul is the capacity or potency corresponding to the actual function or *energeia* of the person.

As for the soul as mentioned in the *Ethics*: when Aristotle talks about an activity of the soul here, he is as much talking about an activity of the person; but at least part of the point he wants to make is that human as opposed to mere animal activity need not be gross physical activity in the ordinary sense—men can think and act according to reason, as animals cannot. In fact, men have a part of their soul (*nous*, usually translated "reason," sometimes "mind," "thought," or "intuition") that Aristotle thinks may in some way not be connected with the body. Hence, in the context of defining the human being, by implicit contrast with every other kind of living being, Aristotle will emphasize capacities we normally call mental when he is thinking of the human rather than the animal soul.[5]

---

[5] Aristotle's arguments, mainly in *De Anima* III, for a faculty of the soul separate from the body seem to pose a problem for my view of personal identity as a special case of substantial identity for Aristotle. If there is a problem, it is a problem with Aristotle's definition of the soul and not with my interpretation of that definition. I

Note, finally, that not just any old performance by a hand or its owner counts as fulfilling its *ergon*. There are some things hands are not supposed to do. As Aristotle goes on to say in *Nic. Eth.* I 7, just below the passage quoted, the standard for definition is that which performs excellently: we must look to the expert harpist, not the hack.[6]

It is now generally clear what it means to say that Aristotle considers the soul to be that which, as a formal "cause," makes a man a man in the same general way as a certain feature makes an axe an axe or a threshold a threshold. He

---

shall show in Chapter Six that the definition is not threatened, as Aristotle thinks it is, by the special nature of characteristically human thought and action. In particular, the function that the disembodied faculty of reason could least well serve would be that of individuating persons, as it is itself not individual.

[6] I have said little about the teleological aspect of form; and although I do not think it is the most interesting aspect of form from our point of view, it is important enough from Aristotle's viewpoint that we should at least not ignore it. As *Met.* H 3 and related passages indicate, the purpose of something is often at least part of its definition. This is clearest in the case of artifacts, which are built for some purpose extraneous to themselves according to the deliberation of the manufacturer; but it is no less importantly true in the case of natural substances, which by growing approach their actuality as one would approach a goal, except that there is no literal deliberation in such growth. This suggests, what there is otherwise reason to believe, that persons and therefore their souls are most correctly defined by reference to the perfect fulfillment of their potency, and it helps explain the priority relations between a person and his parts: as Z 10-11 show, such items as hands are what they are insofar as they contribute to the achievement of (not their own goals but) the state which is definitive of the substance and towards which the substance strives—though not, except perhaps in the case of man, deliberately. So Aristotle's view of the best possible life as contemplative inevitably affects his description and definition of the soul; and in assessing the philosophical merit of his conception of the soul, one may accordingly have some reason to take Aristotle seriously as saying that the soul is *whatever* is characteristic of persons rather than to lay emphasis on what he says about what is in fact characteristic of persons.

has worked out what predicate must be true of the appropriate sort of matter in order for the matter to constitute a man, and he is suggesting what it is that must persist in order for it to be possible to say that this person (rather than this flesh and bones or something else) is the same as that was; that is, Aristotle is saying what goes into the "this" that picks out a person. His language and procedure show that the problem of identity through time, taken into a new and more difficult area, becomes the problem of personal identity. Aristotle is therefore a precursor of those contemporary philosophers who believe that the problem of personal identity is a special case of the problem of spatio-temporal continuity.

According to Aristotle and his modern successors, personal identity and continuity are a matter of bodily identity and continuity. A person is a body. But Aristotle makes clear by his careful discussion of essential predicates that the continuity of a material substance through space and time requires that at each moment it have, and indeed be, a particular essence. As Chapter One showed, Aristotle denies that matter is a "this," that it can be properly referred to. For the same sort of reason, one cannot attribute continuity to anything but essence when one is talking about material objects. So in order to talk about continuity, one must first define the continuant and thus set the conditions of its continuity. Aristotle defines a body—not a corpse, but a genuine *and therefore live* body—by a very full specification of the functions it can perform. According to *De Interpretatione* 11 21a21-23, a dead man is a man in name only; and at various points Aristotle rules that bodily parts are not bodily parts unless they are alive. The same must be true of the body, which is a substance *par excellence*, as Aristotle notes at *De An.* II 1 412a11f. Just as the axe is no more and is not what my father gave me three years ago if it is blunted beyond repair, so Fenwick's living body is no more and is not what Fenwick's mother produced thirty years ago if it is dead. This corpse is not only no longer Fenwick; it is not the body it was an hour ago, when Fenwick was alive.[7]

This much is clear: the chief difficulty for the bodily criterion of personal identity would seem to be that the body can go on existing (as a corpse) after the person has stopped existing. This is not a problem for Aristotle. He can say that if the body is dead, it is no longer a body; it no longer exists. And this seems a reasonable position. To repeat: talk of continued existence must make reference to a form. In the case of the body, that form has a name. It is called the soul. If it persists, so does the body, and vice versa.

II. A PROBLEM: THE LOGICAL RELATION BETWEEN SOUL AND BODY

The soul is the form or first actuality of a natural body potentially having life, Aristotle says (*De An.* II 1 412a20f., 27f.); and in the same chapter (b5f.) he says it is the first actuality of a natural body that has organs. So a person is a (living) body whose identity remains intact through time as long as the soul (the form or essence) does—that is, as long as the body continues to meet the criteria for personhood and does not suddenly undergo any radical or total change in matter. My aim is to show that this is a reasonable view.

There is, however, as J. L. Ackrill has noted,[8] a problem about how Aristotle expresses the view. Ackrill argues that Aristotle does not and cannot find any way of talking about the soul and the body as distinct from each other. According to Ackrill, the contrast between form and matter makes good sense only if one can conceive of the matter in question as being able to exist in the absence of the form; but

---

[7] For an illuminating treatment of this and other topics touched on in this section, see G.E.L. Owen, "Aristotle on the Snares of Ontology."

[8] In "Aristotle's Definitions of *Psuche*," cited in Chapter Two, note 24.

on Aristotle's account one cannot conceive of the matter in question—in this case, the body and its organs—without its form. The person is, one might suppose, a form with some matter; the soul is the form, the body the matter. But if a corpse is a human body in name only, then the body is not the matter of the person but is instead identical with the person: the criteria of existence, identity, and persistence are the same for each. Nor can Aristotle solve this problem just by stipulating that flesh and bones are the matter of the person; for even they qualify as flesh and bones just in virtue of their role in the economy of the organism. The criticism deserves some discussion, not least because what Ackrill says is largely true. The question is, does the truth in Ackrill's account imply the uselessness of Aristotle's? I think not.

To begin with, for whatever it may be worth in defense of Aristotle, there are too many concepts available for the situation; Aristotle does not need both the concept of person and that of human body. And there is a similar inflation on the other end: as David Wiggins notes,[9] if the form axe makes something an axe, the form soul should make something not a man but a soul. Wiggins concludes that "for Kallias then, *psyche* and *man* must come to the same. . . . [Aristotle must] give up speaking of Kallias *having* a soul. He is one. (Cp. *Met.* 1037a9)." Part of the confusion must surely be the result of the ontological extravagance Aristotle finds in ordinary speech and traditional psychology, which are for the most part dualistic. Aristotle wants to reduce the status of the soul from independent entity to form of a substance; so he finds himself saddled with a separate noun where there is no separate entity for it to denote, and therefore with the only form in his ontology that has its own name.

I agree with Wiggins against Ackrill that a person is the same as his soul, because I think it is Aristotle's view that

[9] *Identity*, p. 76, n. 58.

a thing is identical with its form.[10] To be sure, Aristotle denies that the soul is identical with any sort of body (414a20); but his more careful statement of the relation between soul and body is this passage in the first chapter:

> One must not ask whether soul and body are one, any more than whether the wax and the shape of it are one, or generally whether the matter of the thing is the same as that whose matter it is; for "one" and "be" are said in many ways, of which the actuality is primary. (412b6-9)[11]

Although the relation between a particular form and a particular bit of matter is not precisely strong identity, Aristotle is not willing to rule out all sorts of identity for this case. It is a case of accidental identity, or coincidence, which does allow that a form may be the same as a piece of matter in the same way as a musical person may be the same as a white person. One thing may be denoted by alternative descriptions, in Aristotle's view; but a thing under different descriptions is one thing only in the accidental sense.

Now the relation between soul and body is not a case of the relation between form and matter: the body is strictly speaking not matter, since every real body is alive. There is no difference between the existence of a body and that of a person; and I believe, against Wiggins, that the body and the person have identical principles of individuation. But Aristotle does frequently, and confusingly, treat the body

[10] Ackrill does not believe this is Aristotle's considered view. See "Aristotle's Definitions of *Psuche*," esp. p. 122.

[11] It is at least conceivable that a more accurate translation would have Aristotle saying that one *need* not ask whether soul and body are one. Even so, I think the point of the passage would be that either an affirmative or a negative answer would be an oversimplification. Aristotle has in mind the point made in the famous passage at the end of *Met.* H 6, that form and matter are (somehow) identical. The question presented in that chapter is, what unites the form and the matter of a substance? The question incorrectly presupposes a sort of non-identity that does not hold between them in the first place.

as matter. Moreover, a problem remains even if we give up talking about the body as matter and talk instead of flesh and bones as the matter of the person, because Aristotle defines flesh and bones too by their contributions to the life of the organism and as therefore no longer really flesh and bones when they are parts of what is dead (Ackrill refers to *Mete.* IV 12 390a14f. and *Gen. et Corr.* I 5 321b28-32).[12] No doubt it is a mistake for Aristotle to tie the definition of the organ quite so tightly to that of the organism; as Ackrill suggests,[13] that a carburetor removed from an engine cannot inject fuel hardly proves that it is not then a carburetor.

Ackrill correctly identifies some of the sources of Aristotle's difficulty. For one thing, the artifacts that make the best introductory examples of matter with form have components or materials that last throughout the lifetimes of the substances and possibly thereafter as well. But in true substances, living things, the material is often transformed by chemical or biological operations so that it has quite different characteristics in its informed condition; so one is rather at a loss to point out what counts as the matter in such a case. Flesh and bones are like that: they have in themselves emergent characteristics that can be explained only by some reference to the final, informed state they achieve. There is no independently identifiable stuff that underlies the process from beginning to end and beyond. One might say that the four elements underlie the process, but they lack the required feature of being potentially the thing they constitute: Aristotle clearly says earth is not potentially a man (*Met.* Θ 7, 1049a1-16);[14] and the soulless body is not potentially alive (*De An.* II 1 412b25-27).[15]

A related problem is that, in many cases other than the simplest ones, the essence of the thing turns out to be its ability to perform certain sorts of action, as in the case of the person. If the form is the functional capacity, then the shape and structure will be part of the matter; and it would

[12] "Aristotle's Definitions of *Psuche*," p. 129.
[13] *Ibid.*, p. 128.   [14] *Ibid.*, pp. 130f.   [15] *Ibid.*, p. 132.

seem to follow that the existence of this sort of matter is a sufficient condition of the existence of the form too, since the functional ability is a consequence of the materials and structure of the thing.

Recall that *Met.* H has it that the shape and structure of the substance or quasi-substance are not in every case its form, that instead the role of form or essence may be played by location or time or some other property normally considered accidental. But in most such cases it is possible for all the material or accidental properties to be present while form is absent; so although these cases of form and matter do not fit the usual pattern of structure and stuff, they do not raise the problem of the matter being a sufficient condition of the substance. Here, as generally elsewhere, it seems to be characteristic of matter that it falls short of substance: that is how in the threshold case the structure of the thing can be part of the matter. But there is one case, by now familiar, in which, without problems, matter is sufficient for substance.

The discussion of the road up and the road down (Chapter Two, Section III) showed that Aristotle is willing to distinguish two entities, which he calls only accidentally identical to each other, by virtue of the fact that there are at least two different descriptions through which it/they can be identified. What is important about this example for present purposes is that he is holding out for two quasi-entities, the road *qua* going up and the road *qua* coming down, and for only accidental identity even though each entity is a necessary and sufficient condition for the other. A long strip of packed-down dirt or some other hard surface, which might seem to be the matter of a directionally defined road, is in fact a sufficient as well as necessary condition of two roads defined that way. Chapter Two has shown that the relation between form and matter is in effect a special case of the relation between accidentally identical entities determined through two compatible descriptions—one of them, in this case, the essential description, the one that will remain in force for exactly as long as the substance abides through time. But sometimes a non-essential description turns out to imply an essential one. This happens in the case of roads; it happens in the case of bodies and persons too. It is not fatal.

Form is not in general entirely independent of matter. Form puts certain demands on matter in all but such simple cases as the bronze disc, where form and matter are as independent as their crude names suggest they ought to be. You cannot make a house out of porridge, or breakfast of bricks; and natural substances have certain required components and materials too. It should not be surprising that, particularly in those cases in which the essential description is not merely a description of the structure of the thing, the demands made on the matter by the form may be so severe as to render the matter a sufficient condition of the form. For if you want to define some sort of thing by what it can do, you will probably consign everything else about it to its matter, and the latter may include enough to be a sufficient condition of its ability to do what it can do. That is what happens in the case of the person: he is defined by his psychological abilities, and the machinery that makes them possible is regarded as the matter.

It is only a minor misfortune that in these cases there is no description that captures just the proximate matter of the substance. The important things are that Aristotle is simply giving two descriptions that may seem at first glance not to imply each other but in fact turn out to do so, and that a person and his actions may be described in various ways that may or may not reduce to or imply each other.

This is the answer to Ackrill's problem. He believes form and matter must be logically independent in order to be really useful concepts; but once it is understood that the relation between the form of something and its matter is just the relation of a thing considered under one description to the same thing considered under another that may or may not imply the first but is always compatible with it, then the mystery of how form and matter are (and are not) the same is dispelled, and their independence is not impor-

tant.[16] Moreover, an understanding of Aristotle's unreliable
and half-conscious tendency to identify and distinguish
through descriptions will help lay to rest Ackrill's worries
about how a body can be a soul; for any substance is something considered under an essential description, and an essence too is something considered under an essential description.

Chapter Four will argue that Aristotle seems to permit—
indeed, perhaps even require—the matter of an event, including a psychological event, to be at least a causally sufficient condition of the form of the event. So he is a kind
of materialist. But then how will the matter and the form
differ? As in the case of the matter and the form of the
person, there will be one item variously described; but in
the case of the mental event, there will be a difference in
the ways in which it is explained, and that difference will
constitute the difference between the form and matter of
the event—that is, the event described and explained by the
dialectician or, on the other hand, by the natural scientist.
I shall argue that Aristotle divides events as he does substances into aspects that are not in the strongest sense identical, but of which he will not flatly deny identity. There,
as in the case of substances, he has not developed a fully
adequate notion of contingent identity and so says that one
ought not to ask whether the form and the matter are the
same, even when each is sufficient for the other.

III. AN ARISTOTELIAN DEFENSE OF
THE BODILY CRITERION OF IDENTITY

In making the soul the principle of individuation and
continuity for the living body, Aristotle seems to bypass

---

[16] To be sure, this mystery gives way to that of contingent identity,
about which so much controversy remains that one has no right to be
patronizing towards Aristotle. But Aristotle was surely mistaken in
treating contingent identity and the form-matter relation so nearly
alike.

serious consideration of the mental and its somewhat mysterious nature as a problem in personal identity.[17] He treats personal identity as a special case of spatio-temporal continuity in making a person a substance (with, therefore, form and matter) with standard conditions for continued existence: the live human body remains the same substance and therefore the same person as long as it meets the persistence conditions implied by its being a member of the species man, since identity is tied to species. If this body stops being a man—or, more properly, if this piece of matter stops being a body—it is dead, and there is no soul to it any longer, and the person is dead and is no more. As long as this body continues to exist, this man—the same man—continues as well.

Aristotle considers neither the possibility that a body might switch minds and therefore house distinct persons at different times nor the possibility that a mind might switch bodies. If the soul is, as Aristotle does not believe it is, an immaterial substance causally related to a body, then there would be nothing logically strange about its being causally related now to one body, now to another. What might count as evidence that a switch of this sort has taken place? The best evidence would be that a certain body undergoes a radical change in personality, memory reports, intelligence, and other mental features, while a second body takes on the features the first body had until this time. On Aristotle's view the first body goes right on being the same person, and so does the second body. For him it is as close as anything can be to a logical impossibility that a body could switch souls.

Two questions press. First, can Aristotle's bodily criterion of personal identity be defended? Second, does Aristotle himself give any signs of understanding what the problems are? I shall try to answer both questions together, in this way: Aristotle's position is defensible, and Aristotle himself makes some remarks that can be used in his own defense;

[17] I shall say more in the fifth chapter about Aristotle's rather thin treatment of these problems.

but the defense finally fails under the weight of considerations of which Aristotle himself is to some small extent aware. I want first to discuss some apparent difficulties with the bodily criterion of identity and then show how these difficulties can be evaded. Next I shall present some difficulties that Aristotle cannot escape, but along with them some accommodations Aristotle seems to make to a conception of the soul of which he might have been thought to be quite ignorant.

There is a certain sort of objection to the bodily criterion of personal identity to which Aristotle can give a firm and convincing reply. It is not the only sort of objection, but it is important in that the story it tells is a plausible one, which does not require a strenuous effort of the imagination. Sydney Shoemaker[18] offers us a puzzle about an unfortunate operation. In delicate surgery two men, Robinson and Brown, both have their brains removed from their skulls. An inept intern switches the brains, so that Robinson's body gets Brown's brain and vice versa. Then only the man with Robinson's body and Brown's brain survives, and he acts and thinks and remembers as Brown. Surely we should be inclined "to say that while Brownson has Robinson's body he is actually Brown. But if we did say this we certainly would not be using bodily identity as our criterion of personal identity. To be sure, we are supposing Brownson to have *part* of Brown's body, namely his brain. But it would be absurd to suggest that brain identity is our criterion of personal identity." This argument against the bodily criterion and, in effect, in favor of a criterion that takes into account memory and other mental properties and capacities as individuators of persons is especially attractive because it involves a certain amount of explanation of how Brownson has—let us say—Brown's mind, and because that explanation does not require any Cartesian assumptions about the mind being distinct from the body and causally

[18] *Self-Knowledge and Self-Identity*, pp. 23f.

related to it in a way a materialist would find unacceptable. But Aristotle has a way of replying to Shoemaker.[19]

In *Met.* Z 10 Aristotle considers whether a definition of a substance should contain definitions of the parts of the substance; and this in turn leads him to ask himself what parts of a thing are prior to the whole thing. The question is more than one of necessary condition: matter is a necessary condition of the existence of an ordinary substance, but it is not normally prior to the thing unless it is a particular sort of matter or a particular piece of matter without which the thing cannot be what it is. The answer to the question is that the parts of the definition (some of them, anyway) are prior to the whole definition, whereas the parts of the matter of the thing that are not also parts of the definition are posterior. Aristotle concludes that the parts of the soul are mostly prior to the animal as a whole, and that the parts of the body are posterior to the soul and not constituents of it; so they are parts of the matter and not of the form. The finger, for example, is posterior to the whole person, apparently because its being a finger is dependent upon its being attached to and a functioning part of a person, as what makes a gear-shift lever what it is is its being attached to the transmission of a car. (In the next chapter Aristotle notes that, while a hand cannot be defined independently of man, a man cannot perform his characteristic and defining functions without the aid of such bodily parts as the hand.) Some parts of the body, then, are prior and some posterior. But "some are neither prior nor posterior but simultaneous, such as the things that are dominant and in which the formula and the substance are immediately present, such as the heart or the brain—it does not matter which one" (1035b25-27).

[19] It is a sign of Aristotle's greatness that he provides answers to questions that in his time were never asked, as a great scientist might invent a cure for which there is as yet no known disease. This particular answer is found and identified by Wiggins, *Identity*, pp. 50f. and n. 58 (p. 76) and 61 (pp. 77f.).

Aristotle regarded the heart as the motor of the body, and he thought that the main function of the brain was to cool the blood; there is evidence that he regarded the heart as the center of consciousness (see Chapter Five, Section V). He says here that the definition and substance of the person are in the heart or brain immediately, and thereby suggests that it is the heart or brain that makes the person a person rather than just a corpse. The word *kuria*, which I have translated "dominant" and followed Ross in so doing, is of little help here. It appears in *Met.* Δ 27, where Aristotle is defining mutilation: the point is that if something cannot survive the loss of a piece of itself—if, that is, the piece is one of the *kuria* of the substance—then that loss does not constitute a mutilation. The examples given for the case of the human being are the flesh and the spleen. Surely they are not that in which the definition and substance first inhere; they are only necessary conditions of the existence of the thing, and they are posterior to the thing at least in the sense that they would not be what they are if they were not contributors to the human body. (Compare the example of the finger, remarked upon in passing a page ago.)

The heart and the spleen differ in that the heart is neither prior nor posterior to the soul; therefore it is neither prior nor posterior to the person either, whereas the spleen is posterior. The distinction cannot be put in terms of necessary and sufficient condition; strictly speaking, the spleen's existence is a necessary and sufficient condition of the existence of the person (sufficient because without the person it would not be a spleen and so the spleen would not exist). But the spleen is a causally (efficient) necessary but not sufficient condition of the person, while the person is a logically (formal) necessary but not sufficient condition of the spleen; that, anyway, seems to be what Aristotle would say. Now the heart is a causally necessary condition of the person, which is in turn a logically necessary condition of it.[20]

---

[20] It may seem odd to speak of things as being causally sufficient conditions for things. The purpose is simply to use Aristotelian

But the heart cannot be a causally sufficient condition of the person, because a heart without a spleen and other things does not (causally) produce a person; that has been established.

What other sense might there be in saying that a finger, despite its functional importance, is posterior to the whole person, aside from its being a finger only if it is attached to a particular body that functions? Perhaps it is in one important ontological respect on a par with an accident like color: if the argument of Chapter One is correct, then Aristotle holds that the being of a non-substantial particular is dependent upon substance in that its very identity is dependent on the identity of the substance it qualifies; so a particular instance of white is identifiable and reidentifiable only as long as and insofar as its owner is identifiable. Aristotle might well say that about a finger. For if a finger is a quasi-substance by virtue of its being a piece of a person and has a quasi-essence in virtue of the same fact (here remember the doctrine of focal meaning as giving life to quasi-substances and quasi-essences), then the conditions for its *persistence* are similarly parasitic upon the person. In that case it is *the same finger* over a period of time just in case it is, say, the left index finger of Brown, who in his turn must keep living up to a certain persistence conditions. This is a matter of necessary, not sufficient, conditions. If Brown had his left index finger cut off and transplanted to Johnson's left hand, then it would no longer be the same finger; but it does not follow that this finger is now the same finger as the one Johnson used to have on his left hand.

This is precisely what Aristotle does not want to say about the heart. Its identity is not parasitic upon that of the person, nor vice versa. In addition to saying that neither can exist without the other, he appears to say that the heart does not borrow its principle of individuation from the body—

---

terminology where possible. And one should remember that formal and efficient causes cannot be wholly separated, particularly in the case of the soul.

that is, from the rest of the body—that contains it. This means that a switch of heart is possible without our saying that the "new" heart is really the same heart. Add this to the fact that the heart is a causally necessary and logically sufficient condition of the person (logically sufficient because the person is a logically necessary condition of it), and the result is that *this* heart is a causally necessary and logically sufficient condition of *this* person. In other words, it is the heart that counts in individuating persons.[21]

Aristotle is therefore able to reply to a point like that made by Shoemaker that brain (heart) identity is indeed a proper criterion of bodily and hence of personal identity, and the reply is not an *ad hoc* one. Even if it is a bit strange to say that sameness of heart amounts to sameness of body, the solution that can be distilled from Aristotle's views is a sensible one. It is surely better to explain Brownson's being Brown by reference to his having Brown's brain than by reference to his ability to act and think like Brown and to give Brown-like memory reports, for two reasons. First, the former circumstance actually explains the latter. Second, the ability to behave in a Brown-like way is a characteristic that it is logically possible for more than one person to share, and identity with Brown is not. The second consideration will turn out to be crucial to the argument, various in its forms, that bodily identity is what counts for personal identity.

The Aristotelian reply to Shoemaker's puzzle only begins to establish the bodily criterion of personal identity. If what I (and Aristotle, on my interpretation) have said so far is correct, then continuity of a persistently living human body (that is to say, at least a working brain or heart) through space and time is a necessary condition of the con-

---

[21] Does it follow that the heart is identically the person? Very strictly speaking, that is true, but it would almost certainly be misleading to say it. What makes the heart identical to the person is that it is not truly a heart unless it is equipped with arms, legs, and the rest of the body.

tinuous existence of a person. But one might well ask whether it is sufficient. The concept of a person involves certain characteristically human activities, including some we call mental activities; Aristotle is clear on that point. But as is evident from Chapter Two, these parts of the essence are to be characteristic of the species man, not of the particular person. So, on Aristotle's account, if the activities of a certain body, including memory, thought, speech patterns, etc., while remaining characteristically human from time t_1 to time t_3, cease at time t_2 to be characteristic of Socrates and begin to be characteristic of Alcibiades, the body has not ceased to be Socrates or begun to be Alcibiades, provided there is no brain transplant. That is what one would expect if persons are Aristotelian substances.[22]

Aristotle would not deny that the ability to remember is part of man's essence, though it is most unlikely that he would rule out of the species an amnesiac who had not lost the innate capacity to remember, any more than a sleeper who for the moment could not see. Nor is there any good reason to believe he would individuate persons by what they remember. To do so is in any case difficult. Take the example just considered: how can we say the person who suddenly acts like Socrates does in fact remember being Socrates, doing what Socrates did, and so on? A necessary condition of his remembering being Socrates is that he have

[22] Wiggins (*Identity*, pp. 43-58) seems to believe that the concept of a person, which covers claims of personal identity (somewhat as form or essence might be said to cover any claim of entity or identity), involves the capacity to remember some sufficient amount of one's own past. It would follow that continuity requires acting in a certain way relative to the way in which one has previously acted, as part of the essence of the person. Thus the essence remains tied to the species, but each member of this species has the capacity to report on a substantial amount of what has actually happened to him in the past. But then someone with total amnesia would not only be a person different from the pre-amnesia person, but in fact not a person at all. In our example, the body that after t_2 behaved as Alcibiades would not be a person. That is absurd.

been Socrates; so an argument for identity that rests on the ability to remember is circular, since it presupposes just the identity it seeks to establish.[23]

One of the reasons why Aristotle does not regard a person as definable by a certain unitary pattern or process of living characteristic of that person herself as opposed to anybody else is that he allows that a substance may have as its essence an *energeia* but not that its essence may be a *kinēsis*[24] (I shall translate the terms "activity" and "process," respectively). I have written as though *energeia* in *Met.* H (as opposed to Θ) were the term for the form or essence of something defined by what it does, but even in that context there is more in the term than just that. The state of full exercise of the characteristic and definitive powers of substances of the sort explained in *Met.* H, including the person, is called *energeia* rather than *kinēsis* presumably because it fits the criteria for activities and not for processes.[25]

[23] This famous argument by Bishop Butler is quoted by Wiggins in *Identity*, p. 75, n. 55. Wiggins's reply appears to make my remembering something dependent on "a parcel of matter" still a part of me having been there. The right way to deal with this reply is Aristotle's way: identity of matter is a poor way to account for substantial identity through time.

All the same, I do not think Butler's argument devastates all criteria for personal identity but the bodily one. If necessary, the defender of a different criterion can talk about a mental state causally related to some past event in a way that can be described in some detail without our presupposing that the body whose mental state it is was present at the past event. Of course this apparent memory, as we can call it, does not in itself provide a sufficient condition of personal identity, but only evidence for it.

Aristotle's theory of memory, which I shall treat in Chapter Five, seems to make identity of heart, but not of matter, a necessary condition of identity of memory, since numerically the same *phantasma* cannot appear in more than one heart.

[24] What follows owes something to Fred D. Miller, Jr., "Did Aristotle Have the Concept of Identity?"

[25] Along with Miller and many others, I am in debt to Terry Penner's "Verbs and the Identity of Actions." I shall make use of his findings again. See Chapter Four, Section III.

Activities are not defined according to the stages from and to which they progress; they are homogeneous states; when one is undergoing an activity one *ipso facto* has undergone it (see especially *Met.* Θ 6 for the full list of criteria). So these substances are what they are by virtue of attaining and remaining in a certain essentially homogeneous state. Thus the state that makes a person a person is not marked by a progress through stages definitive of a species; nor, *a fortiori*, can one distinguish between one person and another on the basis of sorts of activity separately characteristic of each. What makes one a person is that one is in a state of being humanly alive.

In the case of a process, Aristotle says the whence and the whither constitute the form, and therefore the criterion of identity (along with sameness of substance involved and time). But Aristotle does not combine process and substance to get four-dimensional process-things. Neither does he regard a person as something like a human life, to be distinguished by its natural course from birth through three-score and ten to death, much less by a career peculiar to it and no other of its sort.[26] All the more reason to take the Aristotelian view of personal identity to stipulate that a radical change of personality and memories in a body does not make that body a different person.

There are, however, some arguments for denying that a person is identical with his body. The most familiar is that the body, being the matter of the person, may outlast the person. It is clear what Aristotle's reply is: if it lacks the characteristics that define a human being, it is not a body but only a heap of flesh and bones. Moreover, the very notion of a corpse is parasitic on that of a person: it is what it is because it was a person; the less it resembles a person, the less we are inclined to call it a body. Of course in one important sense Aristotle does not regard the person as

[26] See Miller, esp. pp. 486ff. Here particularly he seems to be right against Nicholas White in "Aristotle on Sameness and Oneness." Miller cites *Met.* H 2 1043a27, b. 35f.; Θ 6 1048b6-9; Θ 8 1050b2f.

primitive and has not even the language to do so. He lacks the notion of a person as being anything that is capable of certain (typically vaguely characterized) self-ascriptive statements;[27] instead, he shows how human beings are and are not related to other species in the genus and thus avoids some of the confusion engendered by Cartesian distinctions between what is mental and what is not.[28]

It would be misleading to say that what we call the body Aristotle calls flesh and bones. "Flesh and bones" is a sort of mass term; a body is an organized whole made of flesh and bones. So it is odd to deny that a body is a substance. (I mean what we, but not Aristotle, would call the body; a corpse would qualify. Let us call it the body$_2$.) But if it is, then what is a person? Is it identical to a body? Surely not if the body$_2$ is dead. A body$_2$'s being a person is not like a person's occupying an office.

Suppose, then, we revert to the example of the road up and the road down and invoke the principle that to be identical is to have the same history. The body$_2$ and the person (what Aristotle would call the body, when he is speaking strictly) are accidentally identical and co-material, but they are not the same three-dimensional object because they do not have the same history: they are like Roosevelt Boulevard and U.S. Route 1, in that they do not entirely coincide. The trouble here is that one is forced to say that a person is to a body$_2$ as a monument is to a pile of stones, and a body$_2$ is not what Aristotle would call a mere heap: it has a definite structure. Therefore we might say that the person and the body$_2$ are co-material substances.

This conclusion avoids both making a person a titular entity and making the body$_2$ mere matter, but it is not satisfactory from Aristotle's point of view. We may be more willing to carve the world into substances according to pragmatic considerations than Aristotle is. His ontology

---

[27] Cf. Sydney Shoemaker, *Self-Knowledge*, p. 15.
[28] On the confusion see Bernard Williams, "Are Persons Bodies?" p. 139.

does not encourage co-material substances. He does not believe nature is organized that way, and he does believe a close study of nature will make it possible to say which the true subtance concepts are. Aristotle seems to share some of our intuitions about the sort of thing that is typically matter; for example, he would probably agree that something is matter if it remains what it is even after the shape has been radically changed or the parts jumbled about, or if you can break it in half and get two of it. On the other hand, he is strict about drawing the line between substance and proximate matter, even when he is talking about substances that are not substances in the primary sense. As I noted in discussing *Met.* H (above, Section I), it is a bit odd to make the spatial or temporal position of a thing essential to it; but Aristotle does not hesitate to say that a certain piece of wood ceases to be a threshold if it is removed from its place before the door or that a certain bowl of porridge ceases to be breakfast and becomes lunch if, having been left untouched in the morning, it is reheated and served at noon. Aristotle clearly believes that the porridge and the eating time are related as matter and form and not as substance and property. Our intuition is likely to differ, since we should be uncomfortable denying that this porridge is identical to breakfast; but, more importantly, it may seem a matter of indifference whether this porridge, if it is eaten in the morning, *is identical to* breakfast or *constitutes* breakfast. The distinction between the matter-form distinction and the substance-attribute distinction can be made out clearly only if it is possible to say clearly where to draw the line between form and matter, or essence and accident. Aristotle is more optimistic about this possibility than most contemporary philosophers would be.[29]

[29] Williams ("Are Persons Bodies?" p. 152) wonders how, persons not being bodies, it can make sense that bodily properties will be ascribed to persons rather than to bodies$_2$. If the Aristotelian view is right, then any bodily$_2$ property will be a property both of the body$_2$ and of the person. Surely a material object and its matter may share material properties.

Hence the question whether the body₂ is identical to the person or constitutes him is not of first importance. It is more important to see in some detail what the relation is between the body₂ and the person than it is merely to characterize it as a matter-form relation or a substance-attribute one. What is important is to decide whether materialism is true and whether what we should consider bodily identity is a necessary and/or sufficient condition for personal identity. (See further Chapter Four, Section III.)

IV. FURTHER ARGUMENTS FOR THE BODILY CRITERION

The rest of this chapter is devoted to further considerations against the possibility of bodies switching souls, then to considerations against making bodily continuity the overriding factor for all questions of personal identity and survival. The conclusion will be that Aristotle is wrong on certain points, for reasons not entirely beyond his grasp.

On one important point Aristotle is right. It does not make sense to talk about a self that is some third thing in addition to a body and the psychological properties and events it suffers. Now it may seem that there must be a self that is the subject of mental attributes to which they belong immediately, as they do not underivatively belong to the body. For however one may correctly describe the whole universe without the use of token-reflexives, there is no way for me to say that *I* am some particular person in the world, whereas I might have been some other person. That is, having given a *very* full description of the world, I might add, "and *I*, this ego, am in fact identical to Edwin Hartman rather than to, say, Henry Kissinger." Now I might wish I were Henry Kissinger; the wish seems to be coherently expressible. But what would count, after all, as me becoming Henry Kissinger? If Kissinger and I switched completely—if I came to have all his physical and psychological characteristics and he mine—then at the very least nobody, including Kissinger and Hartman, could know about it. Surely nobody would want to hold that it could happen without either of us knowing about it. One struggles to say what would count as this happening. In fact, I cannot convey to you in language this notion that I am Edwin Hartman rather than anybody else; and that is evidence that it is not a coherent notion.[30]

This innocent-sounding argument has important consequences. It strongly suggests that a Cartesian view of the mind is incoherent, because it makes it difficult to see how one could identify and talk about a mind that bears only a causal, not a logical, relation to a body. There seems little point in believing in anything that cannot be identified or talked about. Aristotle does not believe in such a thing, and it is not clear to me that he ought to. At the same time, his failure to consider what at first blush seems to most of us (as it probably seemed to Plato) a compelling and natural view of the mind is a bit surprising. Instead of going through the hard work of defeating this time-honored conception of the mind, Aristotle seems simply to ignore it; one is bound to wonder whether he arrived at some of his most sensible views by good luck. I shall have more to say about this matter in Chapter Five.

If the argument of the previous paragraph but one is sound, then the notion of bodies switching souls is, strictly speaking, absurd. The closest thing to it that is conceivable is switching personality, apparent memories, and other psychological properties. If your body gets my old personality and apparent memories and my body gets yours, the Cartesian will probably take it as evidence that our bodies have switched souls; but one can more parsimoniously say that this is all that switching souls amounts to. It is clear now what Aristotle would say if this switch came about as a result of the transplant of the central organ, but that is an easy case for people of almost any persuasion on the issue.

[30] For a similar argument see Thomas Nagel, "Physicalism," pp. 353-356.

The hard case is the one in which it somehow happens without a change of brain (or heart). The Cartesian side will hold that this body has a new mind, whether the switch is evidence of a new mind or (as a sort of neo-Cartesian would say) just what having a new mind is. The Aristotelian side will say that nothing could count as a body's getting a new mind. There is one mind, which is to say one person, per body. How can one begin to settle this argument?

In an influential article that ranks among the best defenses of the Aristotelian point of view on this question, Bernard Williams[31] adopts a strategy that seems to come as close as any to making the problem of personal continuity both serious and tractable: he focuses on how self-interest might choose among certain alternative futures. Suppose you and another person were to be put into a mysterious machine from which, after an interval, would emerge a person who looked like you—that is, had your body—but acted and remembered as Jones, and a person who had the body of Jones but acted and remembered as you would be expected to. If in advance of the experiment you were given the choice as to which of the emerging people was to be given a large sum of money and which was to be tortured to death, which would you choose? Most people say they would choose to reward the person psychologically similar to themselves and torture the one with their "old" body, if anybody must be tortured. Williams notes that this would not be an idle question: there would seem to be a real risk involved that one would make a mistake and get tortured oneself. Perhaps, though, this feeling of riskiness rests on the unexposed and unwarranted assumption that there is a unitary self, that mysterious third thing, which accompanies either one's psychological properties or one's body but obviously not both.

On the Aristotelian view, as long as a particular body keeps having psychological properties characteristic of hu-

[31] "The Self and the Future."

mans—not of a particular human, remember, but of the species—it is the same substance, the same person. Features that at a particular time distinguish one member of the species from another, including differences of character and memory report, are accidental rather than essential.

If this seems wrong, consider the following story, also from Williams. You are told that you are to be hypnotized very thoroughly indeed, so that your intelligence and personality and memory reports radically change, perhaps to match those of another person. Then you are to be tortured. How does the prospect strike you? It does not sound very appealing, I suspect. But how is that situation different from the more popular alternative presented in the previous story? Surely it is not different; and that ought to be considered a strong intuitive argument in favor of the Aristotelian view that bodily continuity is all the personal identity there is.

It is worth emphasizing again that personal characteristics are logically repeatable. Aristotle will allow any number of things to be one in color, or size, or in any of the accidental properties without being one in number. So there might be some other person with all or virtually all of your psychological properties who is nevertheless not you; and the existence of such a person from the moment of your death (let us call it) would seem not to be the survival of you, even though your replacement would sincerely claim to be you, would make all the appropriate memory reports and so on, and would probably be convinced that you—that is, as far as he is concerned, he—had survived. But what good would that do *you*? So it seems that Aristotle is being reasonable in denying that that is a case of sameness in number, of identity.

Aristotle's conception of the identity of the person as being a case of the identity of a substance is admirable in avoiding the mysterious self that is neither body nor psychological properties, but he benefits in this case from a failure to attend with sufficient care to the epistemological and metaphysical problems caused by the apparent special nature of mental events. So, for example, he does not think what counts in survival is the persistence of psychological properties in part because he does not consider the possibility that the self might be a center of consciousness that endures through time in a kind of perfect self-identity unlike any other.

V. PROBLEMS FOR THE BODILY CRITERION

But there are some reasons for believing Aristotle to be wrong. First I consider some reasons to deny that identity of body over a period of time is necessary and sufficient for survival; next, reasons to say that identity of body at a time is, like identity of body through time, inadequate for unity of person. The result will be that there are cases for which Aristotle's conception of the soul as the individuating essence of the body will be false or beside the point.[32]

The first set of reasons has been most powerfully formulated by Derek Parfit.[33] If one could split a brain down the middle and transplant each half into a vacant body with the result that there were now two people with the same memory reports, personality, and intellectual abilities, it could not be said that both resultant persons were identical with the original, nor that one was rather than the other (on what basis could the distinction be made?); but though the original person is no more, it seems that it would be irrational

---

[32] The two philosophers whose work I shall present in evidence against Aristotle's views are not the first to challenge the bodily criterion of personal identity at a time or through time. I choose Derek Parfit and Thomas Nagel because they argue well and clearly, because their views are representative of important and widely held positions, and because their arguments do not depend on considerations that are merely barely conceivable. Aristotle did not concern himself with remote logical possibilities in defining his central concepts; so criticism of him should in fairness work from within the bounds of the plausible.

[33] See particularly his influential "Personal Identity."

of someone contemplating getting split in that way to regard it as death. Indeed, it is more like having the length of one's life doubled, with the terms running concurrently. It would seem to follow that in the absence of a particular person's continuing to exist there may yet be *survival*, to use the word in a sense that does not involve identity. What counts in the first instance is what Parfit calls psychological connectedness, which means roughly a carrying-over of at least some of what but for the requirements of identity would be called memory, intention, and other things that define a person. A lesser degree of survival is psychological continuity, which holds between A and C just in case B is psychologically connected with A and C with B; it does not require that A be psychologically connected with C.

The relation that matters most is psychological connectedness, and it is a matter of degree. Jones today and Jones tomorrow are very closely connected: Jones today and Jones twenty-five years from now are more distantly connected. Jones today and Jones at age one are connected almost not at all; in fact, they are probably only psychologically continuous: it is unlikely that the older Jones remembers the life of the younger or carries out the baby's intentions, though some psychoanalysts might argue otherwise. Parfit concludes that it is psychological connectedness and continuity that give identity its importance; where they are absent identity has none, and where they are present in the absence of identity one ought rationally to be as concerned about them as one is accustomed to be about identity.

It follows that Parfit will take a rather different line about the transfer of those multiply transferable mental features that the Aristotelian view disqualifies as criteria of personal identity. Parfit holds that so long as there is some causal relation between a person and his subsequent mental twin, the resultant psychological connectedness holds and is worth worrying about.[34] The important thing is that there be in the world a person of such and such a psychological de-

---

[34] There seems to be no restriction on the sort of causal relationship there might be. This is nearly always left vague.

scription. One should worry about survival for the same reason one worries about whether after one's death there will be someone to carry on one's work, or about whether one will be survived by a worthy son or daughter.[35]

This view may seem unsatisfying. What is troublesome is that the replica will not clearly be myself. The replica will not be a substance identical to me. But why should I not regard it as a survival of me? What one wants to say is that *I*—not this body nor this brain nor this collection of features, but this ultimate subject that may inhabit this or that body—shall in that imagined situation not be inhabiting any body. But—again—this notion of a single, underlying, no doubt immaterial substance is indefensible.

From Parfit's point of view, Aristotle is missing something. The continuity of a person through time is a subtler matter than Aristotle has thought. If he is right in saying that the unity of the person just amounts to the unity of the body, a substance, then he must rule out arguments that take seriously the possibility that a single body could successively house different persons, or that one self could turn up in different bodies.

Nor could Aristotle allow that one body might house different selves at the same time; for two substances cannot occupy the same place at the same time, though a substance and its matter of course do. Here the second set of reasons mentioned above comes to the fore. The notion of two souls in one body is not so fantastic as one might think. Again, one's ability even to think of such a possibility rests on one's having a conception of a mental realm, which Aristotle does not much emphasize. Could anything count as the partition of this center of consciousness within a single body at a particular time? It is just possible that something could.

Thomas Nagel[36] discusses some findings by psychologists who have studied patients who seem to exhibit multiple con-

---

[35] A number of people have argued for this sort of view. See, e.g., Jeffrie G. Murphy, "Rationality and the Fear of Death," esp. p. 197.
[36] "Brain Bisection and the Unity of Consciousness."

sciousness in the same body. In the case of a person whose corpus callosum in the brain has been split, usually as a cure for epilepsy, the two sides of the brain may dominate disparate activities of opposite sides of the body in such a way that one side of the brain does not always know what one side of the body is doing. An example: what is flashed by a tachistoscope to the right half of the visual field or is felt by the right hand can be reported verbally. What is flashed to the left half of the visual field or felt by the left hand cannot, though if the left half is flashed the word "hat," the left hand can in response pick out a hat from a group of objects. This is because the left hemisphere sees what is in the right visual field and alone controls speaking; and it is unaware (if I may speak that way) of what the right hemisphere is aware of and can show it is aware of by the action of the hand it controls. Another example: two spots on different sides of one's visual field cannot be compared for color. The subject can know whether they are the same color only if they are within the purview of the same hemisphere.

Our conception of a person as a unified entity is more complex than body-that-behaves-in-a-certain-way, which is, roughly speaking, Aristotle's way of conceiving of the person. For to know what a person is is to know something about the person's special behavior with respect to himself. Persons are unitary beings because they can coherently introspect, act intentionally, and in general have (relatively to other observers) easy access to knowledge about themselves. This ability is definitive not only of personhood but of the unity of the person. You and I are different not only because we are two different material objects but also because my knowledge of what you are sensing and feeling and thinking and what you are going to do is likely to be much less complete than yours. The importance of Nagel's example lies in its impairment of our confidence that we can count minds or even persons by counting bodies, because a mind (or a person) is supposed to be related to itself and not to other selves in certain familiar but nevertheless complex ways.

So it is possible that animated bodies with brains split at the corpus callosum cannot be called individual persons because they do not clearly and unambiguously have one mind. To be sure, they do not have two each: most of the time they are perfectly normal; and were it not for carefully controlled experiments that create unusual and artificial inputs, nobody would have the slightest reason to suspect there was anything double about them; nor, accordingly, is there any reason to count them as two for normal situations. On the other hand, to say that they have just one mind is either to ignore the radical disintegration of mental functioning that split-brain bodies sometimes display or to deny that the right hemisphere (the non-verbal and less intelligent one) is or produces a mind in itself. But one can assign a mentality to the right hemisphere alone on the strength of its ability to carry on quite recognizably intentional and coherently goal-directed activity on its own. It can integrate input enough to follow instructions; it can do things that demand alertness; it can remember some things; in general, it performs tasks that seem to require awareness and integration of consciousness. And if the left hemisphere were destroyed, there would still be a person remaining.

If, as I believe, some sort of privileged access on the part of the owner is a crucial distinguishing characteristic of a mental event, then a necessary condition of the unity of a mind ought to be that its contents, at least sensory ones, are specially accessible to whatever entity has (or is) that mind. So when a split-brain body denies with apparent sincerity any knowledge of a whole elaborate and well-integrated range of at least partly mental events in which that body is obviously engaged, it is rational to infer that those events cannot belong to the mind on whose behalf the voice reports—one might say, the person on whose behalf the voice reports. There is reason to believe that these integrated activities that are unavailable to the mind that speaks do belong to some mind. I said before that I do not think it is clearly a matter of two minds in one body; but this amounts to approaching that question of the number of minds there are, not by counting bodies, but by assessing the coherence and integration of the consciousness of one body. If that is the right way to do it, then personal identity at a particular time might conceivably be a matter of degree.

Aristotle's treatment of the person as a substance and the soul as its form promises to set the problems of persistence through time and individuation at a time in a familiar and manageable context. If all goes well, personal identity will be no more puzzling than the river whose water is ever different, or the road that goes both up and down. But Parfit and Nagel have shown how attention to some special features of mental events and their owners casts doubt on both aspects of Aristotle's solution. Parfit's arguments suggest that what is important about personal identity through time is a matter of degree; Nagel suggests that the same is true of personal identity at a time, and perhaps it is true not only for a few wild cases. For just as each person's psychological connectedness with his past is imperfect—we forget things, we change our opinions and sometimes our character, etc.— so each person is imperfectly integrated at any time: nearly everyone has had the experience of finding himself saying something he had no intention of saying, of driving a car fairly skillfully while engrossed in conversation, of not feeling the pain until the blood is visible, of self-deception, of weakness of will. So it is not clear that one can tie the concept of person and personal identity to body and bodily identity as Aristotle would like to do. To put the point another way, it is not a necessary truth that there is one soul per body.[37]

---

[37] It is sometimes argued that there is something logically difficult about separating persons and bodies. Strawson, for example, devotes a section of *Individuals* (I, 3, pp. 87-116) to refuting this Cartesian tendency. It is true, as he says, that one ascribes mental predicates to others and to oneself on the same logical basis, with the result that even in our own case we do not ascribe mental predicates to a dis-

VI. THOUGHTS ON THE UNITY OF THE SELF

Aristotle does worry about some of the considerations that have caused this doubt about the unity of the self. He talks both about splitting and about what makes two or more experiences belong to a single consciousness.

Towards the end of the first book of *De Anima* (I 5 411a24ff.) Aristotle says plants and insects continue to live for a time after being divided (the parts have locomotion and sensation) if the souls of the remaining bits differ in number (each part has one) but are of the same species. In *De An.* II 2 he makes the same point again. This is a bit surprising. Surely one of the differences between a substance and a piece of matter is precisely that the latter can be broken down into bits as deserving as is the original of being called that sort of stuff, whereas one does not break a substance in two and get two substances. But here something very like that happens: cut a worm in half and you have two worms. What Aristotle says about plants and insects

---

embodied mind. The person considered as a material object that can take mental predicates does provide a way of imputing experiences to myself and others. So I assign a pain to you because you are the one who reports it (that is, the speech comes out of your body) or who winces or screams, and because it is a result of something that has happened to your body; that is just what makes it your pain. But the necessary truth rests on some contingent matters of fact. It is not inconceivable that A might wince or scream when one bashed B's body, that B could report on what is before the eyes of C, and that C could deliberate about and decide what A would do next. It is not easy to say how much detachment of that sort our present vocabulary and conceptual scheme could handle, but I do not see that our usual way of individuating persons and ascribing mental events makes cases of the sort Parfit imagines and Nagel reports any less plausible or important. I think Strawson would agree. (See *Individuals*, p. 133: "I am not denying that we might, in unusual circumstances, be prepared to speak of two persons alternately sharing a body, or of persons changing bodies etc. But none of these admissions count against the thesis that the primary concept is that of a type of entity, a person, such that a person necessarily has corporeal attributes as well as other kinds of attributes.")

implies that the individuation of souls and thereby presumably of ensouled entities is a more complicated business than my analysis of his theory has so far suggested.

Aristotle is granting separateness to the surviving parts of the insect not only because they are physically separate but also because they do not act together. The passages do allow that the surviving bits of the insect have separate sensations and imagination and even conflicting desires; he has reason for regarding the bits as separate ensouled beings, presumably because having inseparable psychological events is a criterion of psychological unity.

Now what does this inseparability of psychological events amount to? Start with desires. Aristotle's discussions of practical reasoning and particularly of weakness of will in the *Nicomachean Ethics* make it clear that, in his view, normal persons normally act with faculties integrated towards goals that serve their interests. Action in pursuit of a goal seen not to be in the best interest of a person is an aberration that requires explanation and in fact considerable, barely plausible reinterpretation by Aristotle. His view presupposes that individuals normally exhibit a sophisticated integration of psychic functions of a sort that we now know is occasionally conspicuously lacking in split-brain people. The monkey whose paws struggle over a peanut (one of Nagel's examples) is a good example of that lack. Unsurprisingly, it does not occur to Aristotle that division of the corpus callosum could bring about the occasional failure of normal integration of psychic function; but given the importance of that sort of integration to his heavily intentional and teleological account of human behavior, and given his readiness to grant individuality to pieces of insects (one might almost say pieces of insect) in part on the basis of their acting in ways that are integrated enough to make it possible coherently to assign them their own desires, it is reasonable to suppose that Aristotle might have had sympathy with Nagel's treatment of the issues raised by the split-brain people.

There is confirmation for the view that Aristotle uses the notion of access to some mental center as a sign of unity. At *De An.* III 2 426b12ff., in arguing that we perceive differences between and among objects of sense by a single faculty of sense, he says:

Separate faculties cannot judge that sweet is different from white, but they must be both clear to one faculty. If one could [perceive such a difference with two different organs], then that two such entities are different from each other would be clear on the basis of the fact that I perceive one and you the other.

In the absence of some central faculty that senses both together, the situation *is as though two different people were each sensing one of the entities*, and that surely would not add up to the judgment that the two entities are different. Aristotle's comment fits the split-brain person, who cannot tell whether two spots are the same color if they are on different sides of his visual field (run by different hemispheres), but he can if they are on the same side. There must be, and in these cases there is not, something with immediate access to a set of states if these states are to be considered states of one mind. Aristotle talks of there having to be *one faculty* to perceive the relation of identity or difference between things within a person's ken; Nagel suggests that it is because a person can perceive the relations among elements, even simultaneous elements, of his experience that one ascribes *one mind* to him. And Aristotle likens the situation of there being more than one faculty involved to that of there being more than one person. He is thereby developing a notion of the unity of the self that could subvert the view that it is some sort of necessary truth that there are exactly as many souls as there are live human bodies. Of course Aristotle could reply that that is the way nature always works; and he would be wrong.

Consider now some hypothetical cases that can be constructed from Nagel's facts with the help of Parfit's imagination. A man who is about to have his brain split is told that one of his two post-operative centers of consciousness is going to be stimulated pleasurably and the other tortured. He cannot imagine what it will be like to be pleased while he is being tortured—while, indeed, each "he" is relatively indifferent to the other's treatment, though of course the pre-operative person cannot be. Probably no ready intuition will encompass what is about to happen to him.

Now suppose, however, that the brain will be split but that thereafter his environment will be carefully controlled so that both centers of consciousness will have the same experiences. For example, if the left side is having an experience that is communicated to the right side in a normal brain, the environment for the split brain will be arranged so that the right side gets the same data it would have got in the normal case. In that case the subject's experience would be the same as if there had been no brain split; and under those circumstances, if one of the halves of the brain were destroyed (or as much of it as would be needed to produce experiences that could be duplicated by the other half), no consciousness would be lost. Therefore, it does make sense to individuate consciousnesses according to qualitative differences if it makes sense to individuate them at all. It follows that Parfit's view, rather than the Aristotelian one, is correct.

Parfit does not say that persons are universals, but he does say, in effect, that what is most important about survival is logically repeatable. The cases Nagel discusses suggest that the number of consciousnesses cannot always be determined; *a fortiori* one cannot clearly or finally individuate them qualitatively. But the essential point for immediate purposes is that in those cases we are inclined to individuate consciousnesses *within* individual bodies only when their contents are qualitatively distinguishable. Parfit's view is that continuity of consciousness *across time* is a matter of qualitatively indistinguishable contents being carried over from one person to another.

Consider one final point in favor of the line Parfit takes. Suppose a physiologist discovers that the cells in most people's brains do wear out and get replaced, contrary to common opinion. More surprisingly still, the rate of replacement varies widely from person to person. In some people the process is very gradual, and one full replacement takes longer than the average life lasts. In others all the cells are replaced within a year. In a few it takes a week or so. In one percent of the cases the body gets a new lot of brain cells every few hours. In one-tenth of one percent of the cases, every few minutes, and then instantly. But in most cases the new cells bear the traces of those they have replaced, so that memory, intention, personality, character, and so on are carried over. All this would be going on without the people themselves being aware of it, unless they were examined and told. Thus for all I know I might have (what one would surely call) a wholly new brain in my head by morning, or in a few seconds. Is this now a new person? Has somebody died overnight? And if not, how does the case differ importantly from a duplicate brain transplant? But if one does believe that a new brain in a few seconds means a new person, then might we not equally say that, as things really are, a wholesale change of the molecular if not cellular structure of our brains is death? That question cannot be answered by saying that one does not remember having died! Here intuition is surely on Parfit's side: no sane person could fear impending death on these grounds. And if under these circumstances we told someone that his body was to be tortured at some time in the future but that by that time his present brain would have been wholly replaced in the manner described, he would not be much comforted.

What seems to be missing all along in our speculations is the heart of the notion that I want *me* to continue to exist; one wants one*self* to persist in whichever body or with whatever psychological characteristics. But there is no such self. It is tempting to conclude that a certain sort of self-interest ought not to have the grip on our intuitions it has. Just as it is nonsense to say that I might have turned out to be identical to Henry Kissinger (that is, without Henry Kissinger being identical to Edwin Hartman) but am instead identical to Edwin Hartman, so it is wrong to say that the question of my bodily identity versus psychological connectedness is a trivial question for others than myself, but an absolutely vital question for me as I view it *from inside*.

It is perhaps this inside perspective from which we are sometimes urged to view such events as death and pain. It does not follow from anything said so far that one's having a special attitude towards oneself is irrational. But there does seem to be reason to believe that one's self is not what one thinks it is, that therefore its extinction is not what one thinks it is, that survival and death are not the events one thinks they are. If there is not a discoverable phenomenological difference between falling asleep and waking up refreshed and falling asleep and waking up replicated, then we may have to begin to rethink a good many of our dearest moral and prudential opinions.

How far this disturbing and even offensive line of thinking will go is difficult to say, but it may be worth worrying about. If certain views about the soul turn out to form a substantial part of the basis of our morality, as they do for Aristotle, then it will be hard not to find the destruction of those views and the working out of the implications of that destruction immoral. For the moment it is comforting to be able to say that Aristotle's views about personal identity are sound for all situations anyone is likely to encounter. Perhaps Aristotle himself would be satisfied that they should hold for the most part.

Chapter Four

THE HEART, THE SOUL, AND MATERIALISM

ARISTOTLE has two important general points to make against what is recognizably a kind of materialism. The first is that certain events of the soul (primarily thoughts) are unaccompanied by events in the body. I shall deal with those events mainly in Chapter Six. His second point is that certain other soul events do require bodily events as accompaniment but are nevertheless not identical with them. Instead, soul events and bodily events are related as form and matter. That relation is the one I shall be discussing in this chapter and the next. I shall attend to the psychological states that do seem to have sufficient physical conditions, with a view to showing how Aristotle uses the form-matter device to explicate the relation between psychological and physical events. But first it is necessary to say more about how Aristotle relates the soul and the heart.

The problem is that the soul would seem to be the engine, not the essence, of the body; and as it is the heart that plays that role, the soul might well be thought identical to the heart. If Aristotle resists or ignores this view, he will justly be suspected of avoiding the subject, as his account of substance would have been trivial if it had ignored common opinion and common criteria. Again, Aristotle's introductory remarks in *De Anima* II suggest that he has a conception of the soul that is not adequate to account for what the soul patently is and does. But it will turn out that Aristotle's detailed treatment takes him far beyond the general formulas and inadequate arguments with which he begins the exposition.

I shall begin by looking briefly at those introductory

remarks (Section I), and then at the way Aristotle deals
with the undeniable data about the heart as that which controls the body (Section II). Next, I shall discuss Aristotle's
views about the identity of events as applied to the relation
between events of the body and events of the soul (Section
III). Finally, I shall place Aristotle's dualism in the explanation of animal behavior in the context of his dualism in the
explanation of things in general (Section IV).

This chapter is primarily devoted to a particular case of
Aristotle's individuation of things and events according to
the descriptions under which they are introduced. The
extension of the essence-accident distinction to persons and
to psychological events leads him to some dubious positions,
but it has a salutary demystifying effect on the mind-body
relation. Moreover, as with many of Aristotle's views, its
heirs have a vigorous part in modern discussions of this
ancient problem.

I. THE DEFINITION OF THE SOUL

Ostensibly in order to decide whether the soul and the
body are identical, Aristotle starts from scratch in *De An.* II
1 and in a few lines reviews his whole system and its major
concepts in order to give some idea of where the soul fits in:

1. Under the heading of substance we speak of (A) matter, (B) form, in virtue of which matter constitutes
   a particular thing, and (C) the compound of matter
   and form.
2. As received opinion has it, bodies, and in particular
   natural bodies, are what primarily exist. Of these
   natural bodies, some have life, which is the power to
   nourish oneself and grow and so also decay. Therefore,
   every live natural body is a composite substance.
3. Every body thus partaking of life is a substance of
   type C. Therefore, since it is a certain sort of body
   (that is, since it is a body with life),

4. The body is substratum and of type A, and not of type B;
5. Therefore, the body is not the soul.
6. The soul is a substance of type B; that is, it is the substance (in the sense of the form) of a potentially live body.
7. Substance-form is actuality.
8. Therefore, the soul is the actuality of a potentially live body.

The passage has some of the trappings of an argument: the word "therefore" appears repeatedly; some of the statements follow from previous ones; the last line, which embodies an important proposition, is presented as though it were a conclusion. But there are surely some premises missing. It is not to be expected that within a few lines Aristotle can establish a view about the ontological status of the soul that makes it quite different from what anybody has ever thought before. Much has to be taken for granted, including some things Aristotle has said in the first book of *De Anima* and in the *Metaphysics*. But even a reader who accepts Aristotle's ontological distinctions and agrees with him about the deficiencies of certain other definitions of the soul may not be convinced by this enthymeme.[1]

To begin with, what justifies Aristotle's conclusion in step 2 that every natural body is a composite substance? It must have matter in order to change, grow, and decay: that is a firmly settled Aristotelian view. It must have form in order to be itself—that is, in order to be some particular thing—especially a living thing—rather than a lump of stuff.[2] Whether it is truly a compound of form and matter is another question, but it is reasonable to assume it is form with matter.

In steps 2 and 3 Aristotle clearly says the live body is a

---

[1] Rodier, for example, seems to find the whole chapter arbitrary and unconvincing. See esp. pp. 175ff.

[2] So, apparently, Themistius 39. 31.

compound of form and matter, and therefore a certain sort of body. It will have to be a certain sort of body if it is to be a substance: every substance is of a certain sort. But then in step 4 the body is suddenly no longer a compound of form and matter; it is only matter. Not only does this conclusion not follow from the premises stated; it seems to contradict at least one of them, step 3. Aristotle must mean that the body *qua* live is a substance, while the body *qua* parcel of flesh and bones with a certain structure is its matter.[3]

The soul is first mentioned in step 5, which states its nonidentity to the body, apparently in part on the basis of step 6, which states that the soul is substance in the sense of form. What warrant has Aristotle for virtually introducing the conclusion of the argument as one of its premises? Up to that point one knows that the living body is a substance, a particular material object. Now Aristotle believes he has shown in the biological works that living beings sort themselves into species and genera not only according to physical structure but also according to the kinds of life they have. It follows that the sort of life a living being has in common with other members of its species is essential to it, rather than accidental.[4] It is universally agreed that the soul is— whatever else it is—that which is responsible for the life of the living substance. If Aristotle denied that proposition, it would not be the soul of which he would be giving an exposition. Hence it is a necessary truth that the soul is the essence of the living thing. That is really all Aristotle needs to complete the argument; he does not need any premises about precisely how the soul works, only about what its effect is.

[3] So I have argued in Chapter Three, against Ackrill in "Aristotle's Definitions of *Psuche*."

[4] Different sorts of life partly define different species, and genera too. In *De An.* II 2 and 3 we learn that plants have the power to nourish themselves and grow, animals to sense, and men to think. Each more sophisticated capacity involves the presence of all the less sophisticated ones.

The soul is not identical with that effect. In this opinion too Aristotle has the support of common sense: the soul's effect is or may be intermittent, but nobody would say that an animal has a soul only while it is awake, or a plant only while it is growing. Therefore, while the soul is the actuality of the body, it is potential with respect to the activity characteristic of the appropriate species.[5] Given that the soul is by definiton whatever produces this activity, it would not be expected that the soul just is the activity. The eye need not at each moment be seeing in order to be an eye, and the axe need not always chop. Most importantly, there is nothing in this account to tell against the possibility that there is a relation of efficient cause between the soul and the activity for which it is responsible. If the soul is by definition what is responsible for the activities essential to a body of a certain sort, it is to be expected that that responsibility is a causal one. Why not?

Aristotle concludes the chapter with some lines that are sometimes thought troublesome. It is clear, he says at 413-a2ff., that the soul cannot exist apart from the body, and in some cases that the parts (that is, capacities) of the soul cannot exist apart from certain parts of the body. This is a corollary of the view, advertised in the *Metaphysics*, that form makes demands on matter. But it is possible that certain parts of the soul are not actualities of any body, and it is not clear whether the soul is the actuality of the body as the sailor is of the ship.

There is no problem in the statement that the soul cannot exist without the very organs and parts whose activity is the second actuality of the live body, nor without the organs and parts necessary for that activity, for they cause the activity that makes the organism a human being. Their necessity is compatible, I shall argue in Chapter Six, with the fact (it is no mere possibility, as Aristotle diffidently suggests here) that certain parts of the soul are not actualities of any body. There is a causal basis for thought; but

[5] Cf. II 2 414a4-14.

while the workings of certain bodily organs are necessary for acts of intellect, they are not sufficient. That is the respect in which the intellect is separable from the body.

II. THE SOUL AS FORMAL AND EFFICIENT CAUSE[6]

But the third suggestion Aristotle makes here, that the soul might for all he has said be to the body as the sailor is to the ship, is widely believed to present difficulties. It is not obviously an intrusion. A ship cannot fulfill its defining function of carrying goods across water from A to B without a pilot; and a person is a pilot only by virtue of having the task of guiding a ship and so causing it to perform its essential function. So there is a logical relation between ship and pilot, but a causal one as well. That is how it is with the body and the soul.

Aristotle says at *De An.* II 4 415b8ff. that the soul is the efficient, formal, and final *aitia* of the body. Whether and how it can be all three is a bit of a puzzle. If the soul is just the heart, then the soul is the efficient cause of life; if the soul is the formal *aitia* of the body, then it cannot very well be identical with an organ of the body. This difficulty has led Nuyens[7] and others to argue that the soul as efficient cause of behavior is incompatible with Aristotle's notion that the soul is the form of the body and that therefore Aristotle's statements on the two sides of that issue must have been made at different stages of his thought. Hardie, Block, and others[8] have argued that Aristotle saw no incom-

---

[6] My use of the usual translation of *aitia* and *aition* is not meant to suggest that they must always mean "cause."

[7] F.J.C.J. Nuyens, *L'Évolution de la psychologie d'Aristote.*

[8] W.F.R. Hardie, "Aristotle's Treatment of the Relation between the Soul and the Body," and *Aristotle's Ethical Theory*, Chapter V, Appendix. Irving Block, "The Order of Aristotle's Psychological Writings," pp. 5off. Block holds that the notions are compatible; Hardie does not. Charles Kahn argues in "Sensation and Consciousness in Aristotle's Psychology" that Aristotle's account of the func-

patibility between the two notions. I think he was right in seeing no incompatibility.

The passage most often quoted in aid of the view that Aristotle saw no incompatibility between the soul being in the heart and the soul being the form of the body is in *Met.* Z 10:

> Since the soul of animals (for this is the substance of an ensouled being) is their substance according to the formula, i.e., the form and the essence of a body of a certain kind (we shall define each part, if we define it well, not without reference to its function, which cannot belong to it without perception), so that the parts of the soul are prior, or anyway some of them, to the compound animal . . . some parts are neither prior nor posterior to the whole, i.e., those which are dominant and in which the formula, i.e., the essential substance, is immediately present, e.g., perhaps the heart or the brain; for it does not matter which of the two has this property. (1035b14-27)

The essence of the body is present in this part of it because this organ is the primary efficient cause of its acting in the way that is characteristic of the sort of animal it is.

There is no doubt about the soul's causal and logical roles in *De An.* II 4:

> . . . soul is an *aitia* in three senses of the word we have outlined. The soul is the *aitia* of animate bodies in that it is itself the origin of motion; as final *aitia*; and as substance. That it is an *aitia* in the sense of substance is clear; substance is the *aition* of being for everything; and for living things being means living, and it is the soul which is the *aitia* and origin of life. (415b10-14)

---

tional unity of the soul rests in part on his account of the physiological basis of psychological activity, and in particular of the function of the heart. I am in debt to Father Theodore Tracy, S.J., for showing me his paper entitled "Heart and Soul in Aristotle," from which I have profited.

There are certain activities the capacity for which constitutes life, which is the essence of the person; and there is within the person an efficient cause of those activities. Thus the relation between the capacity for life and the internal efficient cause of life is surely identity.

This is no *ad hoc* device designed to rescue Aristotle from possible contradiction. It is consistent with the notion that the soul is a *physis* (usually translated "nature"; see *De Part. An.* I 1 641a28ff.) and with what Aristotle has said about *physis* in *Met.* Δ 4: "nature in the primary sense is the essence of things which have in themselves, *qua* themselves, a source of movement; . . . nature in this sense is the source of the movement of natural objects, inhering in them in some way, either potentially or in actuality" (1015-a13-19). So *physis* in the primary sense is what is at once the essence and the internal source of movement of a natural substance. Now the essence and the source of movement can be the same only when the activity of a substance is involved in its definition; and Aristotle appears to believe that this is the case for all natural substances that move on their own. Most clearly it is true for persons, and it is clearly persons and their souls Aristotle has in mind in the last few lines of the passage just quoted.

It does not follow either that there is or that there is not a particular organ that is the primary efficient cause of characteristically human behavior. That sort of behavior is highly complex, and it involves the cooperative labor of many parts and organs. So Aristotle argues at various places that the soul pervades the body at least in the sense that the whole body is alive and that its parts contribute to the life of the whole (*De An.* I 5 411b15ff.), and that moreover there could be no soul without the contributions those parts make (II 2 414a25ff.; cf. *Met.* Z 11 1036b24ff.). Still, he locates the soul primarily in the heart in the metaphysical works (e.g., *Met.* Z 10 1035b25ff.), in the biological works (e.g., *De Motu Animalium* 3 699a14ff.), in the *Parva Natu-*

ralia (e.g., *De Somno* 2 455a12ff.), and in *De Anima* (e.g., I 4 408b1ff.).

How can the essence of something be a part of it? How can the formal cause of something be identical with its efficient cause? Since Nuyens the topic has had more than its share of discussion, to which I want to add what I think is suggested by a familiar sort of analogy Aristotle uses to show what the relation is among the heart, the soul, and the human being. At *De Motu Animalium* 10 703a28ff. Aristotle compares the place of the heart in the body to that of the ruler in the polis. Clearly the relation of ruler to government to state is analogous to that of heart to soul to man.

Aristotle does not push the analogy very far, in part because he does not see a need to defend the way in which he unites formal and efficient cause in his accounts of the soul. The elaboration that follows is mostly my defense of Aristotle's position. The relation of government to state is not a perfect example of the form-substance relation, but it is close. The government is a necessary and sufficient condition of the state, and it makes a collection of people and other items in a certain area a state as a formal cause makes some matter a substance. The people may come and go, the area may shift its boundaries somewhat, but the state persists. Officers, institutions, and laws may change within limits, but we should probably say the state persists so long as it retains the same general form of government: a revolution is a substantial change, a constitutional amendment an accidental one. But there is a certain sort of state in which there is slightly less leeway for accidental change. That is the absolute arbitrary dictatorship; and that is the analogy Aristotle needs. In this case the controlling power of the state, the power to coerce, which is also the feature that creates a state, is vested in one person. A new ruler would amount to a new government. The sense in which the government is in this person is not difficult to grasp; and, as it happens, the sense of "in" used here is suggested by the sixth of eight senses Aristotle lists in *Phys.* IV 3: "as the affairs of the Greeks are in the king, and in general as things are in their first mover" (210a22ff.). The same meaning appears in a helpful passage in *Met.* Λ 10:

> We must also investigate how the nature of the universe contains the good, i.e., the best: whether it is separate and by itself, or by virtue of its arrangement. Perhaps both, as in the case of an army. For its goodness is in its arrangement and its general, perhaps especially the latter; for he does not depend on the arrangement, but it depends on him. (1075a11-15)[9]

The heart is to the person as the general is to the army or the dictator to the state. The latter analogy would be clearer if it were customary to speak of the dictator as just being the government, as we sometimes refer to an army by its general's name ("Meade retreated"). No doubt that would be the usual practice if all governments were dictatorships, as all men are "governed" by a heart. But even if all governments were dictatorships, it would be best to say that the government is that which (whatever else it is) is the sufficient condition of something's being a state and functioning as a state does; for it would be purely contingent that this capacity for functioning as a state was centered in one person. An Aristotelian analysis of government would make it a matter of definition that government is what makes the state a state. It would then turn out that in every case it is the dictator who, by use of the instruments of coercion, causes people to perform in ways definitive of statehood. Now Aristotle contends that the soul must be primarily located in one part of the body. But his physiological arguments for that assertion are dubious. (He has *a priori* arguments for there being one central faculty of perception. More on that in Chapter Five.) At any rate, that the soul is primarily located in one part of the body is, Aristotle

[9] Alexander Mourelatos reminded me of this passage.

believes, reason enough to concede to dualistic common opinion from time to time and call the heart the soul. (But recall that in the crucial Z 10 passage he says it makes no difference—presumably, to the definition of the soul— whether it is located in the heart or the brain.)

All this may help explain the temptation to identify the heart with the soul; and though Aristotle does not explicitly do that, he says some things from which this identification follows.[10] At the same time, the analogy with government illustrates the pervasiveness the soul has. The government is in the dictator but also (less clearly) in the army, in the department of transportation, and in other agencies under the dictator's authority. These facts are nevertheless compatible with the government's being located primarily in the dictator.

One of the problems in identifying the essence of something with a part of it is that the essence of a substance is supposed to be identical with it; so I argued in Chapter Two. That argument would suggest that the heart is identical with the person. Is that claim anywhere close to the truth? Consider again the analogy to the state. Had Louis XIV of France been correct in saying *L'état, c'est moi*, then he would have been a necessary condition of the existence of this French state, though not of the French nation.[11] The King of France is a sufficient condition of the monarchic state of France, for he is actually a king only if there is a state—in particular, a monarchy—of which he is the king, and he is King of France only if France is a monarchy. But the *person* who is King of France is not a sufficient condition of any state. So it is with the heart: it is a heart, rather than just a collection of flesh, by virtue of its function within the body, which is in turn an actual human body by virtue of the function of the heart. So the heart,

---

[10] As I shall show in the next chapter, he repeatedly talks of the soul when he clearly means the heart, especially in *Parva Naturalia*.

[11] Mary S. Hartman assures me that Louis XIV did not make this statement.

like any essence, necessarily involves a certain sort of matter. Moreover, as we know from Chapter Three, Aristotle would probably agree that the heart is what individuates the person, in that sameness of heart is tantamount to sameness of person.[12]

This interpretation does not make Aristotle's conception of the soul fit perfectly into his ontology, but I trust it shows he is not wallowing in random contradictions. His psychology as a whole provides an illustration of an Aristotelian tendency noted previously: a simple model becomes enormously complex, and initial definitions prove inadequate to account for all the data Aristotle brings forward.[13] But even if Aristotle needs to learn as he discusses the status of the soul that formal and efficient cause may overlap, it does not follow that he must essentially change his fourfold classification of explanation. The world is full of overlaps, borderline cases, and exceptions to neat rules. Part of Aristotle's greatness—it is also part of the difficulty of reading Aristotle—is that he neither ignores the refractory details of the universe nor abandons his main beliefs and concepts at the first sign of difficulty for them.

As it happens, recent conceptual analysis of certain psychological states, in particular desires and intentions, has led to controversy about their relation to behavior. Aristotle tries to say how the soul can be both the form of the body and the efficient cause of its actions. For some recent philosophers the problem has been similar. Given that an intention to perform action B is by definition a psychological state that is normally followed by action B, how can the intention cause the action?[14] For a causal relation is contingent, not necessary. But surely the intention must be the cause of the act one performs. What makes an intention

[12] Sameness of dictator is of course not tantamount to sameness of state.

[13] So G.E.L. Owen, "Tithenai ta phainomena."

[14] The argument I use in the following lines is adapted from Donald Davidson's "Actions, Reasons, and Causes."

truly explanatory of a certain act is precisely the causal connection, for it is clearly possible to have an intention to do something and then to do it unintentionally. But now we have, what one would have thought impossible, a description of a cause that is not logically independent of the description of the effect.

But if a single event or state can have various true descriptions, then there is no problem in there being some description of the cause that logically involves the effect. Indeed, that will be true in every case of cause and effect, since one can always rename the cause of B "the cause of B" and say "the cause of B caused B." It would certainly be possible to find some description of each state of intention that does not have any logical connection to its fulfillment. Now in order for A to be the cause of B, the connection between the two states or events must be an instance of some universal law. But though there is no universal law according to which an intention to perform an act is always followed by the performance of the act, there are descriptions of these states under which they are instances of some law; and such is all that is required.

It is clear from *Met.* Δ 5 and any number of passages in the *Nicomachean Ethics*, particularly those dealing with the practical syllogism and weakness of the will, that Aristotle defines desires as efficient *aitiai* of actions towards ends.[15] What is not so clear is whether Aristotle could use anything like Davidson's defense of the possibility of both logical and causal relations between states or events, for that defense depends on our being able to give various descriptions of individual states or events, as well as of things. This, unfortunately, is just what Aristotle is loath to do, as I argued in Chapter Two: he individuates things and

---

[15] See Richard Sorabji, "Body and Soul in Aristotle," esp. p. 81, n. 4. Sorabji seems to believe it is not possible for two states or events to be both logically and causally related in this way, and in that I think he is wrong. But I am happy to acknowledge my debt to his excellent essay, in which I have found much with which I can agree.

events by their descriptions. But my purpose has been only to show that there is some plausibility in Aristotle's view that the soul is both engine and essence, not that he has a full defense of it.

I want to go on now to discuss psychological events and their relation to physical events. Aristotle denies that that relation is identity, for reasons that tell us something about his standards for identity and a great deal about the sense in which the soul is the form of the body. Aristotle's view is that the mental event is the form of the physical event.

III. PSYCHOLOGICAL EVENTS AND PHYSICAL EVENTS

It follows that Aristotle does not believe that each mental event is strictly identical to some physical event; in fact, he believes that no mental or psychological event is strictly identical to any physical event.[16] Since he accepts a physiological theory that gives prominence to the heart, it is natural that Aristotle should take as a paradigm of materialism the notion that certain mental events are identical to certain movements of the heart. That much he suggests at *De An.* I 1 403a3ff. The question he is trying to answer there is whether the *pathē* (this may mean properties, actions, or passions) of the soul apply also to what has the soul; or is any of them a property of only the soul?[17] The question

[16] This is true, remember, even of those events that have nothing to do with *nous*, the faculty notoriously unconnected with the body.

[17] I am not now trying to distinguish between psychological events and mental events. If there is a distinction, it probably lies in the epistemological peculiarity of mental events: the person whose mental event it is can make authoritative reports about it. The notion of a psychological event is broader, as it includes events that might be more easily discerned by a psychiatrist than by their owner. Some of what I say towards the end of this chapter and in Chapter Five could be roughly summarized in this way: Aristotle says much more about the psychological-physical relation than the mind-body one.

In any case, the notion of a physical event is elusive, and it tends to take its color from what it is being contrasted to. From an Arisis not a simple one, as Aristotle goes on to show; for there are degrees of dependency. In that chapter he uses the unfortunate analogy of a straight line to show that something may be inseparable in fact from that from which it is separable in definition—from some matter, for example. But even if psychological events are not by definition inseparable from certain physical events, they are inseparable in fact, and in a way in which mathematical objects are not; for they are possible only with matter of a certain definite sort. Aristotle might better have used an ordinary substance as an analogy, since its form will make certain demands on the matter of which it is made, as I argued in Chapter Two.

It is clear from *De An.* I 1 that no psychological event is possible in the absence of any physical event whatever. When one is in a state of anger, tenderness, fear, pity, courage, joy, loving, hating, ". . . simultaneously with these the body suffers something" (403a18f.). This is true even of thought (8-10), which cannot happen without imagination; but imagination is only a necessary condition for thought, and not sufficient. The interesting question, then, is this: are certain bodily states sufficient as well as necessary for certain psychological states?[18] Does Aristotle believe there is a one-one or many-one correlation between sorts of bodily state and sorts of psychological state? The passage just quoted is compatible with, say, fear and courage being correlated with the same bodily state. But the context shows

---

totelian point of view on psychological events other than thoughts, the physicalist or materialist is the one who believes that every psychological event is identical with some physical event, that a physical event is the sort of event a natural scientist would be likely to investigate, and that a natural scientist usually explains events by reference to efficient causes, at least when discussing the actions characteristic of animate organisms.

[18] If they are—if, that is, a certain sort of psychological state can be correlated with a certain sort of physical state—that is (inconclusive) evidence in favor of the identity of bodily and psychological states. If many different sorts of psychological state can accompany one sort of bodily state, that is evidence against identity.

that that is not Aristotle's intention. His reason (stated in lines 19-25) for saying that each psychological state is accompanied by a physical state is that one may be angry or afraid without good reason, or unafraid in spite of fearsome circumstances. It is reasonable to infer that he means that whether one is afraid or angry depends, in the first instance, not on the circumstances, but rather on the state of the body involved. Moreover, if all this goes to show, as Aristotle next says it does, that psychological events are formulae with matter (*logoi enuloi*), what remains to distinguish fear from anger is only that they accompany and are in fact constituted by different physical events.

Now Aristotle gives what looks like it is supposed to be an adequate definition of anger: "being angry is a certain movement of a certain sort of body or some part or faculty of it, brought about by something or other, for the sake of something or other" (403a26ff.). The definition involves more than just the physical state of the person; it involves both the cause and the purpose of the state, though it is reasonable to suppose that the external circumstances standardly connected with the state need not actually be present in every case.

The natural scientist would define anger as the boiling of the blood and hot material around the heart, the dialectician would define it as something like a desire to retaliate; so the first gives the matter of the event, the second the form (403a29-b1). That the physical event is called the matter of the psychological event does not imply that different psychological events might accompany this physical event. If my interpretation is correct thus far, the matter (the physiological event) is in fact, but not by definition, a sufficient condition of the form (the psychological event). There is no logical connection between one's being in a state of fear and one's heart being in a certain state: that is, the two descriptions under which the states are individuated are different, and they do not imply each other. Therefore the states are at most accidentally identical, and not strongly identical. To borrow an expression Aristotle uses in another context but could have used here as well, the two are the same in actuality but not in being (*De An.* III 2 425b25ff.; cf. Chapter Five, Section III). For event identity Aristotle wants mutual logical dependency, and he does not have it here.

But there is a famous passage in I 4 that argues that movement of the heart, at any rate, is not even a sufficient condition of what we call mental events. Aristotle notes that the soul is thought to move; for it is said to exult, to be in pain, to fear, to be angry, and to be in many other such states; and all these are movements.

> [But] even if it is true that feeling pain or joy and thinking are movements, that experiencing each of these is being moved and that the movements are due to the soul; even if being angry, for example, or being afraid is a particular movement of the heart, or thinking is a movement of this or some other part (some of the movements being loco-motion, others qualitative change—the sort and the origin don't matter); nevertheless, speaking of the soul as being angry is like saying that the soul is weaving or building. Surely it would be better not to say that the soul pities or learns or thinks; better to say the man does it with his soul. This means not that the motion happens in the soul but that the motion sometimes reaches to the soul and sometimes starts from it. So perception starts in particular objects; memory, on the other hand, starting from the soul, is directed at movements or traces in the sense organs. (408b5-18)

Aristotle has a problem. On the one hand, he argues in the first chapter for a one-one correlation between psychological states and physical ones by pointing out that one can be afraid or angry in the absence of the appropriate circumstances. In the fourth chapter, on the other hand, he argues against attributing anger and fear just to the soul by pointing out that these and other psychological states bear essential reference to things and circumstances outside the person; perception, which requires something that gets perceived, is a perfect example.

What Aristotle needs to do, and does not quite manage to do, is to distinguish between (a) those mental states that are defined in part by reference to their usual causes or effects (for example, pains, desires, and certain emotions) but can sometimes exist in the absence of those causes or effects, and (b) those mental states that are necessarily accompanied by the circumstances definitive of them (for example, perception and memory). Then he could say that one's body's being in a certain state is a sufficient condition of one's being afraid, whereas one is perceiving only if there is actually something there that bears a certain causal and evidential relation to one's sensory state.[19]

In any case, even where Aristotle is ready to allow that the state of the body is a sufficient condition of the psychological state, the relation between the states is not identity, for the descriptions of the states are independent. The denial of identity in this case is of a piece with his general approach to identity, about which something more needs to be said, this time on the relation between *kinēsis* (movement, or process) and *energeia* (activity). Aristotle has a detailed and coherent position about the identity of *kinēseis* —the word is usually taken to mean "movements," but it is broader and subtler than that.[20] He believes movements can be individuated in a way partly derivative from the way in which we individuate substances; and in *Phys.* V 4 he gives some criteria for identity of movements, particularly local movements. The thing moving, the place, including termini

---

[19] Aristotle is not reluctant to define entities by saying what they do always or for the most part. For a contemporary example of a definition by reference to usual causes or effects, see David K. Lewis, "An Argument for the Identity Theory," pp. 163ff.: pain is what is typically caused by damage to the flesh.

[20] In much of what follows I am in debt to Terry Penner's "Verbs and the Identity of Actions"; see esp. pp. 412-414 and 438-441.

and route, and the time must all be the same—thus 227b23ff. At *Phys.* VII 4 249a17ff. he suggests that the means of locomotion must be the same as well, though it would surely have to be if all the other respects were the same. The place in which the movement happens is its form (or genus, Aristotle sometimes says); so two movements over the same route are the same kind of movement, but distinguishable according to the mover and the time somewhat as matter or accident distinguishes things that are the same in form.

The sort of event with which movement (*kinēsis*) is often contrasted is actuality (*energeia*).[21] Aristotle distinguishes between *kinēsis* and *energeia* mainly in two ways: (1) in the case of an *energeia* to be ϕing is to have ϕed, whereas in the case of a *kinēsis* to be ϕing is not to have ϕed because one has not finished one's ϕing; (2) one can sensibly be said to perform a *kinēsis*, but not an *energeia*, quickly or slowly. (See *Met.* Θ 6 1048b18ff. and *Nic. Eth.* X 3 1173a29ff.) The idea is that a *kinēsis* is a process from one place or condition to another, whereas an *energeia* is just being in a certain essentially homogeneous state or condition as opposed to not being in it. Performing a task and walking somewhere (all walking is walking somewhere) are *kinēseis*; seeing and having pleasure are *energeiai*. Now an *energeia* and a *kinēsis* can happen in the same place at the same time, but they cannot be the same event. So, for example, a *kinēsis* that one enjoys performing is not identical with the pleasure (an *energeia*) that one gets from it, though the pleasure is not some different event over and above the movement and caused by it (see *Nic. Eth.* VII 12 and X 5).[22] Moreover, the exercise of a human faculty is regularly an *energeia*, but the bodily events that are necessary and jointly sufficient for that *energeia* may be *kinēseis*; and if the passages in *De An.* I 1 and I 4 are any indication, they

21 From now on I shall use the Greek terms, since the usual translations may obfuscate some issues.
22 Cf. Penner, pp. 441f., n. 40.

are the matter of the *energeia* and not identical to it.[23] In some cases an *energeia* could be more like the matter of a *kinēsis*; so, for example, one could be using one's legs just for fun and thereby (perhaps even unintentionally) win a cross-country walking race from A to B. And since *energeiai* are homogeneous and lack the criteria for identity that individuate *kinēseis*, it is to be expected that they would more readily function as matter than as form.

But two *kinēseis* can be related somewhat as form and matter, or at any rate as items that are accidentally identical, if they are presented under different descriptions. So my hand's moving in a certain way and my waving are both *kinēseis* and are only accidentally identical. That is how it will be in every case in which the thing moved, or perhaps even any part of its movement or its route, is described differently.[24] It is this relation of accidental identity that holds between a psychological event and its accompanying physical event. Sometimes the physical event is a sufficient condition of the mental event; but even then they are not strongly identical. Their being, as Aristotle says in *De An.* III 2, is different.

[23] This seems a good way to make sense of some of what Aristotle says in *De An.* II 5 and 6 and III 2. See further Chapter Five, Section III.

[24] Though what Aristotle says about *energeia* and *kinēsis* indicates that the recently fashionable distinction between behavior and bodily movement would not be entirely foreign to him, I am not convinced by D. W. Hamlyn's attempt to assimilate the distinctions in "Behavior." Hamlyn argues from the completeness of *energeia* that its final cause is not separate from it, and from the incompleteness of *kinēsis* that "no movement is in itself and by itself intelligible." Since, Hamlyn believes, a piece of behavior is intelligible in itself in that it does not normally make sense to ask for the efficient cause of an activity, whereas we do ask for and give efficient causes for bodily movements, it makes sense to say the former is complete but not the latter. But I think Hamlyn is wrong about what completeness means; Penner makes that clear. If anything, *kinēsis* is more like what we call behavior and *energeia* like bodily movement—the inside, one might say, of a *kinēsis*. How can Hamlyn explain that thinking is an *energeia*, learning a *kinēsis*? See *Met.* Θ 6 1048b23ff.

As I have argued in Chapter Two, Aristotle's standards for identity are too high, for both things and events. Nearly all contemporary philosophers would agree with me against Aristotle on things; concerning events there is less agreement. Aristotle's demand that strongly identical things have the same definition and description has the absurd consequence that no individual can have multiple descriptions. That consequence does not seem so clearly absurd in the case of events and states, but I think it is a problem. One may be misled because facts are tied to propositions and thus descriptions, and facts seem little different from states. The fact that I own a Plymouth is not identical to the fact that I own a blue Plymouth, and it may be that my being the owner of a Plymouth is not identical to my being the owner of a blue Plymouth. But surely the state (or state of affairs) by virtue of which it is true that I own a Plymouth is identical with the state of affairs by virtue of which it is true that I own a blue Plymouth, and your theft of my Plymouth is identical with your theft of my blue Plymouth.[25]

Moreover, I think Aristotle is wrong in denying that a particular bodily state is identical with a particular psychological state on the grounds that there is a further condition of their co-occurrence (for example, that there be an object of perception or that there be an event one is remembering). The events might not have been identical, and events so described may not always be identical; but I do not believe they are therefore non-identical in this case.[26]

There are, then, occasions on which one might wish Aristotle had held out for one event or state with two or

[25] For a sample of good work on two sides of the current controversy about the identity of events, consider two papers in Nicholas Rescher, ed., *Essays in Honor of Carl G. Hempel*: Donald Davidson, "The Individuation of Events," and Jaegwon Kim, "Events and their Descriptions: Some Considerations."

[26] See again *Met.* E 2 1026b31ff. and Chapter Two, Section III. For Aristotle strong identity is necessary identity, and necessary identity is eternal identity.

more sorts of description and explanation. But perhaps that judgment takes Aristotle out of the context that helps to give his words their sense. If the distinction between form and matter has any use at all, it is supposed to undercut the stultifying notion that we can in every case straightforwardly say of entities that they are or are not identical: either to identify or simply to distinguish form and matter or mind and body is to fail to understand the categorial distinction Aristotle takes such pains to draw. So every time Aristotle says that form and matter are after all not identical or that they are after all not distinct, the statement must be understood in light of his detailed rulings about the relation between form and matter. More important than whether Aristotle does or does not believe in the identity of soul and body is that he sees the necessity of the system of description and explanation built on the classification of certain things and events as characteristically human, goal-directed, open to assessment from a moral or a prudential point of view. If Aristotle warns us in the first chapter of *De An.* II not to try to say that the soul is or that it is not identical to the body, he will be equally ready to warn us against affirming or denying the identity of every psychological event with a physical event. What counts most is that, in all respects in which materialism is an interesting thesis, Aristotle is a materialist (except as concerns *nous*, which I shall take up in Chapter Six). No dualist—Cartesian, religious, or otherwise—could take much comfort in the reasons Aristotle gives for denying that anger and boiling blood are strongly identical.

IV. VARIOUS KINDS OF EXPLANATION

Before going on to talk about how the Aristotelian view of mental events and the explanation of human behavior has fared in recent years, I want to pause to emphasize how well Aristotle's conception of the status of certain mental events and states fits with his general way of seeing things.

The crucial question for many philosophers who think about the explanation of behavior is whether there are alternative ways of organizing the data of experience depending in part on the questions one wants answered— whether, to put it crudely, there is "room" for psychological explanation. Aristotle sees that there are indeed alternative ways: explanation by reasons and explanation by causes are not in competition, since one thing or event may have as many as four different sorts of explanation.[27] But whereas for recent philosophers this is a truth hard won back from the pretensions of natural science, for Aristotle it is a truth natural science itself can teach us.

Human beings, after all, are natural substances; and things happen for purposes throughout nature, not just among animate beings. Aristotle's argument for that last proposition, presented in full in *Physics* II 5-8, is essentially the following. If events happen in such a way as to serve certain ends, they do so either by chance or by necessity. If they do so by chance, then they do not do so regularly; for what happens by chance is precisely what does not happen regularly. But, contra Empedocles, certain end-serving events do happen regularly; for example, men always or for the most part are born with teeth well suited for the various stages of eating. Therefore the occurrence of end-serving events is a regular and necessary part of nature. So it makes sense to say that a full explanation of at least some events requires mention of the end for which they happen, for to explain an event by giving only the efficient cause is in effect to say that it is just a coincidence that it serves a certain purpose.

Aristotle therefore has two reasons for holding that the typical natural scientist's explanation of a psychological event is inadequate. First, the explanation by efficient cause

---

[27] This ignores, as Aristotle often does, the point mentioned towards the end of Section II above: if things or events are described by reference to different sorts of explanation, they are not strictly the same thing or event.

leaves unanswered a certain pertinent sort of why-question. There are not only causes for behavior, but also reasons for it.[28] Second, as I noted at the end of the first chapter, Aristotle does not believe one could predict everything that happens in the world just by virtue of knowing all the efficient causes there are; for there is no law-like regularity but rather genuine spontaneity at the level of the components of objects in the world. Regularity is imparted to the world by the imposition of form on matter, and sometimes form involves purpose.

Clearly this dual explanation of psychological events is a reflection of Aristotle's view of the way in which natural science at its best should explain physical events as well. This is in part a consequence of his view of nature, which he likens to a doctor treating himself (*Phys.* II 8 199b30ff.). His use of the notions of potency and actuality, rather than the notion of a law of nature, makes it hard for him to distinguish clearly between a dispositional property and a desire and thus hard to resist the temptation to use the latter as an analogy to the natural power of an inanimate object. So psychology looks very much like biology, and the relation between mind and body is assimilable to that between form and matter. Aristotle has made it a bit too easy. Moreover, as I noted in the previous chapter in discussion of personal identity and unity, the mysterious "private" aspect of the mental never strikes Aristotle as a particular problem. (This is a matter I shall mention in the next section, then discuss in some detail in the following chapter, as it has to do primarily with his treatment of the nature of

---

[28] There is a distinction here I am not sure Aristotle grasps. In some cases the end of human behavior seems to be the person's conscious reason for action; in other cases it is just the person's well-being or survival. In the latter case we explain an event or a state by showing why it is good that a person should be in that state, or should be capable of that sort of state; it does not follow that the person is in the state voluntarily. *De An.* I 1 seems to run the cases together.

perception.) There are, then, at least two good reasons for expecting something like the sort of view this chapter has discovered in the programmatic statements in *De An.* I 1 and 4 and II 1 and 2, where Aristotle argues that the relation of mental to physical events is not quite identity.

As before, Aristotle has propounded a view for which there is much to be said, though he is unaware of some of its limitations and difficulties. In the discussion of Aristotle's metaphysics it was necessary to admit that Aristotle was naive in believing that any possible rational science would accept the view that there are in nature substances with potencies, irreducible to their constituents, and events inexplicable just by reference to laws governing the behavior of matter. But from a certain point of view Aristotle has been vindicated: substances form a keystone of any conceptual system we can think of, even if for the scientist's purposes there are not tables but clouds of molecules. Much the same can be said for Aristotle's views on the soul: he holds out against something like the identity theory on grounds of distinctness for events that many recent philosophers would not accept, and he does not contemplate the possibility of a conceptual disruption, based on the progress of neurophysiology, that could reach all the way to the cognition of what we now consider the very basis of all our empirical knowledge. This sort of conservatism is itself dubious; but then so too, in my opinion, is the radical claim that the eventual complete erasure of our present classification of certain events as mental is genuinely possible. Again, Aristotle's vindication is a matter more of how we must normally see things than of a certainty that things must be as we normally see them. Aristotle is wrong about the limits on any possible good scientific explanation of human behavior, but he is right on two matters it is not easy to get right together: one sort of explanation we give of mental entities is ineliminably important; but the mental is all the same not *sui generis*, a surd element in an otherwise complete and coherent picture of the world.

V. ARISTOTLE AND HIS HEIRS ON
PSYCHOLOGICAL STATES

There is much more to be said about Aristotle's treatment of the mind and its states, but his view even as so far described is an important one with influential advocates in contemporary discussions of the mind-body problem. It is time to say a bit more about those discussions, and in particular about some philosophers who take a recognizably Aristotelian side in them.

Broadly speaking, there are two arenas in which arguments about the relation between mind and body are now carried on. One has something to do with epistemology: philosophers have argued that what is special and unquestionably true about certain mental events is that their subjects have some kind of private access to them, as they do not have to physical events. The other involves explanation: the explanation of the behavior of entities with minds is quite different from that of inanimate entities. It is sometimes argued that the best possible explanations of human behavior require the postulation of characteristically mental states, which are not identical with physical states. Aristotle is active mainly in the second arena; he has so little to say about the first sort of problem that there are those who deny that he has anything to say about what is now called the mind-body problem. This seems to me incorrect, if not entirely wrongheaded. However, it is a topic better discussed in Chapter Five, where Aristotle's views about perception will be scrutinized. Here it is appropriate to compare Aristotle's position on psychological events with that of some contemporary philosophers who attend to problems other than that of the privacy of mental states and events. What is good about Aristotle's view, and that of his modern counterparts, is the hospitable attitude towards various sorts of explanation, in particular towards psychological explanation, as opposed to an insistence on taking only one sort of explanation seriously. What is wrong is the inference that materialism is false. As I have already indicated, I think Aristotle has unnecessarily high standards for identity, especially for event identity. So have some of his philosophical heirs, including Jerry Fodor and Hilary Putnam, whose views on the mind and psychological explanation suit them well for comparison with Aristotle.

Fodor and Putnam[29] have argued that the fact that certain events can be described and explained in various ways is the beginning of a sound argument against materialism. According to Fodor, psychological and physical explanation are the counterpart in a theory about explanation to mind and matter in a theory about nature. Fodor tries to show that these two sorts of explanation, while they do not reduce to each other, do not conflict either, but in fact complement each other. The outcome of this approach is monistic in one way and dualistic in another: the mental and the physical are two in that they admit of two different sorts of explanation; they are one in that the one sort of explanation rests on the other. Exactly how the one rests on the other is a difficult question, but we shall look at Fodor's answer in due course.

Fodor begins with a view about explanations that Aristotle would find congenial: "Roughly: the appropriateness of an explanation is determined not by the phenomena it seeks to account for but by the question it seeks to answer."[30] An explanation of a fire might satisfy a chemist but be of no interest to an insurance adjuster. An explanation of behavior that would satisfy a physiologist might not satisfy a psychologist. Fodor's point is that there are two sorts of explanation of any behavioral phenomenon because there

[29] Fodor: "Explanations in Psychology"; "Materialism." Putnam: "Minds and Machines"; "Robots: Machines or Artificially Created Life?"; "The Mental Life of Some Machines"; "The Nature of Mental States."

[30] Fodor, "Explanations," p. 165.

are two prominent sorts of question one can ask about behavior, and not because behavior defies classification and description in a scientific way.

Quite aside from the claim that a genuine explanation of action requires reasons and not causes, the dualist may argue that psychology of the physiological kind can explain only bodily movement and not behavior, which requires interpretation, which as a rule is to be kept out of the observation-base. Even learning theory requires interpretation of bodily movements; for responses are classified according to functional equivalence or lack of it, and the determination of that also requires interpretation. So it seems that "the requirement that we characterize the events upon which the confirmation of a theory depends *only* in terms of their immediately observable properties may render the systematic explanation of these events impossible."[31]

In the present state of psychology and physiology, it is claimed that a science purely of the motions of organisms is no more possible for us than it was for Anaxagoras, whose mechanistic explanations Socrates deprecated, according to the *Phaedo*, just because he thought they were not capable of predicting behavior accurately.[32] Instead, we must identify motions of organisms as constituting this or that act in part by their relations to hypothetical states like needs, drives, and so on. The explanations that make behavior intelligible to us cannot be had only by appeal to causal chains and laws.

What, then, is the form of psychological explanation? According to Fodor, it is a two-phase process. The first phase of the explanation is the development of a theory of internal states of the organism (desires, fears, drives, etc.).

[31] *Ibid.*, p. 169. Fodor might have added that the notion of a property that is naturally immediately observable is most difficult to make out. I shall return to this topic in Chapter Five.

[32] He thought bodily movements were necessary but never sufficient conditions of rational action. *Phaedo* 98C-99C.

The terms of the theory that refer to these internal states and not to behavior are functionally characterized: that is, the theory characterizes the internal states of the organism only in respect to the way in which they function in production of behavior. And the theory can predict the behavior of the organism given knowledge of the current stimuli. The evidence that such states exist is this: the assumption that they do is the simplest way to account for the behavior of the organism. The second phase of the process of explanation is to uncover the details of the mechanism capable of realizing the functionally defined internal states postulated by the first phase of the theory. The phases may proceed hand in hand; so the psychologist may be able to construct his first-phase theory with an eye to what the neurological facts are, or are likely to turn out to be. I confess I do not understand how a first-phase theory will correspond to a physical theory, or fail to correspond. Surely all it needs to do is correspond to—that is, account for—the behavior of the organism. In fact, it could fail to correspond to a physical theory only by failing to correspond to the behavior for which that theory is supposed to account—that is, the same behavior for which the first-phase theory itself is supposed to account.[33]

The two phases of the complete explanation (or the two different sorts of explanation) cannot be reduced to one, and each is indispensable.

> In microanalysis one asks: "What does X consist of?" and the answer has the form of a specification of the microstructure of Xs. . . . In functional analysis, one asks about a part of a mechanism what role it plays in the activities characteristic of the mechanism as a whole. . . .[34]

> . . . psychological terms are . . . names for functions, psychological states are not available for microanalysis and

[33] Stephen P. Stich, "Grammars, Psychological Theories and Turing Machines," p. 10.
[34] Fodor, "Explanations," p. 177.

theoretical revision could identify them only with other functions, not with mechanisms.[35]

> The remark "A drive is not a neurological state" . . . expresses a necessary truth.[36]

Much of what Fodor says is, as he acknowledges, elaboration of Putnam's views. Putnam contributes to the analysis of the mind-body relation the analogy of the relation between the program of a computer (or, more generally, the logical states of a Turing machine) and the mechanism (transistors, etc.) that makes it work. The example is a bit more elaborate than Fodor's example of the camshaft, but the point is much the same. Putnam does argue, though, where Fodor seems only half-heartedly to assert, that a (functional) state of the organism, which is analogous to the psychological state, is not identical with any physical-chemical state.

> We cannot discover laws by virtue of which it is physically necessary that an organism prefers A to B if and only if it is in a certain physical-chemical state. For we already know that any such laws would be false. They would be false because even in the light of our present knowledge we can see that any Turing Machine that can be physically realized at all can be realized in a host of totally different ways. Thus there cannot be a physical-chemical structure the possession of which is a necessary and sufficient condition for preferring A to B, even if we take "necessary" in the sense of *physically* necessary and not in the sense of logically necessary.[37]

So in normal cases the logical or functional state can exist in the absence of any one particular physical-chemical state. Can the particular physical-chemical state exist without the logical or functional state? That depends on how fully the physical state is described; but surely in some cases the

---

[35] *Ibid.*, p. 179. [36] *Ibid.*,
[37] Putnam, "Mental Life," p. 192.

would-be description of the state would have to be extended to take account of so much of the environment in order to constitute a sufficient condition of a logical or functional state—including, probably, facts about languages—that it might seem odd to speak of it as just a description of the physical state of the organism. Still, if an organism may have relational properties, then a particular physical state can suffice for the existence of a particular mental one. What I said in Section III about Aristotle's denial that perception is an action of the heart applies here as well.

One might object that the definition of mind might turn out to depend on what can instantiate the program and what cannot. To this Putnam would reply that we have a definition of the mind already; we just do not know what it can and cannot be housed in.[38] And of course that reply rests on a clear notion of definition that cannot change no matter how much information we may get in addition about something, as well as a notion of the definition of something as opposed to fact about it—that is, the analytic as opposed to the synthetic.[39]

---

[38] Recall *Met.* Z 10 1035b27: "the heart or the brain; it doesn't matter which. . . ."

[39] There are in any case doubts about the analogy between functional states and mental ones. To begin with, even if we were clear about what a functional state is, there would be a question about why we should believe every mental state, including a flash of pain, is a functional one. Is it only because most are characterized through their normal causes or effects? Why does that make them functional? Again, what are the criteria for the functional isomorphism of two states? Whether two states or two mechanisms are functionally isomorphic is as easy or as difficult to determine as whether two things do the same thing; and whether two things do the same thing will depend on the criteria one uses for sameness. Where are these criteria spelled out, and how are they to be defended? (See further Richard Rorty, "Functionalism, Machines, and Incorrigibility.")

It is not easy to see just how far the machine-program analogy is supposed to go. If its point is only that one must distinguish between physical states and functional ones, then Aristotle's analogy of the axe is just as powerful. But what is interesting about a computer is that there is some reason to suppose that it can do what one might

Now Putnam nowhere gives any good reason for doubting that a particular functional or psychological state can be identified with some mechanistic state, nor therefore for saying that materialism is false. It is true enough that there is no particular sort of mechanistic state, as described narrowly and in detail, that is necessary for some functional state: the "realization" of pain, for example, varies between species. But it does not follow that either my being in pain or a squirrel's being in pain is non-identical to my brain state or its, respectively, just because our brain states are different. That a Pinto is a Ford and a Torino is a Ford does not prevent this Pinto from being identical to some Ford.[40] To be sure, the *fact* that I am in pain is different from the *fact* that my C-fibers are firing; but then the fact that I am driving a Ford is not the same as the fact that I am driving a Pinto. Nor is the property of being a Ford driver the same property as that of being a Pinto driver. There is, I think, a sense of "state" that amounts roughly to "property"—as a state of being red, which is not the same as a state of being colored. (See Section III of this chapter and Chapter Two, Section III.) That is not the sense I have in mind here, nor is it the sense that I consider pertinent to

---

have thought only men can do: that is, think. Given that it can, and given that its carrying out a program is an example of its thinking, then lo and behold a certain form of materialism is true (unless, as Putnam has suggested, materialism is false for machines too). There are, to put it very mildly indeed, a number of shortcomings in that use of the analogy. It needs some argument to show that what the computer does is really thinking, that thinking is essential to the mental life in a way in which sensation and other capacities aren't, that a Cartesian mind cannot emerge from hardware. It would be at best enormously difficult to show that on the one hand the computer is a good analogy to the human mind while on the other hand there is no mind-body problem with computers; I know of nobody who has even begun to do it. It is probably true that the manufacture of robots indistinguishable in behavior and superficial appearance from ordinary humans would convert a good many people to materialism, but it is not clear that anything interesting follows from that.

[40] I owe the example to Simon Kirby.

materialism. If it were, as the functionalists give indications of thinking it is, then a mental state would be different from a physical state only in the sense in which the state of a bridge being unsafe would be non-identical to any structural state described in terms of atoms and the void alone. In fact, if we use mutual logical dependency as a criterion for the identity of states and events, then Gerald Ford's headache is not the same as the thirty-eighth American president's headache. So I am inclined to agree with this statement of Putnam's: "If Materialism is taken to be the denial of the existence of "nonphysical" attributes, then Materialism is false even for robots![41]

There are widely varying degrees of reducibility; so there are likely to be various strengths of materialism too. I have suggested standards for event identity much less strict than those assumed by some other philosophers, notably Aristotle. It may be that the best way to assess criteria for identity is to see whether the results of using the criteria make sense in quite different contexts. Putnam is in effect suggesting high standards for identity, but then denying that strict identity need be involved in a reasonable sort of materialism—namely, the sort that permits materialism to be true for robots, bridges, or tables. That form of materialism would presumably be ready to deny that a material object must be identical with its matter. Aristotle, rather like Putnam, has high standards for identity but does not insist that a material object is identical with its matter—indeed, he holds that it is not, that furthermore the material object under one description is only accidentally identical to the material object under some other description. It is precisely because his standards for identity are so high that one can say that, in modern terms, Aristotle is a materialist, at least on the topics under discussion in this chapter. For materialism does not require identity as strong as what Aristotle considers full identity.

What does it require? If the physical-chemical state or

[41] Putnam, "Robots," p. 72.

event, however fully described just in physical-chemical terms, is no sort of sufficient condition of the functional-logical or psychological event, then materialism is false. That is, materialism means that the fully described physical-chemical state is a sufficient condition of the psychological or functional-logical state. The converse need not be the case. So a one-to-one or many-to-one relation between the physical states and the psychological states spells materialism, whereas a one-to-many relation indicates that materialism is false. But that last would be hard indeed to pin down; for if we came upon a one-to-many relation, it would be rational for us to believe we had not explored the physical basis of the mental events sufficiently thoroughly.[42] I am not sure this criterion would be useful in other contexts, but for materialism it seems to work. Note that it is loose enough to allow the state of a thing to be no more than a state of its matter, since a complete description of the state of a thing's matter in the terms meaningfully and truly applicable just to the components will determine the state of the substance as a whole; but the matter itself will not be the same as the thing, since the existence of the matter does not entail the existence of the thing, nor vice versa.

Nothing I have said is intended to show that we should give up the practice of attributing intentions, drives, and other propositional attitudes and psychological states to persons. On the contrary, materialism is compatible with our usual ways of explanation of human behavior and our restriction of these ways of explanation to animate beings. Furthermore, materialism is compatible with ethical and other concerns of our lives, just as determinism is compatible not only with our incorrigible experiences of having

[42] This is a successor to the old view that a one-to-one relation between sorts of physical event and sorts of mental event spells materialism. It is further supposed that a one-to-many physical-to-mental relation makes for materialism and that a many-to-one physical-to-mental relation is incompatible with materialism. See, e.g., Herbert Feigl's "The Mental and the Physical," esp. pp. 374ff.

desires and making decisions but also with our having less free will if we are in prison than if we are not.

Some materialists do betray a scientistic bias in describing what the increase in scientific knowledge will or should do to the concepts we use. Thus Quine:

> An example is the disposition called intelligence—the ability, vaguely speaking, to learn quickly and to solve problems. Sometime, whether in terms of proteins, colloids, nerve nets, or overt behavior, the relevant branch of science may reach the stage where a similarity notion can be constructed capable of making even the notion of intelligence respectable—and superfluous.[43]

In order to establish this claim, one would surely have to show how the notions to be substituted for intelligence will be at least equally useful in all the contexts in which intelligence figures. They almost certainly will not be, as no set of structural properties of bridges will ever do the job now done by unsafeness. The materialist need not be bothered by this fact, but neither should he forget it.

The withering away of our mental concepts would not obviously follow on the acceptance of materialism. For even if one regarded pain as a certain sort of neurophysiological event, there would be moral reasons for sorting neurophysiological events according to whether they are (or constitute) pains. Indeed, within science certain mental events or processes seem to take an ineliminable place: surely science —or knowledge of any sort—is possible just because there is some isomorphism between the realm of entities we now call mental and that of physical ones; hence to deny the importance of the standard taxonomy of mental entities is to deny the very possibility of knowledge, which is itself a mental state.[44] So the trouble with refusing to attribute

---

[43] W.V.O. Quine, "Natural Kinds," p. 22.

[44] That science is a human enterprise seems to have parallel consequences for certain (perhaps unnecessarily strict) sorts of determinism: decisions too seem not eliminable from doing science. See

mental properties is that it would be self-defeating: the utopian science that suggests such a course must be one that has pulled the ladder up behind it. Whether one finds interesting only a materialism that denies that truth depends on one's interests.

I find Aristotle's position, and therefore that of Fodor and Putnam, about the relation between psychological and bodily events most interesting for its failure to take into account an essential feature of mental entities.[45] Materialism is harder than it looks from an Aristotelian point of view, as the next two chapters will demonstrate.

---

further Bernard Williams's "Postscript" to D. F. Pears's anthology, *Freedom and the Will*, pp. 132f.

[45] Putnam does briefly discuss the epistemological peculiarities of the mental in "Minds and Machines" and "Robots," but it is clear that he does not regard them as puzzling or particularly important.

Chapter Five
PERCEPTION AND MATERIALISM

I F Aristotle's conception of the mind and its relation to physical nature is at all like that of any contemporary analytical philosopher, the similarities will surface in the discussion of perception. For analysis of perception usually draws one's attention to internal representations of sensed items, and these representations are thought to be characteristically mental entities. I think some philosophers have misunderstood them, and in particular our knowledge of them, to the detriment of a possible rational materialism. But the immediate question is not whether materialism is true, but whether Aristotle thinks about the features of the entities that lead some philosophers to bifurcate nature into the mental and the physical (Section I). Aristotle's discussion of special sensibles gives some evidence that he is conscious of the importance of these features. He says that one is an infallible authority on one's special sensibles, and he suggests that the perceiver acquires empirical knowledge by inference from immediate knowledge of them. But the account of these sensibles is confused, and on balance they seem not to be much like what many philosophers since Descartes have considered the paradigmatically mental entities that play a mediating role in perception (Section II). Aristotle does believe, however, that perception is a kind of assimilation of perceiver to perceived, and therein he agrees with both common sense and traditional epistemology. But he has some puzzling ways of describing this assimilation, and the evidence is that he has an essentially materialist theory of sense perception as a special case of physical change because he cannot clearly say what sensation is over and above ordinary physical interaction (Section III). His account of *aisthēma* in *Parva Naturalia* adds to what he has said in *De Anima;* but *aisthēmata* are not clearly mental entities in the Cartesian sense, and they do not fully answer the question, what is perception but interaction (Section IV)?

But there are some promising things in Aristotle's account of perception. One of them is his description of the workings of the common faculty of sense, which is a device drawn up to help unify consciousness. The success of the device is far from complete, but it does show that some good questions are getting asked (Section V). That Aristotle is on the track of reasonable answers to these good questions is likely, for his doctrine that a psychological event is the form of a physical event is to a great extent true, wrong though it be in some details (Section VI).[1]

I. PERCEPTION AND MENTAL ENTITIES

Discussion of perception is one important source of both confusion and enlightenment about materialism and views opposed to it. But Aristotle's theory of perception is sometimes thought to be a counterexample, for what is most significant about it seems to be that Aristotle has nothing interesting to say about the special status of the immediate objects of perception, which are mental if anything is. This view of what goes on in the second book of *De Anima* has been disputed, but there is something to it. Aristotle really does not see the problem of what is sometimes called the privacy of certain experiences or reports. Despite this shortcoming—indeed, maybe because of it[2]—Aristotle takes some positions that are importantly right.

Aristotle gives an account of perception that begins with

---

[1] I have profited from the commentaries of Hamlyn, Hicks, and Rodier, though I shall seldom cite them specifically.

[2] The point is that those who stress the privacy of mental entities have been misled into believing that that feature of them makes it impossible for them to be physical entities. Since Aristotle fails to ponder privacy carefully, he fails to be misled by it.

a description of the action of a perceived object on a sense organ but does not end there; yet precisely what more he thinks perception is than the reflection of an object in an organ is controversial, no doubt in part because Aristotle himself vacillates on the question. And well he might, for it is a most difficult one, disputed even today. Given that a certain physical event takes place in my eye when I see, given that the event is caused in part by what I see, what more must be the case in order for there to be seeing? Something must happen in the brain too—in the heart, Aristotle says—and that is important. But one may believe that any description of the physical states of the participating organs leaves something out. From what may seem a common-sense point of view, or a Cartesian one to those who do not share those intuitions,[3] what is most interesting about perception is the mental event or state that the physical events cause in the appropriate circumstances; and the description just of those circumstances omits any mention of what is the most important part of perception, namely, what is directly available to the perceiver's consciousness. A slightly different objection, characteristic of some contemporary philosophers who reject Cartesianism, is this: no description purely of the physiological processes involved in perception can adequately characterize what is in fact a psychological process. Even if there is no separate mental event caused by the physical processes, this question remains: given that something happens when a person sensibly apprehends something, such that that person's sense organ is in a certain state, what is it about that state that justifies one in saying that the person is in a state of perception?

A materialist might try to meet the demand for an ade-

---

[3] In *The Concept of Mind* Gilbert Ryle urged that the standard bifurcation of things into physical and mental was a Cartesian trick. (See Hampshire's review of Ryle for an early dissenting vote.) Ryle's view that unseduced common sense is uncartesian will be impressively supported if Aristotle does not notice these mental entities that are supposed to be so evident. I shall return to this point towards the end of Section III.

quate characterization of perception by describing the mechanics of perception in causal and/or evidential terms. So, for example, to say that someone is perceiving an object that is ϕ is to say among other things that there is between the object and him a relation, essentially involving one or more of his sense organs, such that he is in a state that typically causes him to believe that there is a ϕ object before him. The state he is in can be described in physical terms, but some such causal and intentional (the latter because belief is involved) characterization must be true of it if it is to be a state of perception. Of course what we know about the possibility of error makes it clear that one can be in a state otherwise indistinguishable by the owner from perception even when the state is not being caused by the presence of a ϕ object, and/or causes no such belief. So the sort of state that could count as a sense impression of a ϕ object need only be the sort of state that is normally caused by a ϕ object, so that a person in that state would have a reason, but not always an overriding reason, to believe that she was perceiving a ϕ object.[4]

It may be that this state is still not adequately characterized as a state of perceiving, for it has a further property that distinguishes it from certain other states persons often have: in most cases the perceiver can know beyond doubt and without inference that he is in that state, and it would normally be unreasonable for anybody to refuse to believe his sincere statement that he is in that state. If I say I am in that visual state characteristically caused by my seeing a green apple, it would be reckless for any other perceiver to contradict my statement or not to believe it, except on grounds of my insincerity, even if it is probable that I am not looking at a green apple. The point is not that one's noninferential report (which I shall hereafter just call a report) is infallible, but that it is incorrigible by the unaided efforts of persons other than the reporter.[5] Now this last condition

[4] See Chapter Four, note 19.

[5] See further Richard Rorty's "Incorrigibility as a Mark of the Mental."

encompasses much of what people mean when they say states of perception are mental states.

The view that most deserves to be called traditional is that certain states are immediately and unproblematically present to our awareness and that these states, which themselves form the basis for all our knowledge, require no basis and are of unchallengeable genuineness, as are certain of our beliefs about them. One of the most important contributions of recent analytical philosophy has been to clear a way for materialism by showing that one might be wrong about the contents of one's own mind, despite one's authoritative status with respect to them.[6] One learns, usually as a child, to report one's mental events; and the reports cannot be any more accurate or adequate than the explanatory theory implicit in the vocabulary one is taught to use. It is at least conceivable that one could be taught that grass is red and that fire engines are green, with the result that one would report the presence of a red mental item when looking at grass in normal circumstances. More importantly, somebody could conceivably be taught to report with great accuracy that certain c-fibers were firing, rather than that she had a toothache. It is not, in general, true that the descriptions we are taught to give of mental states and events are naturally the best suited to them, despite our intuitive certainty about the accuracy and fitness of much of what we are inclined to say.

It follows that our certainty about the accuracy of these reports might be overcome, and our vocabulary of mentalese replaced, if they were available a theory (say, a physi-

---

6 Wittgenstein is often credited with having made the initial successful attack on this flank of Cartesianism. One of the best and most thorough attacks has been that of Wilfrid Sellars, who shreds what he calls the Myth of the Given; see especially his *Science, Perception and Reality*. Saul Kripke has subtly argued in the opposite direction in "Naming and Necessity": "this pain" and "this brain state" are rigid designators; so my pain and my brain state are not identical. But the anti-Givenites are in effect arguing precisely that at least the first of those designators is not rigid, that a given pain might in some possible world not have been a pain.

ological theory) sufficiently better at explaining behavior
and therefore at describing what we now call mental states.
If this is possible, then one of the most tenacious objections
to materialism disappears, namely, that we know as well as
we know anything that what we call mental entities have
properties that exclude their being identical with entities of
which a physiological psychologist might be aware. If this
line of reasoning is correct, the materialist need no longer
be stumped by an objection of the form, "But my sense
impression is yellow, and the brain state to which it is constantly conjoined is not yellow; so they cannot be identical."
He can reply that the mental event and the conjoined physical event share the property of being the sort of state that
normally causes one to believe there is something yellow in
the neighborhood. Hence the one-one correlation between
the so-called sense impression and the brain state will be at
least compatible with the two being identical, though, as
Aristotle rightly believes, not proof of it. That sense impressions are normally non-inferentially and credibly reportable, usually under their causal or evidential descriptions, does not entail that they are non-physical states
unless that sort of characterization or that sort of reportability is logically sufficient for their being mental states and
therefore not physical states.[7] I do not believe it is; I believe
all mental states are physical states.

One might reply that this sort of characterization of mental states makes materialism too easy. In order to convince,
such a reply must bring with it a different characterization
of the mental, and that is not easily found. How is it with
Aristotle? He does not divide the mental from the physical
either in the way I have proposed or in a way congenial to
any recent Cartesians. When he says that some event happens in the soul, he usually means that it happens in the

---

[7] For an argument that they are, and that therefore a materialist
might better show that there are no mental events rather than to
try to prove their identity to physical ones, see Richard Rorty's
"Mind-Body Identity, Privacy, and Categories."

heart; and if that were his official criterion, a heart attack would be a psychological event. More generally, he divides events, as he does objects, into matter and form; and when the event is one characteristic of persons, its form is usually the event as characterized in psychological (often intentional or more overtly teleological) terms of partly biological origin and its matter the event as characterized in physiological terms. So Aristotle too is a kind of materialist: at any rate, he does not distinguish physical events from mental ones by stipulating that in the latter case something happens not only in the heart (or, as we should say, in the brain) but also *in the mind*. For better or worse, he has no ready way of saying this in a manner suggesting that certain events happen in some private Cartesian garden into which only the owner-caretaker may ever look. Not only that: Aristotle does not carve out a set of events that are reportable only by the owner. So the overworked distinction between form and matter—in this case, of an event—must be used to answer the question I have raised: given that something happens when a person sensibly apprehends something, such that the person's sense organ is in a certain state, what is it about that state that justifies one in saying that the person is in a state of perception?

One sort of answer that won't do, I think, is that a certain event is mental if and only if it not only has an effect on a certain organ or receptor but also is within the range of awareness of some further receptor that in some way takes in the first one. This simply pushes the problem back one more stage and does nothing towards solving it. No mere proliferation of mechanisms, each processing the output of the previous one, can solve the problem of precisely what makes a certain event a mental one, or one of which the owner is conscious. Consciousness is better analyzed by reportability than by the notion of some sort of introspecting device scanning the contents of the rest of one's mind; one's ability to report the state of one's mind does not depend on one's having any such device. The credibility of one's reports need not be explained by the credibility of anything else: there can be a physiological explanation of one's ability to give reports of this sort, as well as an inductive justification for accepting such reports, but that is as far as we can go. The alternative would be an infinite regress.

Now there is nothing wrong in characterizing consciousness as being in some way layered, so that certain states of organs count as impressions only when certain further conditions of wakefulness or attention obtain. The difficulty comes when one is led to believe that that sort of analysis fully answers the question I have raised. As described in that way, the state is still only a necessary condition of a mental or psychological state. It must be characterized in causal and evidential terms—that is, as the sort of state that normally provides evidence for a certain belief—in order to be a mental or psychological state. But again, I do not believe, as Aristotle sometimes seems to, that it follows that the physical state is therefore not identical with the psychological one.

In common with nearly every philosopher who discusses perception, Aristotle holds that knowledge is possible because there is some relation of similarity between a part of the world and the sensory apparatus of the person. But Aristotle's expository task is made somewhat more difficult by his doctrine that in general the interaction of any two bodies is an assimilation. What is it, then, that distinguishes perception from just any old interaction? On what I have called the Cartesian view, the answer would have the assimilated states of the perceiver in a mental realm; on a typical materialist view, seeing a green apple would not give rise to anything straightforwardly green or apple-shaped in the perceiver. Aristotle uses a number of striking formulas to characterize the relationship: the perceiver and the perceived are the same in actuality; the soul receives the form of the perceived object but not the matter; the sense becomes like the sensed object. In themselves these formulas are not very informative, and they certainly do not indicate whether Aristotle adopts or is aware of anything like the traditional or Cartesian conception of the mind. What they mean in the context of Aristotle's thought is the primary topic of this chapter. What it is that distinguishes perception from ordinary interaction is the primary question that must be kept in mind throughout the discussion.

II. SPECIAL AND COMMON SENSIBLES

A good way to begin to get clear on the status of the mediators in perception is to look at Aristotle's doctrine of special sensibles. These seem to have some of the characteristic features of mental entities, and some of what Aristotle says about them suggests that his concerns are ours. And some of it does not.

A special sensible is an item that can be directly perceived by exactly one sense: thus sound is the special object of hearing, flavor of taste, and sight of color (*De An.* II 6 418a11ff. and *passim*). The word "directly" is meant only to rule out the sort of minimal inference that goes on when, for example, I see that something is sweet because I recognize it as sugar (III 1 425a22). A common sensible is an item that can be directly perceived by more than one sense: thus I can apprehend motion, rest, shape, size, number, and unity (III 1 425a16) without that sort of inference.

Aristotle captures the reader's attention by stating several times that one cannot be mistaken about the special sensible one is apprehending.[8] So when I am seeing Diares's son, who is white, I can be wrong about who it is but not about what color I am seeing. Occasionally there is hesitation on this point: at III 3 428b18ff. Aristotle says perception of the special objects is true or has the least possible falsehood, thereby strongly suggesting that some falsehood is possible. But two lines further on he claims that there can be no mis-

[8] See, e.g., *De An.* II 6 418a12, III 3 427a12ff., III 6 430b29; also *De Sensu* 4 442b5ff.

take about the white being present, though there may be about whether it is Diares's son. The same cannot be said of our apprehension of common sensibles: in that very passage Aristotle states the likelihood of error about them is even greater than in cases like that of identifying Diares's son. Indeed, it is not unusual for somebody to make a mistake about the size of something from a distance, or its shape seen from an angle; and though it is not in general harder to discern that sort of feature than to identify its owner, mistakes are more frequent in such cases simply because we more often wrongly think we know.

But surely I can be wrong about what color something is? The point is not entirely lost on Aristotle. In *Met.* Γ 5 1010b1ff., where he is talking about Protagoras and illusions, Aristotle seems at first to concede that perception of special objects is true—though both the text and its interpretation are controversial—but he goes on to note that colors as well as sizes are not always what those far away or sick take them to be. But then, having raised the point, Aristotle quickly drops it. Within a few lines he distinguishes between the spheres of authority of sight and taste: each has its special objects, and the suggestion is that mistake is impossible in and only in the appropriately special circumstances.[9] That *Met.* Γ 5 begins as a discussion of Protagoras gives a clue about how Aristotle views special sensibles: the point of Protagoras's most famous words is that what seems so to me is so *for me*, and there is no such thing as truth for everybody. When something smells acrid to me, there is (in relation to me, in some obscure way) an acrid smell; and thus with a loud noise, a bitter taste, or a white flash. No other person, and no other sense, need apprehend or can contradict what in this special way I smell, taste, hear, or see. But now one may wish to put scare-

---

[9] Some commentators, perhaps reading the passages in *De Anima* with *Met.* Γ 5 in mind, take Aristotle to be limiting severely the scope of infallibility, e.g., to standard conditions. So Themistius, 105, 4f. Sp.

quotes around the perception words, particularly the last: the objects of perception may now seem to have become not material objects or even their properties, but items that have the subjectivity characteristic of sensations and other mental entities. This point is significant; for if it is true that one important characteristic of the mental is some sort of credible reportability without inference, which seems to be what characterizes my report that something looks white or smells acrid, then perhaps Aristotle is talking about typical mental events.[10]

This inference is too hasty. Note that Aristotle denies infallible availability to shapes and sizes; and if he were talking about colors-as-seen and smells-as-smelled, purely subjective entities, he could say of shapes-as-seen and shapes-as-felt what he says of the others. Moreover, he claims a relation of accidental identity between the white infallibly apprehended and the son of Diares; and as I argue in Chapter Two, that is precisely the relation between a substance and each of its properties. So it would seem that this white that one apprehends is a property of a white object rather than of a soul.

But then why should Aristotle say that I can report the color of something infallibly (particularly when he also denies it at *Met.* Γ 5 1010b5f.)? The answer lies in Aristotle's view about the relation between the property of the object and the item in the soul. It is captured best in a famous passage in *De An.* III 2:

> The actuality [or, activity] of the object of sense and of the sensation are one and the same, but their being is

---

[10] At *Sens.* 4 442b5ff. Aristotle says the reason we are not infallible about the common sensibles is just that they are common to more than one sense; we infer that mistakes can be detected because one sense can correct another. Not so with the special sensibles: only smell can authoritatively judge how something smells, and objections from other senses (e.g., to the effect that it doesn't look as though it would smell fishy) can be rejected. This is an argument for incorrigibility, not infallibility.

different. I mean for example actual sound and actual hearing: for it is possible to have hearing but not hear, and what has sound is not always sounding. Now whenever what can hear becomes active, and what can sound sounds, then actual sound comes to be at the same time as actual hearing; and one might call one of them sounding and the other hearing.[11] . . . The actuality [or, activity] of what makes sound is sound or sounding, that of what hears is hearing or hearing [*akoē* or *akousis*]: for hearing and sound are ambiguous. The same account goes for the other sensations and their objects. For just as acting and being acted on are in the patient rather than the agent, so the actuality both of the object of sense and of the sense itself are in what senses. (425b25-426a1, 426a6-11)

Aristotle locates the actuality of the sense object in the patient, in accordance with his standard view: so in *Phys.* III 3 202a13ff. he says that movement is plainly in that which gets moved. Because it is a corollary of a general view about action and passion, of which Aristotle says with some reluctance and considerable elaboration that perception is a special case (see Section III), one cannot be certain that it is Aristotle's final answer to the question, where is the color of an object? (In the mind? On its surface?)[12] But it is nicely compatible with his view, expressed just below the passage quoted, that there are potential but not actual colors and flavors and sensations when there is no seeing or tasting.

[11] Here Aristotle uses *akousis* and *psophēsis* for "hearing" and "sounding." No natural translation indicates that they are new words in the discussion; rather, they are derivatives of the words he has been using.

[12] At *De An.* I 4 408b1ff. the emphasis is quite different. There Aristotle criticizes the usual practice of saying that it is the soul that perceives, feels pain, is angry, etc.: it is the man who perceives, through the soul, in that the characteristic motions may reach to the soul or start there. How much, then, is included in the location of the event of perception? It is not clear to Aristotle, nor to me; but

This is not the first time Aristotle has distinguished between actual and potential sound in this way. At *De An.* II 8 419b4ff. he has stated that something solid and smooth like bronze can be said to have sound because, unlike wool, when struck it can make a sound—that is, it can with the help of hearing make an actual sound. So there are three stages of increasing actuality of sound: the solid and smooth thing not being struck, the thing being struck, and the thing being struck while somebody listens. There is the same hierarchy on the side of the percipient: the organ that cannot hear, the organ that can hear but for the moment does not, and the organ hearing. (See *De An.* II 1 412a20-28, 412b18-25.) The last two stages are, respectively, the second and first actualities of hearing; and no doubt the last two stages of sounding are the second and first actualities of sounding.

When Aristotle says that the *energeia* (in this context "actuality" is a better translation than "activity") of the object of perception and that of the sense or sense organ are one and the same but their being is different, it may seem a clumsy way to make a point about identity; but we know what the point is (see Chapter Four, Section III). Aristotle is drawing on his doctrine of event identity put forward most succinctly in *Phys.* III 3, of which I have just noted another echo in the passage in *De An.* III 2 quoted above. A certain event of hearing and a certain event of sounding may be related as the road up and the road down (that example too is from *Phys.* III 3) in that each is a necessary and sufficient condition for the other, though they are not strongly identical because they are identified under different descriptions. The link between the doctrine of the *Physics* and the corollary in perception we have before us now is the view that psychological events have form and matter (*De An.* I 1 403a11-30), which is to say in effect that there is, from a reductive point of view, one event that

if it is misleading to say that the soul perceives, then it is no less so to say that something's being actually white or redolent is located in what senses.

can be described in two different ways, one way involving the essence of the event. From Aristotle's point of view, the events are accidentally identical. Now the present case is not about descriptions one of which is material (that is, physiological) and the other formal (that is, psychological); both are, as one might say, on the same level. Hearing and sounding are both of epistemic and psychological import; they are not related precisely as matter and form or as *kinēsis* and *energeia*, for Aristotle says the *energeia* is the same. But the events are still not strongly identical, even though neither is possible without the other, because their definitions are not the same.

In Chapter Two I argued, against Aristotle, for permissive standards for event identity. But when the talk is about sounding and hearing, there is a difficulty about identity; for surely they have distinct locations, one in the object and the other in the perceiver. The problem is not unique to perception. One who is inclined to say that Johnson's death is the same event as Mrs. Johnson's being widowed may have some difficulty locating this one event if Johnson died in Cleveland while Mrs. Johnson was at home in San Diego.[13] Now it is neither necessary nor possible to locate every event with precision; for example, everybody's getting older has no obvious location. Where the discussion is about an *energeia* rather than a *kinēsis*, exact location is not clearly an individuating factor; so Aristotle would be free to say that the actuality is in the area between and including the object and the perceiver. In the case of secondary qualities, which are lineal descendants of special sensibles, it is best not to identify the state of mind characteristic of seeing white with the whiteness of the object, but instead to take secondary qualities to be properties of white or noisy objects. One can still define them by reference to seeing and hearing and other human ways of discrimination, but they remain (highly complicated disjunctive) physical prop-

[13] This particular example of what Peter Geach calls "Cambridge changes" was suggested to me by Mark Sagoff.

erties.[14] It will follow that, though there would be neither sound nor color if there were never any perceivers at
all, there can be sound and color at a particular place and
time even if there is nobody there to see. On this account
Aristotle would be wrong in saying that actual color is dependent upon actual sight, and sounding upon hearing: the
secondary quality is in first actuality just in case somebody
is in second actuality with respect to it.[15]

The view that actual sound requires a hearer follows logically from the view that hearing and sounding are two aspects of the same *energeia* and, as I shall argue in the next
section, relates closely to the claim that in perception the
perceiver takes on the form of the perceived object without
the matter. As I have indicated, I think it needlessly com-
plicates Aristotle's account of the apprehension of special
sensibles. Moreover, it seems to obscure some important distinctions among sorts of secondary quality. A different account might have helped Aristotle to see these distinctions,
for he barely misses them. Just after the passage quoted
from *De An.* III 2 above, Aristotle says:

But in some cases, both actualities have a name; for example, sound and hearing. In other cases one or the other is
nameless: for seeing is what we call the actuality of sight,

[14] Many very different configurations of light can be perceived as
one color. See Edwin H. Land, "Experiments in Color Vision."

[15] This view has problems, or at least complications, of its own.
The relation between secondary properties of objects and the mental
states that normally attend them is both causal and logical: the
properties are defined by the mental states they cause. So a particular
white causes a certain sort of mental state but is not identical with
it; but it is a particular *white* because it causes states of that sort.
To make the situation more complicated: the state of sensing whitely
is itself not a white state, nor an awareness of some mental item that
is intrinsically white. A sensation of white is of white by virtue of
its normal evidential relation to the belief that there is something
white in the nearby environment and so indirectly by virtue of its
being the normal effect of there being something white in the nearby
environment. (See further Section VI below.)

but that of color is nameless; and tasting is the actuality of taste, but that of flavor is nameless. (426a12-15)

Is this an accident of the Greek language, as Aristotle seems to think, or a linguistic clue to a conceptual distinction? That it is the latter we may gather from a parallel feature of English: a noisy object makes a sound, a redolent object gives off an odor; but we would not say that an object makes or gives off a color. Why not? Perhaps because all objects are colored, or because we do not think of color as being able to linger in the air after the object is gone (nor does Aristotle think so, according to *De An.* II 7 and 8), or because sight is not restricted to color in the way in which smell is restricted to odor or hearing to sound.[16]

If something's actually being white is identical with its being sensed as white, then it is not absurd to say that the special sensibles are both mental states and properties of objects. Aristotle's restriction of actual color to what is being seen is no mere thoughtless blunder. It helps explain my infallibility about the color of Diares's son when I apprehend it: his having that color just is my sensing that color. The strong implication in *Met.* Γ 5 that everyone is authoritative concerning the color he perceives might, in aid of making Aristotle consistent, be taken as a remark, not about what is ordinarily called color, but instead about what Aristotle when he is being careful calls actual color, which exists only as it is being seen. But the resulting view causes problems, as Aristotle himself suspects. How, on this account, can any particular thing be counted on to have one color no matter how many people are looking at it? At *Sens.* 6 446b15ff., accordingly, Aristotle finds himself stuck

---

[16] Indeed, it is more plausible to say that color is primarily a property of an object than that sound or odor is; so the previous footnote must be taken with caution. Some philosophers still wonder whether what standardly causes one to have a red sense datum really is itself red, in addition to looking red. I know of none who wonders whether what causes one to smell a foul smell really is itself foul.

with a hard question about how two people can perceive the same thing: the bell or the incense you and I hear or smell may be one, but the particular affection is numerically different for you and for me; there is one for each of us, one in each of our souls. Aristotle does not want to adopt this position, for it is impossible for each of the particular hearings or smellings to be accidentally identical with the sound or odor the thing makes, as his theory requires. So we cannot say that the theory is satisfactory though eccentric, for it is not quite coherent. Aristotle cannot consistently make the special sensible both a property of the object and an event in the sensor, as he seems to want to do.

This is to say that I do not think a consistent account of the status, in particular the relative status, of special and common sensibles in Aristotle is possible. Not only do special sensibles tend to function both as sense impressions and as secondary qualities, but they seem—primarily, I suppose, in the former role—sometimes to mediate in the inferential perception of common sensibles, which one would have thought immediately perceivable.

Some of the trouble arises from Aristotle's way of defining the senses primarily by their objects:[17] it is not a matter of straightforward empirical fact that we do not see odor or smell color. *De An.* II 4 415a14-22 and 6 418a7f. set out this way of definition quite clearly, and at *Sens.* 5 444b7ff. Aristotle draws the correct conclusion: it is possible that an animal might perceive odor even if it cannot breathe, for the perception of odor is smell no matter what organ is involved. But if that is true, then of what is sight the perception? The answer is supposed to be color, but it is a dubious answer for two related reasons. First, as noted above, color is not related either to the colored object or to the perception of it as odor and sound are to the odorous and smell or to the noisy and hearing. Second, color is not all we see in anything like the way odor is all we smell.

[17] On this point see Richard Sorabji, "Aristotle on Demarcating the Five Senses."

Aristotle recognizes this second point in saying that the common sensibles are just those properties of objects that can be apprehended by more than one sense, and shape is such a property.

Now if Aristotle really has problems about whether a special sensible is a mental event or a property of an object, if he is genuinely tempted in the former direction, then there will be signs of that temptation in his treatment of the relation between the special and the common sensibles. If an actual special sensible is a necessary and sufficient condition of being appeared to in a certain way, and if in consequence one cannot be mistaken about a special sensible if one is in its presence, then Aristotle will betray a tendency to consider the apprehension of a common sensible somehow indirect, perhaps an inference from a special sensible, or to say we infer the presence of a physical entity from awareness of a mental one. There is indeed evidence that he is tempted that way. Starting with a view of the special sensible as the sort of thing about which one cannot be mistaken, he sometimes allows himself to consider the apprehension of a common sensible somehow indirect, perhaps an inference from a special sensible, and to say we infer the presence of a physical entity from awareness of (what is virtually) a mental one.

But the interpreter must be cautious on this point. It would be anything but cautious to read *De An.* II 6, in which Aristotle says we apprehend both common and special sensibles in their own right (*kath' hauta*) but physical objects like persons accidentally (*kata symbebēkos*), as saying that we do not directly perceive physical objects. That view probably rests in part on the mistaken notion that any description of a mechanism of perception implies that one sees, not the apparent object of perception, but some piece of the causal process, perhaps the nearest end of it. If so, one can never perceive that for which there is a mechanism of perceiving. Thus if Aristotle says something's being colored necessarily involves the perceiver's being in a certain condition, whereas something's being the son of Diares does not, the interpreter may leap to the conclusion that we do not really perceive the son of Diares, or that we do not directly perceive him (that is, we do not perceive him just as we do color). That one is infallible about the color seems to clinch the point. But Aristotle says there is an accidental connection between *that which one perceives* and the white (418a22f.); that is, the white and what we perceive are accidentally identical. There is, to be sure, a higher order of identity between Diares's son's white and my state of sensing white than between the son himself and my sensation: the son can actually exist without being sensed. Moreover, the sensor is not affected by the sensible *qua* the sort of thing the sensible is (23f.): again, the actuality of the son of Diares does not coincide with the actuality of my sensing him, whereas the actuality of his being white does. Nothing in this view, however, has the least tendency to show that I do not unproblematically perceive Diares's son.[18]

But the last sentence of the sixth chapter is puzzling. Aristotle contrasts special sensibles with common sensibles by saying that it is the special ones that are primarily sensible. What does this mean? Is color prior to shape in capacity to be sensed except in that actual color is by its nature sensed whereas shape is not? Some other passages suggest that Aristotle has in mind that one does not after all perceive the common sensible directly. Consider *De An.* III 1 425a14ff.: "Nor can there be a special sense organ for the common sensibles, which we perceive by each sense incidentally; e.g., motion, rest, shape, size, number, unity; for all of these we perceive by movement. . . ."

This seems to contradict not only the opening lines of II 6 but also the next few lines of this passage. For Aristotle

---

[18] This point is widely misunderstood. Even Themistius, who gives a generally good explanation of this passage as well as of III 2, which states an essential part of the theory on which II 6 is based, says flatly that Diares (his example, not the son) is not an object of perception (107, 1 Sp.).

goes on to deny that the relation between a sense and a common sensible is like that between a special sense and the sensible special to a different sense (for example, sight and sweetness). That it is not is said to be evidence that we do not have a special sense for the common sensibles; for if we did, we should perceive them incidentally by senses like sight, and we do not. There seems to be a contradiction, but one could avoid it by reading "which we perceive by each sense accidentally" as part of the rejected hypothesis.[19] The sentence is a little odd, but it makes sense. But *Sens.* 1 437a4ff. makes it plain that Aristotle just cannot resist saying that special sensibles are mediators of our (less direct) perception of all other items. He says there that we perceive the common sensibles by sight because all bodies have color, through which we perceive shape and the other common sensibles. This must mean that we perceive color immediately and then somehow infer that the colored object has a certain shape. The inference is not the same as that by which we see that sugar is sweet, but it is anyway some sort of inference.

Why might Aristotle want to say that we infer from color to shape as we do from color to flavor? In part because it is color that we are infallible about and that there-

---

[19] As Charles Kahn does in "Sensation and Consciousness in Aristotle's Psychology," pp. 53f. He follows Theiler, Rodier, Themistius, and Simplicius. The alternative method of rescue would be to insert a negative into the line, as Torstrik, Susemihl, Neubauer, and Moerbeke do.

One might think Aristotle's next statement, that we perceive the common sensibles by the mediation of movement, suggests that we infer to the common sensibles by the movement in the soul of the special sensibles. This is Barrington Jones's view. But Aquinas (lect. 1, n. 577) seems to have the right idea: the motion is just the action of the sensible on the sense, as usual. A common sensible and a special sensible do affect the appropriate sense organ(s) by their movement; an incidental sensible does not—for example, the sweet does not affect the eye. For a defense of this interpretation, see Stanislas Cantin, "La perception des sensibles communs au moyen du mouvement d'après Aristote."

fore serves as a court of appeal to which all claims of empirical knowledge may be finally referred. So on this occasion, at least, special sensibles perform a task that has since been assigned to sense impressions, whose status as mental entities well suits them to be a firm basis on which to build empirical knowledge.[20]

This is not to say that special sensibles, as Aristotle describes them, and their functions qualify as unquestionably mental (if anything is) as sense impressions do. For Aristotle explains the infallibility of our beliefs about them, not by reference to anything like the privacy characteristic of mental events, but instead by reference to the fact that something's being actually white just is its being sensed as white. There is no error because, logically, there is no room for error. But one can still say that Aristotle sometimes grants infallibility to our judgments about some items that have features characteristic of mental entities. Had he clearly separated mental entities from properties of objects, had he been clearer about the nature and extent of our privileged access to those entities, had he been consistent about that access and what it applies to, then it might have been correct to say that he had a view of the mental much like some contemporary views. Had he then asked how this sort of event can be accidentally identical to any physiological state of the (or any) perceiver, he would have had something more like what we consider the mind-body problem. As things are, Aristotle is a materialist in this sense: he takes every state of the soul to be accidentally identical to some state of the body.

For that last statement, which was an essential part of the conclusion of Chapter Four, the rest of this chapter will argue. The particular question that will occupy us is this:

---

[20] This is not to say that Aristotle's interest in describing perception is to show how knowledge is justified, or that he has a view of knowledge as resting on the solid rock of infallible intuition. As I shall argue in the next section, it is an important feature of his theory that it is not primarily about justification.

what is perception other than the effect on a sense organ of an object outside the person? The answer will lie in understanding the relation between the form and the matter of an event and in seeing perception and its physical basis as constituting a special case of that relation.

III. SENSING AS ASSIMILATION

The view that sounding and hearing are in effect accidentally identical events is compatible with a wide range of possible accounts of the mechanics of perception, though not necessarily with every detail of the account Aristotle actually gives. That account makes perception a sort of assimilation: the sense becomes in a way one with its object. At the same time, sensation is a case of taking on the form of something without its matter. So what happens when one perceives? And what is it about what happens that justifies saying that the event is a perception, and not just an ordinary interaction of bodies?

To a first approximation, Aristotle states in *De An.* II 5 that perception is a change in a sense organ such that it becomes like the object or objects perceived. He seems to regard perception as a case of an agent (the perceived object) working on a patient (the percipient), and at the same time as the actualization of a complex faculty, but he puts most of the emphasis on the first of these two aspects in his analysis of what happens in perception.

Having said (II 5 416b33f.) that *aisthēsis* consists in being moved and acted upon—and having thus left open the question whether perception is identical with being moved and acted on—Aristotle reminds the reader that, as he believes, like is acted on by like: the talk of assimilation thus comes in at the very beginning of the account, as a feature of any action of one item on another, and not something peculiar to perception. Aristotle's reminder at 417a1f. presumably refers to *De Gen. et Corr.* I 7, where he has argued that a hot temperature affects a cold one and a hot thing causes a cold thing to be hot. So perception would be an object of a certain sort affecting an organ and making it somehow like the object. If that is so, then one's having a perceptual sensation of a certain sort is just one's appropriate sense organ being in that sort of state.

Aristotle goes on (417a14-17) to equate *paschein* (being affected), *kineisthai* (being moved), and *energein* (being actualized) for present purposes. In defense of this view, he notes that *kinēsis* is a sort of *energeia*, though incomplete. This is an important passage, for it equates some things Aristotle knows are not really identical. In fact, sensation is not a *paschein* of any previously recognized sort (417b-2ff.): it is not, as in the usual case, a destruction of a certain state of affairs; it is just the fulfillment of a potential, as in the case of a builder who is caused to build or a thinking being who is caused to know. Much later, in *De An.* III 7, Aristotle puts his reservations more strongly: it is incorrect to talk of the faculty being acted on or changed, since it is only activated and, again, the process is not a movement in the usual sense.

It is tempting to say Aristotle is simply sharpening his account as he goes along: action and passivity according to the account given in the physical works will not well describe what happens in perception, though there is a similarity useful for introductory purposes. But Aristotle's detailed discussions of what happens to the five senses when they operate do involve affection and assimilation on the standard model. So, for example, the liquid in the eye becomes colored when one perceives a colored object. This important point is never clearer than when Aristotle tries, in *De An.* II 11 and 12, to say just why the standard model is inadequate—to say, that is, what is characteristic of the assimilation in perception, as opposed to the sort of assimilation one would expect to find in insensate beings like plants. Having reiterated at 424a1 that sensation is a sort of assimilation, Aristotle infers that we do not perceive what is as hot or cold, soft or hard as are our organs of touch, but only what is hotter or colder, softer or harder. The reason is that if the object is the same temperature as the percipient, then there will be no such process as the potentially so hot becoming actually that hot; nothing will happen, and the organ will be in the state it was in before it was in touch with the object. In view of a passage like this, it is hard not to take the assimilation model literally.[21]

In *De An.* II 11 (424a3ff.) and III 2 (426b5ff.) Aristotle tries to help matters by putting forward an inchoate doctrine of perception being a mean. If the doctrine adds anything to what I have summarized in the previous paragraph, I do not know what it is. I offer two speculations: the organ at rest is in a state intermediate between (say) the temperature of the object about to be perceived and one of the two possible extremes of temperature, and the sense organ works only if when activated it reaches a temperature between the extremes; alternatively, the physical basis of any state of perception is, like the physical basis of the music made by a harp, delicately balanced and will not produce what it is meant to produce unless it is affected properly. But neither of these speculative interpretations, nor any other of which I know, is of help to Aristotle in solving the difficult and important problem to which he has brought his exposition at the end of *De An.* II 12.

That problem is this: what is it about the effect of a certain sort of item (for example, odorous air) on a sense organ that makes for perception, when there is no perception but only the standard sort of assimilation where the item is in contact with an inanimate object? The question is an excellent one. If perception is just a special case of being affected, then why doesn't the plant smell the air? There

---

[21] Cf. also 424a28ff. and III 4 429a29: excesses in the objects of sense destroy the senses. The literal interpretation of the process of assimilation has an influential sponsor in Thomas J. Slakey, whose "Aristotle on Perception" argues against the possibility of our finding in Aristotle's account of sensation any promising account of what more than assimilation sensation might be.

must surely be more to it than that. Were Aristotle a sort
of unreflective Cartesian, he would no doubt answer the
question this way: in the case of animate objects, and in
that case only, there is produced, in addition to the physical
likeness of the sensed object, a mental one, the object of some
sort of immediate awareness. Not only does Aristotle not
resort to this sort of explanation, he explicitly rules out
something rather like it. In III 2 (425b12ff.) Aristotle prof-
fers and rejects a story according to which one (for example) sees, and thereby gets one's eye assimilated to, the seen
object and then has some further experience of being conscious of the condition of one's sense organ. Before the
reader can be enlightened concerning the nature of this
consciousness, the theory is dismantled in the face of the
laudable objection that one is making a demand on perception that can lead to an infinite regress of states each needing
yet another state to be conscious of it.

The answer Aristotle does seem to think adequate is this:
in the case of an animate organism, the form of the perceived object is taken on without the matter. What does
this mean? It cannot be taken literally: whatever has a form
is a substance of a certain sort (with, by the way, matter
of a certain sort). And when Aristotle elaborates briefly
on the doctrine in II 12, he seems to say no more than that
the sensible form of something is a property of it, and so
of the organ that apprehends it. Thus one runs up against
the assimilation doctrine again; and that, straight from the
physical works, is just what one had hoped to get beyond.
It is time to try some other suggestions.

First, it may be that the formula "without the matter" is
supposed to indicate that when one perceives a house, there
is in the organ of sense a house that is not physical but
mental. The suggestion has a certain intuitive appeal to
those who are accustomed to divide the world into the
material and the mental. The interpretation is of venerable
origin: Philoponus, whose commentary dates from the sixth
century, says "not that the eye becomes white or black but

that the senses receive in themselves cognitively the forms of the objects of perception without the matter."[22] The interpretation prospered under the Scholastics and was welcomed by Brentano as a version of his own doctrine that mental entities have "intentional inexistence."[23] In *Die Psychologie des Aristoteles* Brentano writes:

> Yet it is not insofar as we are cold that we perceive the cold—otherwise plants and inorganic bodies would perceive too—but rather insofar as the cold exists in us objectively, that is, as an object of awareness, thus insofar as we receive cold things without being the physical subjects of them; the subject can capture this or any other form only by being altered.[24]

In a footnote he calls this a precise characterization of Aristotle's doctrine, and he links his use of "objective" with that of the Scholastics.[25]

But I know of no evidence showing that the distinction between *esse naturale* and *esse intentionale* is what Aristotle has in mind, nor do I think it is in itself a helpful distinction. If *De Anima* is an attempt to distinguish the mental from the physical, then it succeeds only if Aristotle explains in detail what it means to say that a sense or a sense organ is hot or white in some analogous way. Brentano does give detailed explanations of intentional inexistence; but that feature, refined by Chisholm and other distinguished successors to Brentano, has not worn well as a distinguishing

[22] Hayduck edn., 303.4-6.

[23] See "The Distinction between Mental and Physical Phenomena." This piece is a translation of the first chapter of the second book of the first volume of Brentano's *Psychologie vom empirischen Standpunkt*. Brentano takes Aristotle to hold that perception is the act of a physical organ (he refers to *Sens.* 1 436b7 and *De An.* I 1 403a16), though the object of perception is mental.

[24] P. 80.

[25] For a recent interpretation along the same lines, see Jonathan Barnes, "Aristotle's Concept of Mind."

characteristic of perceptual states, as opposed to thoughts and intentions. Brentano just asserts and does not argue that this distinction is what Aristotle has in mind. It is not the only time a philosopher has espied his own views in Aristotle's vague words.

Another possible interpretation is that the organ in perception becomes identical with its object, if the object be considered the color, the odor, or some other special object rather than the material body one sees or smells. And we do know Aristotle says that the full actualization of sounding and that of hearing coincide; and so with the other senses and their special objects. The colored or noisy item is, in the absence of a perceiver, only potentially colored or noisy. It is actually colored when and only when there is somebody seeing it. On the perceiver's side the situation is much the same: the sense organ is a thing of extended magnitude (literally, a size: see II 12 424a26), but the sense is not essentially a size but instead a *logos* and a faculty (*dynamis*). Sense organ is to sense as matter to form, or potency to actuality: it is another case of accidental identity. There is a sense of sight when and only when an eye is in a particular state of activity. That eye is in an appropriate state of activity just in case it is being stimulated visually by some colored object, which in turn is actually colored just in case it is stimulating a live eye appropriately. There being an object that is, strictly speaking, potentially white is a necessary condition of there being an object that is actually white; and there being a sense organ that is potentially sensing is a necessary condition of there being a sensation. Each of these relations is as form to matter, or potency to actuality. But there being an object that is actually white is a necessary and sufficient condition of there being a sensation of white.

If this interpretation is correct, then the full actuality of the object's being white and that of the perceiver's sensing white are the same actuality; and that is what Aristotle says in *De An*. III 2.[26] Depending on the individuating concept used, one could say that there is one event here or that there are two. There is one *actuality*, which consists of (but is not identical to) two *movements*. Aristotle's views about the identity of events, explored in Chapter Four, apply in this case. In particular, the alteration of the sense organ as it ceases to be transparent and becomes colored, or changes in temperature, is not identical with the sensation it accompanies: it is to that sensation as the matter of an event is to its form. As I noted in Chapter Four, the passages in *De An*. I about the relation between a psychological event and its physiological basis provide this interpretation. Indeed, the puzzle about whether perceiving is an alteration is much less mysterious if one is clear on the relation between *kinēsis* (movements) and *energeia* (actuality), which I claimed to be in some instances a special case of the accidental identity of events as presented under different descriptions. There are movements in the sense organ, in the medium, and in the organ. They may happen quickly or slowly; they can be located fairly precisely; they are truly processes, with termini. On the other hand, as we know from Aristotle's standard examples, sensing is not done quickly or slowly, nor does it have termini: at a given moment one is seeing or one is not. One might say a sense is created (*energeia*) when a sense organ is changed (*kinēsis*). Sensation is opposite to the case in which a builder exercises his building art and thereby builds a temple, for in that case the *kinēsis* is the form of the event and the *energeia* the matter.[27]

The special sensible for sight is a particular actual color;

[26] Presumably, if there are several perceivers, then the sensing white of all of them is a unitary actuality identical with the object's being white.

[27] J. L. Ackrill objects (in "Aristotle's Distinction between *Energeia* and *Kinēsis*," esp. pp. 140f.) that Aristotle is simply reluctant to call an actualization of a trained ability, as opposed to its acquisition, a real change. But it is a fact that the psychological event is an *energeia* and its physical basis a *kinēsis*.

it is clear that the potential color is the physical configuration of the material object considered apart from its being sensed. In other words, the physical property of an object that modern philosophers might say is identical to its color is considered by Aristotle not the color but the potential color—that is, related to the actual color as matter to form. (Perhaps the potential special sensible would include the condition of the medium as well; but whether or not it would does not affect the point at issue.) Now in vision the eye does not take on the potential color, the physical property; it takes on only the actual color, in the sense that the eye being in a certain state is part of there being an actual color. The eye is in (second) actuality just in case the color is in actuality. The actuality of each is necessary and sufficient for the actuality of the other. In that sense they are, as Aristotle says in the famous passage in *De An.* III 2, the same in actuality but different in being. This view, which can be called the unity-of-actuality doctrine, is consistent with the form-without-matter doctrine, at least in that the form *of the color*—that is, its actuality—is apprehended in perception.

This interpretation has some difficulties. To begin with, it applies only to special sensibles. Aristotle would surely not argue that something is only potentially square when nobody is perceiving it. Furthermore, Aristotle states that it is the form of the perceived object, not the form of some property, that is apprehended; so this interpretation has him misstating his position. Again, in III 2, the chapter in which we are given fullest account of the *energeia* of perception, Aristotle says that it is because the sense organ receives the form and not the matter of the object of sense that sensations and images remain in the sense organs even when the objects sensed are no longer present to the perceiver (425b24f; compare 426a17ff., however). But if the presence of the sensation in the sense is identical to the actuality of the special sensible that is the object of sense, then how can the actuality be present in the organ when the sensed object is gone? And the doctrine is supposed to be not only compatible with this circumstance but an explanation of it.

If the assimilation doctrine is taken literally, there is no problem: the after-image is just the eye's remaining white even after the white object is gone. The fact is, Aristotle thinks that the assimilation doctrine and the unity-of-actuality doctrine are the same doctrine, or that at most the latter is a refinement of the former. They are not. For to say that a hot item makes a sense organ hot presupposes that the item can be hot independently of its affecting the sense organ, and that is just what the unity-of-actuality doctrine must deny. One would like to say that the assimilation doctrine should not be taken too literally, in particular that it really amounts to the unity-of-actuality doctrine in the case of special sensibles. The importance of the case of sensations remaining after the object sensed is gone is that the assimilation doctrine explains it only if that doctrine is not identical with the unity-of-actuality doctrine.[28]

Finally, in an important sense the unity-of-actuality doctrine is not even an advance over the assimilation doctrine, for both tell a story about perception that is true of ordinary physical interaction. The unity-of-actuality story comes right out of *Phys.* III 3 too. Therefore it cannot by itself tell us, as the assimilation doctrine cannot tell us, what is so special about perception as opposed to ordinary interaction. That is what the form-without-the-matter doctrine is supposed to do. So the unity-of-actuality doctrine is not an adequate interpretation of it, though it is itself an interesting and plausible doctrine as far as it goes.

There is, I think, an interpretation of the form-without-matter doctrine that has a chance of taking Aristotle a little more literally than unity-of-actuality does and getting him

---

[28] If Aristotle had used the assimilation doctrine for common sensibles and the unity-of-actuality doctrine for special sensibles, in a division of labor proposed by some empiricists for primary and secondary qualities, he still would not have solved this last problem.

a bit beyond his account of physical interaction. When I see a white man, I apprehend the form, not of man, or a man, or of his color, but of the particular white man. Callias *qua* man is, as I argued in Chapter Two, a form; but in *Met.* Z 4 Aristotle allows that in the focal sense there are essences of such entities as a white man. They are not true essences, but are in existence and nature dependent on true essences as properties are on true substances. It is this parasitic sort of essence or form that is apprehended in perception: one sees Callias *qua* white; that is, one perceives not that Callias is white, but rather one perceives something white, which is in fact accidentally identical to Callias, who is strongly identical to Callias *qua* man.

An item is seen *qua* red, heard *qua* harmonious, smelled *qua* fishy but not sensed *qua* Diares's son by any of the five senses (II 6 418a20-24). The terms are not very mysterious. The point is just that it is by sight that we discern a certain red that is accidentally identical to a material object, and so with the other senses. What does this add to the doctrine of assimilation? Just that in perception an animal becomes aware of a color or a sound and so of an item under a description like red or clanging. It does not follow that the animal entertains a thought or a belief, though fairly often Aristotle attributes something more than mere discriminatory ability to sensation. In anticipation of some conclusions for which the rest of this chapter is in effect an argument, I would say that I think Aristotle is on the right track in holding that what is distinctive about a state of perception is that it has something to do with a judgment about the perceived object. It is not itself a judgment, nor does it entail one; and insofar as Aristotle thinks otherwise, he is off the right track. (See further Section VI.)

Aristotle's view seems to be that there is nothing about psychological events considered just in themselves that gives a good clue as to why they are psychological. In particular, Aristotle does not believe there is a distinct mental event that is caused by the physical one when the passive partner is a sensate being. A physical event constitutes a psychological event by virtue of its playing a certain sort of role in the functioning of a live person. That notion can present no difficulty for Aristotle: a physical event, as I argued in Chapter Four, constitutes a psychological event because it admits of a certain sort of description that makes reference to the behavior characteristic of a human being, or at least an animal. Thus, when he tries to find what is special about sensation by thinking very hard about what happens in the eyeball, he will make little progress. He must step back and consider what contribution this event makes to the economy of the living animal.

And Aristotle has the beginning of an answer in his hand, even as he finishes the second book of *De An.* II.[29] It is quite true that the *energeia* of perception is more than the sum of the movements that constitute it, in just the way form is more than matter; so Aristotle is right to abandon his initial view that perception is nothing more than being acted on. That perception is not the only case in which an *energeia* emerges from *kinēseis* does not render the analysis useless. Of course it is not enough to say simply that perception stands to being affected as form to matter; that would indeed fail to show what is special about perception. But once Aristotle sees that that is in general what the relation is between perception and being affected, he can then go on and give a detailed account of what defines the *energeia* we call perception. Having done so, he will have accomplished what he set out to do. The answer, in rough terms, is this: perception is essentially an event that plays a certain causal role in the acquisition of belief. The more Aristotle can say about what that role is, the better he will have done his job.

[29] I have nothing original to add to the debate about the comparative dating of *De Anima* and *Parva Naturalia*. I agree with Charles Kahn ("Sensation," p. 51) that where the latter goes beyond what is in the former, it can be explained as a new point in a progressive and dialectical exposition.

In doing that job, Aristotle goes into considerable detail about the mechanics of perception; but the detail has more to do with how it works than with how empirical beliefs are justified. No doubt if he had dealt more with the question of justification, he would have found himself pressed to show what, if anything, can serve as a firmly justified basis for our beliefs—or, preferably, a basis that needs no justification. Reflection on this basis, which has often turned out to be made up of sensations, is likely to lead to a requirement—and so to a belief—that one's knowledge of at least this part of the universe is impervious to error and hence immune to correction from any source. Thus philosophers have considered credible non-inferential reportability an important feature of most mental events. Epistemology, especially epistemological skepticism, does not rank among Aristotle's greatest concerns; and when he does verge on it, as in *Met.* Γ 5 and *De An.* III 3, he does not well clarify his position on what seem to many philosophers to be the essential issues. In particular, he feels no compunctions about combining a causal and a justificatory account of perception in answer to the question how we acquire knowledge. Insofar as his account is causal rather than justificatory, he is downplaying or ignoring the mentality of states of perception.

But one might find it strange that Aristotle's relative disinterest in epistemology could lead him to take no account of mental phenomena as they are traditionally understood. Surely they are just *there*, a brute fact of our universe, more obviously present to us than any other sort of thing is? Not so. To the extent that Aristotle's account of certain psychological events in perception does not emphasize the sort of infallible availability that the traditional account attributes to mental events, he is providing evidence that the traditional Cartesian conception of the mental is precisely not the single natural and inevitable conception. And if entities of this Cartesian sort really are not so stubbornly apparent to any possible attentive mind, then it becomes a bit more plausible to say that our beliefs about our mental entities are true just in case they are postulates of a successful theory, and even that what we know without inference is a matter of what we have been trained to know without inference.[30]

However, despite Aristotle's coolness towards epistemology and his unwillingness or inability to mark perception off from ordinary interaction by reference to the former's production of mental entities, certain texts, particularly in *Parva Naturalia*, indicate a commitment to some items that look very much like sense impressions.

IV. AISTHĒMATA

According to Aristotle, when I sense, there is present in me an *aisthēma*, or more than one *aisthēma*, by virtue of which I have cognitive contact with the passing show. An *aisthēma* is a state or property (*pathos*) of the perceiver, according to *Met.* Γ 5 1010b30ff. Remarkably, *aisthēmata*

[30] See note 3 of this chapter. Wallace I. Matson argues in "Why Isn't the Mind-Body Problem Ancient?" that Aristotle does ignore what many philosophers have thought to be the objects of immediate awareness, and that it is reasonable to infer from his obliviousness to them that it is not obvious that they are there at all. The previous section and the following one are intended to show that Aristotle is not clear about the existence and nature of what we might comfortably call mental entities. I thank Mr. Leonard Katz for showing me his interesting paper entitled "Did the Ancients Have Feeling Without Raw Feels? Notes toward a Philosophical Prehistory of Cartesian Dualism," which argues further in the same direction.

In "Concepts of Consciousness in Aristotle," W.F.R. Hardie warns against, on the one hand, reading into Aristotle some conception of consciousness that seems natural to us and, on the other, inferring from his silence on this and other matters that he did not know the right answers or ask the right questions (pp. 405f.). It is difficult to judge from what any philosopher says whether he has what we might consider a common-sense conception of consciousness, for consciousness resists easy description. If philosophers can seriously disagree about whether contemporary common sense is Cartesian, how can we hope to decide whether Aristotle was Cartesian?

are mentioned in *De Anima* only twice, both times in explication of *phantasmata* (images), the productions of *phantasia* (imagination). At III 7 431a14f. Aristotle says *phantasmata* are like *aisthēmata* to the faculty of thought; in the next chapter (432a9f.) he says *phantasmata* are like *aisthēmata*, except without matter.[31]

In the *Parva Naturalia* Aristotle has much more to say about *aisthēmata*. In *De Mem.* 1 450a27ff. he says the *pathos* of the soul resulting from sensation is a kind of picture: there is by virtue of perception a kind of picture in the soul, that is, in the part of the body containing the soul (no doubt the heart);[32] and the having of that *pathos* (that is, presumably, the ability to conjure up that *pathos* in the appropriate circumstances) is memory. The passage has more than its share of difficulties, but apparently Aristotle believes that the *aisthēma* attendant upon and in part constitutive of perception is a likeness of the thing perceived, and that subsequent memory images are likenesses of the original likeness. This position is roughly consistent with what we found in *De Anima*, but it goes further. When one sees or remembers something, not only the special sensible properties of the thing but also the common sensibles are reproduced in one's mind. There are, as I have noted, difficulties about how special sensibles can be reproduced in the soul. With common sensibles the problems are

[31] What this last means we shall discuss in the next chapter. I do not believe Aristotle ever makes out a distinction between *phantasma* and *aisthēma* considered just in themselves. The distinction between them is a matter of their causal ancestry and their accuracy. A *phantasma* is by definition more likely to be false than an *aisthēma*— false, that is, in that the *phantasma* misrepresents what is being perceived. (See further Joyce Engmann, "Imagination and Truth in Aristotle," esp. pp. 262f.) But Aristotle does not claim that every *phantasma* is false; so it is hard to see how a veridical *phantasma* differs from an *aisthēma*.

[32] In a number of places Aristotle talks about events happening "in the soul." Some (including, I think, Barnes in "Aristotle's Concept of Mind") have taken this to be a denial of materialism, but he can in each case be taken to mean "in the heart."

not so great: an item in the soul can have a triangular shape, the same shape as some triangular object one sees.

But despite his reticence in *De Anima* about objects of immediate awareness, Aristotle does have views about them. At *De Insomniis* 2 460b1ff. he goes so far as to apply to *aisthēmata* the term *aisthēta* (objects of perception), which is standardly used for extra-mental items. Moreover, Aristotle now discusses error and illusion in a way familiar to epistemologists, whereas in *De Anima*, especially in III 3, he has emphasized standard conditions, and true belief when conditions are not perfectly standard. In *De Insomniis* he says that because *aisthēmata* can remain after the external objects that caused them are gone, we may be mistaken about our sensations when we are ill or in an emotional state (as indeed was suggested in *Met.* Γ 5).[33] But notice that the false opinions generated in these circumstances are a failure of reason rather than of perception: for example, the coward has the same sort of *aisthēma* the brave person does, but he misconstrues it; so does the lover, or the man with a fever. It is clear that men, if not animals, are supposed to make inferences from these items in order to achieve correct opinions about the external world, though Aristotle does not worry about how in general we can find any good reason for making the inferences we normally do make.[34]

By this time it may be tempting to say that Aristotle is treating the inner objects of perceptual awareness as mental entities. In some ways he is, in some ways not. He does hold that we make (fallible) inferences from *aisthēmata*; so

[33] Matson ("Why Isn't the Mind-Body Problem Ancient?") calls this a "spooky" context (p. 101); but I see no reason to take Aristotle not to hold that there are *aisthēmata* in every act of sensing. Philosophers do commonly introduce the objects of immediate awareness by reference to situations involving error.

[34] It does not follow that Aristotle is clear on the distinction between the act of perception and its (internal or intentional) object. If he countenances internal objects of perception, they are *aisthēmata*; and having an *aisthēma* would be part of the act of perceiving.

they do form a justificatory basis for some empirical judgments. He is on record already in *De Anima* as granting infallibility to certain judgments about special sensibles, and the passages just noted suggest an extension of the privilege to other inner states of representation. He says *aisthēmata* arise in the soul and remain there. How much clearer could he be?

But I believe *aisthēmata* fall short of the criteria for mentality I have suggested.[35] To begin with, Aristotle is not entirely consistent in attributing infallibility. There are some suggestions of reservations in what he says about special sensibles, as we know. In the third chapter of *De Insomniis* (460b27ff.) Aristotle implies that we have *aisthēmata* that we do not notice and are presumably therefore fallible about. This view does not fit very well with what he has said before: for example, he holds at *Sens.* 2 437a27-9 that one cannot see a visible object without knowing that one is seeing it. But it is surely true that we may fail to notice some of our sensations. That an entity is mental does not make it always infallibly reportable, or even necessarily noticeable in any circumstance. Aristotle's apparent inconsistency on this point is not difficult to understand. Many philosophers have had trouble in characterizing exactly our epistemological privileges with respect to sensa.

The fact is, not all states that can be reported immediately and either infallibly or at very low risk are mental states. The classic case in modern literature is of this sort: I can know immediately and without observation what position my limbs are in, and it is not at all clear that I have to draw any inferences in order to know. That kind of immediacy seems to be what Aristotle attributes to reports of what we would call mental items. He does say at *Phys.* VII 2 244b15ff. that the difference between a change in a

---

[35] Richard Sorabji's "Aristotle on Soul and Body" is an excellent treatment of some issues I shall be discussing for the balance of the chapter. As I indicated in Chapter Four, I agree with much that he says.

sense organ and a change in a thing that is not alive is that the former is not unnoticed, presumably by its owner. But at *Nic. Eth.* IX 9 1170a28ff. he compares awareness that one is walking with awareness that one is perceiving, or thinking.

To be sure, Aristotle could be just trying and failing to capture what seems to us intuitively special about the mental. It is possible to agree essentially with Descartes without being able to express oneself adequately. But the passage from the *Ethics* cannot be brushed aside: Aristotle embraces an analogy there that a Cartesian would find to be a difficulty. Moreover, he conspicuously fails to make use of this feature of the mental when he is struggling at the end of Book II and the beginning of Book III of *De Anima* to say what it is about a state of a sense organ that makes it a perceptual state, when an analogous state of a plant is not a perceptual state. He says nothing in those chapters against the notion that a perceptual state is a physical state, with some of the properties of the object of perception.[36] In any case, it is most difficult to read the third chapter of *De Insomniis*, in which Aristotle deals in detail with the movements of the residues of sensations, without concluding that the movements are physical states. For example, they can flow along and then be broken up by obstructions, as whirlpools sometimes are (461a10f.).[37]

A comparison of *Parva Naturalia*, and especially *De Insomniis*, to *De An.* II 12 suggests a problem of interpretation, which can perhaps best be seen if we try to find Aristotle's answer to this question: do plants have *aisthēmata?*

---

[36] Sorabji argues ("Body and Soul," pp. 74f.) that since Aristotle says the actual object of sense inheres in the sense rather than the sense organ (III 2 426a4), he may be taken to hold that the object of perception is in the perceiver in what we should consider a nonphysical way. I do not agree. The sense organ is to the sense as matter to form, as we know from II 12 (see Section III). Insofar as the actual perceptual event can be exactly located, it is in the sense organ.

[37] Cf. *ibid.*, p. 77, n. 42.

If not, then why does not Aristotle mention the fact as a crucial difference between the ways in which plants and animals are affected by perceptible items? And if so—but how can one take Aristotle to believe that plants have *aisthēmata*, picture-like states in the soul? One could simply admit an inconsistency and argue that the *Parva Naturalia* is a later, very different work; but I should prefer not to take that tack unless there is no other way to explain the appearance of disparity. There is, I think, a way of reconciling the passages in reasonable conformity with what I suggested earlier is Aristotle's general answer to the question about what it is that makes assimilation in animals but not in plants sensation. It may indeed be true that states of a perceiver's organ mirror the perceiver's surroundings more accurately than those of a plant, so that what happens in a sense organ might without undue stretching be called a picture of the surroundings; still, that is not what makes the state a state of perception. An artist's picture, no matter how accurate, is not a state of perception. To say that there is somewhere inside one's body a representation of something outside one's body is not to say that one is perceiving —nor, by the way, is it to say that there is a characteristically mental state inside one's body. What a perceiver necessarily has, which a plant importantly lacks, is a mechanism for achieving some measure of knowledge. And so what makes a particular affection of a perceiver an *aisthēma* is, again, that it plays a role in the functoning of that mechanism.

Now it is time to say more about the mechanism in which the perceptual state plays a part.

V. THE COMMON FACULTY OF SENSE

What would be a common-sense, non-technical solution to the question, what makes an affection a perceptual state? Perhaps this: the organism is aware of the state, or at least normally aware of that sort of state. And so Aristotle says in the *Physics*: "the inanimate is not conscious of being affected, while the animate is conscious of it—though the animate may not be conscious of it when the process does not affect the senses" (VII 2 244b15ff.). But Aristotle argues in *De An.* III 2 against the postulation of a faculty, distinct from perception, by virtue of which we sense that we sense by sensing what we sense. Consciousness need not be a state over and above that of which one is conscious; for if it were, and one were conscious of one's consciousness, then there would be an infinite regress of distinct states of consciousness. But then almost immediately, instead of giving us any significant information about how it is we are aware of what we sense, Aristotle puts forward what looks like an argument to show precisely that there is a distinct central faculty over and above the individual senses, and indeed a central organ too: one faculty can no more distinguish good from bad or sweet from bitter than one item can be both good and bad or sweet and bitter.

Now in response to this difficulty Aristotle gives the beginnings of what I consider his final answer, mostly compatible with what he has said thus far and with what he has to say in the *Parva Naturalia*. That which apprehends both white and black is one in number but multiple in being. It is logically divisible, but indivisible in that it by itself perceives distinct objects. To put it another way, it is one in being but multiple in operation, as a single point may be an end of two different lines (if it is treated that way by a faculty that is itself two insofar as it treats the point as two). The point is made diffidently, with interrogatives; and the language is vague. But prior acquaintance with Aristotle's method will permit one to see the main point Aristotle is making. Whether a particular faculty is one or two or many depends in part on the point of view from which it is described. The interlude in III 2 about the relation between the object of sense and the event of sensing (425b26-426b7) provides a point of comparison: the two events are not distinct, but neither are they identical in the strongest sense—as no two entities are identical in the strongest sense if they are identified under distinct descriptions. Now if, as Aristotle has suggested in his discussions of the special senses and their objects, the sense faculty is defined primarily by the sort of object it apprehends, then it would be reasonable to infer that any faculty of cognition is defined by what it apprehends. But then how can one faculty apprehend two or more sorts of thing? That is Aristotle's problem, and it is not surprising that he has that problem when one considers his way of distinguishing items according to their descriptions: anything that has functions that are in any way distinct—for that matter, anything with more than one predicate true of it—will have its unity threatened. So there will be a problem about anything whatever with more than one function, especially where, as in Aristotle's philosophy of mind, items have functional definitions.

It is therefore not to be expected that a faculty that is in any way complex will be unitary without reservation. But it does not follow that the faculty of apprehending white is wholly distinct from that of apprehending the apprehension of white, or even that the faculty of apprehending bitter is wholly distinct from that of apprehending sweet. The first pair are related as the road up and the road down: what makes the action of the sensed item on the sense organ a sensation is precisely that it is happening in an organism that is capable of resultant states of behavior and, in some cases, belief and knowledge. By permissive standards, being affected whitely and being aware of white are the same event; by Aristotle's more restrictive standards, the events are accidentally identical. In any case, they are not distinct events; nor, therefore, could the faculties causally responsible for them be distinct faculties. In the case of the second pair, the situation is rather more complicated, but not essentially different. It is common enough to apprehend bitter without apprehending white. All the same, it is evident that one organism can be in the state of apprehending bitter and simultaneously in the state of apprehending white, or in the state of apprehending the distinction between opposites. It follows that the organism has a faculty that can do that. The faculty must be one because there is one judgment being made and one person uniting the terms of the judgment. That is just how faculties are individuated.

In the previous chapter, at 425a30ff., Aristotle has said that the senses perceive each other's objects incidentally, not insofar as each is itself but insofar as both are one, as when we perceive that gall is bitter and yellow. In some way— the very way, surely, that is explicated in III 2—there is one sense faculty responsible for the simultaneous awareness of these distinct entities and of their relation. Is it the same faculty as that by which we are aware that we are sensing? The discussion, while suggesting that it is, finally gives reason not to answer such a question flatly one way or the other. The ability to apprehend white and the ability to apprehend bitter do not together entail the ability to apprehend that something is both white and bitter. But Aristotle would have some reason to believe that the latter ability entails the ability to apprehend that one is apprehending something white (as well as something bitter), and the latter ability is surely definitive of the second-order consciousness Aristotle is looking for at the beginning of the second chapter. Therefore the relation between the faculty of consciousness of sensing and the faculty of consciousness of difference between sensed items is a high grade of identity. Moreover, these faculties are not distinct from the faculty of mere perception (for example, of white) because they are a necessary and sufficient condition of it: they are necessary because without them the physical event that is the basis of perception would not be perception but only a plain old physical event; and they are sufficient because they require that there be simple sensory events in order for them to play their definitive supervisory role, and so in order for them to exist.[38]

In the course of the discussion Aristotle seems to have slipped from talk about awareness of items to talk about awareness of the truth of propositions (or, as philosophers sometimes say, from awareness-of to awareness-that). It is possible to read Aristotle's account of the perception of the special sensibles as imputing only discrimination, not actual judgment, to the apprehension of white. But now it is clear that the more elaborate sensory faculty is a faculty of judgment. Thus Aristotle says: "For the sweet is different from the white; the same faculty says so. Therefore as it pronounces, so it thinks and perceives" (426b21f.).

The story told in the first two chapters of *De An.* III does not involve any organ of perception beyond the five special ones: it is not primarily a story about the physiological basis of perception, and it is a story that emphasizes the unity of the perceptive soul rather than the variety that characterizes its functions and therefore it. But when Aristotle does a reprise of the story in the seventh chapter, he gives a clue about what the physiological basis of the whole faculty may be: "the air makes the pupil of the eye have a certain property and it does the same to another thing, and the same with hearing; the last is one, and one mean, but its being is many" (431a16-20). What is "another thing"? What is "the last"? Clearly it is a central organ of perception. Aristotle tells at *De Sensu* 2 438b12ff. what happens if the perceptive process does not work all the way to the central organ, as in the case of a blow on the temple:

---

[38] I do not mean to suggest that Aristotle's account is a particularly good one, or even that it has any explanatory value to speak of. The point of all this is really to show how little Aristotle is committing himself to when he postulates the common faculty of sense, and how far he is from giving a robust account of consciousness. See further W.F.R. Hardie's "Concepts of Consciousness in Aristotle."

one is blind. This shows, he argues, that "the soul or the sense organ of the soul" is not on the surface of the eye, but within the body; and we know he is talking about the heart, which he takes to be the central organ.

This line of thought is summarized clearly in a famous passage at *De Somno* 2 455a16ff. Aristotle writes of a common faculty that accompanies all acts of sense,

> by which one senses both that one is seeing and that one is hearing. For it certainly is not by sight that one sees that one is seeing, nor does one—nor can one—judge that sweet things are different from white ones either by taste or sight or both; rather one does it by some part common to all sense organs. For there is one *aisthēsis* and one primary sense organ; but the being of sense is different for each genus—for example, sound and color.

The topic is the one discussed in *De An.* III 2; even the examples are the same. Aristotle continues to hold that perception and the faculty of perception are one or many depending on the descriptions under which they are considered, though he has now added some physiological detail concerning the heart. Notice that he is now denying that, for example, one is aware by sight that one is seeing. Does this represent a change of mind since *De An.* III 2? I think not. In both that passage and this one a particular act of sensation is what it is—a cognitive act—by virtue of its occurring in and making a contribution to an articulated sensory organism; in isolation it is not truly a sensation, as no functionally defined item is what it is when it does not appear in its functional role. But does it follow that the functioning person is not aware by sight that he is seeing? It does just in the rather narrow sense that the faculty of this sort of second-order awareness is not strongly identical to the faculty of apprehending white.[39]

---

[39] On this complex of issues I am indebted to a number of scholars, but I mention in particular works that treat these and related matters helpfully: Rodier II *ad loc.*, esp. p. 266 and p. 352; Kahn, "Sensation

I do not claim to be able to show that the central faculty of which Aristotle speaks is consciousness in the sense in which we ordinarily think of it. Aristotle would have to say more than he does in order to make this interpretation certain. His account of the ways in which faculties are and are not to be distinguished explains how a person is able to make certain discriminations and judgments. It does not require self-awareness or self-consciousness of the sort we think characteristic of humans.

Now the conceptual relation Aristotle describes in detail between the individual act of a special sense and the sensory faculty as a whole does not entail that each individual special sensory act will be processed by the common faculty. That is, there can be sensations of which one is not aware; they are sensations rather than mere affections by virtue of being the sort of event of which one can be aware. In that view I think Aristotle is correct. What is particularly attractive about his story is that it lends itself well to a rational account of the relation between the mental and the physical. Aristotle says in effect that the relation between a certain physical event that accompanies perception and perception itself is not one of efficient cause to effect but rather one of accidental identity. The mental event is something over and above the physical event in just the sense in which the soul is something over and above the body—that is, the sense in which the form is something over and above the matter. At the beginning of *De Anima* Aristotle has claimed that the relation of certain physiological events to certain psychological events is of matter to form. What makes a physiological event a psychological event, as form makes matter something, is its causal and evidential relation to some other event or state of affairs. In I 4 408b5ff. he states that even if we concede that psychological events are move-

---

and Consciousness"; R. Schneider, *Seele und Sein; Ontologie bei Augustin und Aristoteles*, esp. pp. 156-160; Barrington Jones, "Aristotle on Awareness and Sensitivity"; Aryeh Kosman, "Perceiving that we Perceive: On the Soul III, 2."

ments of the heart and/or some other part of the body, it is not just the soul but the whole person that pities or learns or thinks: since the motion begins or ends in the heart, we are inclined to forget that it is only within a certain causal context that the heart's action can be anger—or the eye's action perception. When Aristotle shows how the actions of the senses are states of awareness in virtue of their connection to the central organ of sense and its faculty, he does not emphasize a fact for whose importance we have adequate evidence elsewhere: the heart itself is, as any organ must be, functionally defined. A full definition of the heart requires an account of the nature of the person. It follows that the full definition of sensation too requires an account of the whole human being, who in his actions and purposes provides the essence of such human activities as perceiving.

VI. SENSATION AND THOUGHT: SOME PROBLEMS

There is, I think, a serious deficiency in Aristotle's account of sensation. He fails to see clearly, even in a general way, what the relation is between perception and thought, and in particular how thought is in a subtle way conceptually prior to perception. He has made some good progress, to be sure; and he has gone wrong on a most difficult point, though an important one.

One way of getting at a piece of Aristotle's difficulty is to claim that he illegitimately makes sensation a judging faculty. That is, according to this line of interpretation, Aristotle makes sensation's characteristic mirroring response to its environment a sufficient condition of a judgment about the environment; and indeed Aristotle states at a number of points that an act of sensation is an act of *krisis*, which normally means judgment. But if what I have said about the relation between special sensing and the sensory soul is correct, Aristotle may be taken to mean that being in a state of sensing white, so that one's eye is somehow white, is not all by itself a sufficient condition of judging that something is white, for two reasons. First, one may fail to notice the whiteness, or (see *De An.* III 3) not believe there is anything white in the neighborhood. Second, if the rest of one's sensory apparatus, especially one's total sensory faculty taken as a whole, is not functioning, then one will not apprehend the white any more than a plant apprehends odor (*De An.* II 12).

There can be little doubt, however, that Aristotle does think a faculty of sense can and does judge.[40] Taking something to be white or dangerous is certainly not in every case a matter of entertaining a proposition or reasoning: it is the sort of thing an animal can do, after all. But Aristotle frequently speaks as though perception can entertain propositions about particular substances and properties, in his treatments of practical reasoning as well as in his discussions of sensation in its own right. The common faculty of sense is quite clearly a judging faculty: "The one faculty must say they are different, since sweet is different from white. One and the same thing says so. And just as it says, so also it thinks and perceives" (*De An.* III 2 426b20-22). Now there is nothing wrong with saying that being in a certain physical state such that there is an isomorphism between one's sense organs and one's environment and such that certain other organs are working properly as well is a sufficient condition of being in a state of making a judgment. I think that is true. But to say that is to say too little. Judgment requires the use of propositions and concepts, and no account of it is complete that does not mention this crucial fact about it. In particular, no description of any state of

---

[40] For a severe criticism of Aristotle along these lines, see D. W. Hamlyn, "Aristotle's Account of Aesthesis in the *De Anima*." But cf. Joseph Moreau's "Aristote et la vérité antéprédicative." Somewhere between those two lies Stanford Cashdollar's "Aristotle's Account of Incidental Perception."

the sense organs just in terms of isomorphism to the environment will capture the nature of judgment, or even of sense perception.

This is a difficulty for Aristotle's account of perception because he wants to make judgment a function importantly characteristic of certain perceptual faculties. The problem is that the sensitive soul is supposed to be proper to animals, whereas judgment seems not to be possible for any animal but man. Aristotle says in *De An.* III 3 428a20ff. that brutes cannot believe because they cannot be convinced, because they cannot reason. This is by no means an absurd view: having no language, animals have concepts only in an extended sense and so cannot really be said to think.[41] But the central sensory faculty, which presumably brutes do have, is a judging faculty.

We now need a certain amount of untangling, both philosophical and exegetical, and I propose to proceed as follows: first, an argument for a sort of conceptual dependency of perception on belief; second, an explanation of how brutes can have perception though not belief; third, some remarks critical, particularly in light of the foregoing, of Aristotle's account of the relation between object and perception. I do not promise a rational reinterpretation of what Aristotle says about the judging of the common faculty. What can be saved out of that doctrine will be treated in Chapter Six.

The relation between perception and thought is a subtle

[41] In *De Motu Animalium* 6 and 7 Aristotle does suggest that animals employ something like a practical syllogism. The question of animals reasoning and believing may be downright undecidable. If a dog chases a squirrel up a tree and then circles the tree barking even after the squirrel has quietly slipped away to another tree, does the dog believe that the squirrel is in the tree? Or does it believe that the furry thing is in the brown and green thing? Or that the potential food is above him? How could we even begin to distinguish among those beliefs for the case of a dog?

one,[42] but it is one that must be understood if one is to give a correct account of the relationship between perception and the world. It is true that the senses somehow reproduce what they sense: when I see a white triangle in normal circumstances, whiteness and triangularity in some way characterize me, or a part of me. It does not follow, nor is it true, that anything in my mind is colored white or is triangular in shape. It would be better to say that my mind is characterized by the presence in it of a sensation that is of-white and of-a-triangle, which means at least this: I have a sensation that is of the sort normally caused by a white triangle in standard conditions but occasionally by other items in nonstandard conditions. The point of the "of-" locution is to emphasize that the sensory items stand to each other in relations of entailment and incompatibility that mirror those of physical objects. For example, just as an object cannot be both blue and red all over, so a sensation cannot be both simply of-blue and of-red. (There are limits to these parallels: it may be that a sensation can be of-a-bunch-of-flowers without being of-a-particular-number-of-flowers.) Thus far there is not necessarily anything obviously mental about the isomorphism between the sensations and the environment. It amounts to no more than this: there are certain perceptual states normally caused by certain stimuli, states such that this normal causal relation is a sometimes necessary though never sufficient condition for the organism as a whole being aware of that state of its environment.[43]

[42] My opinions on this issue owe something to the works of many philosophers, but to three in particular: Wilfrid Sellars, *Science, Perception and Reality*; Peter T. Geach, *Mental Acts*; Gilbert Harman, *Thought*. None of the three could be expected to agree with everything I say here or in the next chapter.

[43] A difficulty with this view is that it describes the properties of the mental entities involved in perception as parasitic on those of the perceived objects, apparently incompatibly with the apparent

But a perceptual state bears some conceptual relation, a relation of definition, to its typical effect as well as to its typical cause: we call a perceptual state white or of-white not only because it is of a sort typically caused by the presence of something white, but also because it is of a sort that typically causes one to believe one is in the presence of something white. (It might seem to follow that what typical people typically believe is true; indeed, there is some reason to believe that this is non-contingently so.) It is precisely because this sort of perceptual state can serve as evidence for a nearby white item that we characterize it according to its typical cause; for there are many other ways in which it might have been characterized.[44]

It follows that the causal relation between the item in the environment and the perceptual state it stimulates is not

---

subjectivity of secondary qualities. That objection deserves a more elaborate reply than space permits, but I can suggest the direction that reply would have to take. Our knowledge of the properties of our sense, including color sense, must be acquired *in foro publico*; indeed, color words can be defined only in ways that do not take account of the undiscovered qualitative differences sometimes thought to distinguish my red sensum from yours. I know of no good objection to defining colors as properties of the surfaces of objects, properties that explain some discriminatory behavior of normal perceivers. In fuller explanation of the ability to make color discriminations, one can say that the differences among these surface properties cause perceivers to be in states that can be called of-red, of-white, and so on, by virtue of the perceiver's taking the states to be evidence for the presence of red, of white, and so on. How, anyway, could a state—of a perceiver or of anything else—be white?

[44] If my account is right so far, the way in which we describe our mental events, including those we are privileged to report, depends on the way in which we describe the world. It is not true that our empirical knowledge begins in knowledge of the properties of our mental entities and events; it is the other way around. To see this is to begin to see how it is possible that even our way of describing mental events might be subject to radical revision for the better. So the materialist argues against the Cartesian; and his argument goes against Aristotle as well, since Aristotle does not believe that common sense will be undermined by the results of scientific research.

sufficient for the state being a state of white. The evidential relation to the typical belief is necessary as well. Indeed, the latter relation is closer, in an important way. For if a perceptual state is of a sort that its owner acknowledges to be the sort that typically leads one to believe that here is something white, then it will almost certainly be an of-white perceptual state. On the other hand, its being the effect of some white stimulus is quite commonly compatible with its being not of-white. The "of-" relation applies primarily to the sort of belief, not to the sort of stimulus. (In fact, it is in part because it does that we are authoritative reporters of our own perceptual states.)

As described thus far, this relation between perceiver and world does not necessitate the perceiver's having any knowledge or belief on a particular occasion; but if the sensation is to be a genuine state of perception, it must be of a sort that does at least on some occasions play a part in a process that involves forming judgments. It would seem to follow that the capacity for having a sensation of-white or of-triangular is reserved to just those entities that can (though they do not always) make judgments of the form "This is white and triangular"—that is, those entities that have the concepts of white and triangular, and therefore many others besides. Now having a concept is most easily, if crudely, defined as having the mental capacity that is causally sufficient for having a word in one's vocabulary. How then can an animal have a concept? And how can an animal be said to be in a perceptual state?

I think Aristotle has a reasonable answer to the first question, though I shall save full discussion of it for the next chapter. The sort of belief brutes have is the sort that can, as that of a normal human cannot, be reduced to dispositions to behave in certain ways. Although it might not be strictly correct to say that a dog believes that there is a cat in the tree above him, it is not utter nonsense. It seems quite reasonable to explain animal behavior by postulating perceptual states that cause animals to behave as they do.

The conceptual priority of belief over perception need not entail that in either an individual case or the case of a particular sort of organism the perceptual state actually depends on the state of belief or judgment. It is enough that human perceptions are defined in part in terms of beliefs and that animal perceptions are defined by reference to a functional role that is closely analogous to the role human perceptions play in the human organism.

All the same, the notion of belief is crucial to the definition of perception and to the characterization of particular perceptual states. In cases in which the capacity for thought is not well developed, there is some reason to say that the relation between perception and belief is particularly close. Thus at *De An.* III 3 429a5ff., just after he has denied that animals have beliefs much like human belief, Aristotle suggests that for a brute having a belief about a sensed object is no more than either sensing the object in the usual way or having a *phantasma* of it in its absence. Lacking the power of thought, the brute cannot reflect on the circumstances and withhold belief as men do; so having simple *aisthēma* or *phantasma* that is noticed is just having a belief, if belief be considered a behavioral disposition.

In order to be a Cartesian in the broad sense, one must believe at least that there is some natural rather than conventional relation of similarity or isomorphism between the perceived item and a representation of it that is located within the perceiver, and that the representation is, except in abnormal and temporary circumstances, infallibly reportable by the owner under a description of it as isomorphic to the perceived item and under that description only. It is difficult to be sure whether Aristotle holds to the second of those two propositions, but there can be no doubt that he holds to the first. I think this is a mistake. I have claimed that part of the conceptual priority of belief over perception lies in the fact that a perceptual state is white (or, as I prefer to say, of-white) primarily by virtue of its typical evidential relation to a sort of belief, secondarily by virtue of its causal relation to its typical stimulus; and I have claimed that the isomorphism between perceptual states and the environment they represent is important—that it provides an apposite way of characterizing the perceptual states —only because they bear the evidential relation to belief. The mental state is neither white nor triangular *in propria persona*. Aristotle thinks somehow it is. That is why he finds himself faced with this important and difficult question: what is it about the isomorphism between sense organ and sensed object that makes for a state of perception rather than mere isomorphism? No doubt the question were better posed the other way around: what is it about the relation between sense organ and sensed object that makes it legitimate to say that they are isomorphic in any way? The correct answer to the latter question tells a story about belief.

Aristotle answers the former question, and in so doing he tells a story about more elaborate sensory capacities, which seem on inspection to involve judgment essentially. While it is a mistake to claim some natural isomorphism between sensor and sensed, it is an excellent idea to say that the relation is one of sensing because it plays a certain sort of role in the cognitive economy of the whole organism.

Chapter Six

THOUGHT AND MATERIALISM

THE topic of thought is particularly important to the present enterprise because Aristotle holds that the faculty of thought is the one part of the soul that is separated from the body. He is therefore not finally a thoroughgoing materialist by modern standards; and what is required is an assessment of his reasons for not being a materialist. The reasons have to do with intentionality, the elusive feature that has been thought to characterize human thought and desire and so to make them importantly different from physical states and events. Thought, desire, and other similar mental states have the odd property of making essential reference to what does not exist or, as Brentano[1] says, to what has only intentional inexistence. This is generally held to be true of no physical state. Aristotle locates a problem precisely in the relation between what has since been called the intentional state of a person and his physical state, rather than in the epistemological status of sensations. Much of what Aristotle says, as I interpret him, makes sense from a contemporary standpoint; but it is likely that this or any interpretation that makes Aristotle consistent on the topic of thought is partly speculative.

Some philosophers who have worked on intentionality have made much of the characteristically indefinite nature of the objects of thought. Aristotle emphasizes that feature as well. It causes him some difficulties in his explanation of the place of images in thinking, but his final position is

---

[1] See especially his *Psychologie vom empirischen Standpunkt*, of which "The Distinction Between Mental and Physical Phenomena" is a translation of part of the first chapter of the second book of the first volume.

reasonable. Yet his account suffers because he does not well understand the relation between perception and thought, in particular the conceptual dependency of the former on the latter, a difficult matter for any philosopher (Section I). The same weakness is evident in Aristotle's account of the acquisition of concepts and of the function of the faculty of *nous* (often and somewhat inadequately translated "thought") in that process (Section II). *Nous* turns out to be an immaterial faculty of the soul, according to Aristotle. Though the arguments he advances for the immateriality of *nous* are not cogent, the position itself is defensible on Aristotelian grounds; for the abstractness of thought, as compared to the determinateness of the image that must always accompany thought, makes the one-one mental event/physical event relation on which materialism depends impossible (Section III).

Nous is at work in both cognition and desire, and Aristotle's accounts of the two are similar in structure. From these twin accounts, for all their problems and obscurities, emerge some important points about the intentionality of human thought and deliberation, and about the inadequacy of behaviorism as an account of human as opposed to animal psychology (Section IV). Where Aristotle's treatment of thought has received the greatest attention it has been least successful. *Nous poiētikos*, active (or creative) *nous*, is the powerful but mysterious faculty that is supposed to insure that the concepts by which we understand the world are the correct ones. I believe it is an inadequate answer to a wrongheaded question, but *nous poiētikos* has a certain interest for the historian of philosophy (Section V).

I. THOUGHT, IMAGES, AND ABSTRACTION

Aristotle says that thought apprehends the form of something without the matter (*De An.* III 4). But is that not the function of perception? Aristotle has this in mind: although on a particular occasion one can sense a thing only in conjunction with its material or accidental sensible properties, one can think of (for example) flesh without thinking of the stuff it is made of, or of any entity without thinking of any accidental property of it, even if every entity has some non-essential properties. Over a period of time one perceives many concave things, of which each is in a certain parcel of matter and has certain properties not directly related to its concavity: a snub nose, a concave lens. Now a human being can not only remember a number of these experienced items but also organize them according to certain properties they share. That is, he can come to have the concept of concavity, of which he can thereafter think without first attending to some actually concave object and without thinking of any of the sorts of matter or accident with one of which concavity is always joined. In other words, he can think of concavity, and of other things, in abstraction.[2]

Phantasia (imagination) has a role to play in this story. Recall that it made rather an uncertain appearance in the account of perception. From much of what Aristotle says about the faculty of imagination it would seem to follow that one has some sort of representation inwardly whenever one perceives, and in successful cases it somehow represents what one perceives. But Aristotle has less to say about representations than one might have hoped, and in his discussion of the Protagoreans in *Metaphysics* Γ 5 he seems not to see how they might fit into a reasonable account of perception. In *De An.* III 3 he states that one can have a *phantasia* (image) of the sun as a foot across while believing even at that moment that the sun is larger than the whole world (428b2-5); so exactly what a thought is a thought of is not determined by the *phantasia* (that is, the *phantasma*, which

---

[2] Aristotle discusses abstraction in *De An.* III 4 (429b10ff.) and 7 (431b12ff.), and in *An. Post.* II 19 in less detail. The notion that thinking the forms without the matter is essentially a point about abstraction is not new. See, e.g., Themistius, H. 96, 30ff., and Brentano, *Die Psychologie des Aristoteles*, pp. 113f. and 145ff.

is the word more frequently used for image) that accompanies it.[3]

What, then, is the relation between a thought and the *phantasma* that accompanies it? Aristotle argues in *De An.* III 4 that as perception is to its objects, so thought is to the objects of thought; and this analogy suggests that a *phantasma* is what one thinks of. He holds consistently in III 7-9 that one has *phantasmata* when one thinks, but denies in III 8 that the thought is identical to the image that accompanies it. What one is thinking about is in part determined by the image one entertains while thinking, but the situation is more complicated than that if we can think of abstractions like concavity, and not only of things like a particular snub nose. The point of saying that thought apprehends the form of something without the matter and that *phantasmata* are like *aisthēmata* only without matter is that one can think of a sort of item without thinking of it as having any of the properties some one or more of which every item of that sort has. But surely one could not have an image of a triangle that is not isosceles or equilateral or scalene, if one could not find a triangle that is none of those. Accordingly, Aristotle says:

> Since it seems that nothing has separable existence but sensible magnitudes, the objects of thought [*ta noēta*]— both those spoken of in abstraction and the states and properties of sensible things—are in sensible forms. There-

---

[3] See further K. Lycos, "Aristotle and Plato on 'Appearing'."

It is worth mentioning that Aristotle's conception of the image may be a bit subtler than some commentators have believed, for an image can apparently be a copy of a previous state of mind, rather than only of a thing sensed. At *De An.* III 3 428b10ff., for example, Aristotle calls the motion that is *phantasia* a copy of the perceiving, and not of the thing perceived. One task to which this sort of image seems better suited than the empiricist's sort is an account of remembering how to do something. See Richard Sorabji, *Aristotle on Memory*, pp. 7f. and, more extensively, John Cooper's review of Sorabji, pp. 68f. It will become clear that I think it unduly optimistic to attribute to Aristotle a clear and consistent notion of *phantasia*.

fore without sensation one could never learn or understand anything. (III 8 432a3-8)

This passage suggests not only that I cannot think of a chiliagon unless I have seen one, but also that the content of a thought is determinate because the image one has in thinking is determinate; and it leaves one puzzled about precisely what the process of abstraction does.

A famous passage early in *De Memoria* largely answers the question:

> One cannot think without an image. For there is the same feature in thinking as in drawing a diagram: in this case, though we do not use the fact that the triangle has some determinate size, nevertheless we draw it as having a determinate size. And it is the same with the thinker: though he is not thinking of a size, he puts a size before his eyes but does not think of it as being of a certain size. Even if the object is by nature quantitative but indeterminate, he puts a determinate size before himself, but he thinks of it only as having some size or other [but not necessarily some particular size]. (449b32-450a6)

One can think of things in abstraction even from some of the properties of the images one conjures up when thinking about them. Thus I can think of a chiliagon or a perfect triangle, or think of a triangle without thinking of one that is isosceles, and so on, even if I cannot imagine such a triangle, as Aristotle believes one cannot. The ability to think abstractly would seem to accompany the establishment of the universal in the soul as described in *An. Post.* II 19, especially 100a5-9, which states that it is mastery of this sort of universal, the abstract one, that accounts for *epistēmē* and *technē* (knowledge and skill, according to the usual translations).

That one can have a thought of concavity or triangle without also thinking about a particular instance of concavity or about a triangle that is isosceles is an important feature of thought, a feature it does not obviously share with perception. We express this difference (and more) by saying that thought is intentional. Aristotle expresses it by saying that certain items may be thought of in abstraction. So if a certain sort of thing is always found combined with matter, one can nevertheless think of it without thinking of its matter, or any matter. Aristotle generalizes a bit hastily and states that one thinks of essences and not matter or accidents. That is his way of stating the characteristic intentionality of thought.

Aristotle has a problem here because he does not appreciate fully the propositional character of intentional attitudes. It is all too easy to suppose that when one thinks, one entertains a mental image; and though Aristotle denies that that is all we do in thinking (III 8 *ad fin.*), he has some difficulty about saying what more we do. Indeed, he is tempted to assign a truth value to just having an image either of perception or for thought. He seems fairly clear in the first chapter of *De Interpretatione* about the propositional nature of thought, but in *De Anima* he vacillates: in III 6 he says that a combination of elements is required for falsity, but he conspicuously fails to add that truth requires it; two chapters later he distinguishes imagination from assertion and denial by stating that the latter are true or false. Now one can have a thought about something simply by having a picture of it pop into one's mind, though this happens rather less often than some philosophers have believed. But when you and I both entertain the thought that the sum of the interior angles of a triangle is 180 degrees, what makes it true that you and I are having the same thought is that the proposition is the same in each case (or, if one wants to take a very hard line, the sentence is the same in each case). As you entertain the thought, you may have an image of a triangle; I may have no particular image at all, or one of a chiliagon, or one of a man sleeping.

Recognition of the propositional nature of at least a certain sort or part of thought would help Aristotle deal better with a certain intentional feature as well. Insofar as we think in propositions, images being incidental to the content of the thought, there should be no problem about how one can desire a tiger without desiring any particular size of tiger (for one desires that one should possess a tiger), nor any problem about how one can think about a triangle without thinking about a scalene or isosceles or equilateral one (for one thinks that, say, every triangle has interior angles equal to 180 degrees).

II. CONCEPTS AND THE ACQUISITION OF KNOWLEDGE

More needs to be said about Aristotle's account of the relation between thought and the world, in particular about his account of how we acquire the ability to think about things. In the discussion of his account I shall venture some opinions about the facts of these matters, on which I think Aristotle is seriously mistaken.

I have claimed (Chapter Five, Section V) that one's having knowledge at all presupposes that sometimes one's sensory faculties are in a state somehow isomorphic to the state of the perceived environment and that Aristotle's theory makes the faculties mirror the sensibles. But a sensory item is in fact characterized only in a very derivative way by the property it represents: thus a sensation may be of-white in that it is the sort of state of the perceiver that a white thing standardly produces and therefore is standardly taken as evidence by the person in that state that a white item is at hand. Now the perceiver cannot take a sensory item as evidence for the presence of something white until he has the concept white. So there are grounds for believing that it is because one has the concept of white that one can have of-white sensations, and not vice versa. Therefore it is a bit misleading to say that having white sensations leads to having the concept of white.[4]

It is not enough to argue, as Aristotle does, that perceptive awareness of an object depends on the proper functioning of a central sense organ. For it is an important feature of perception that it is conceptually posterior to belief just in the sense that a full account of it demands an account of one's coming to believe something. But as Aristotle attributes perception but not belief to brutes,[5] it is not surprising that he fails to do justice to that important feature. For even if we could not have the concept we do have of perception without also having something like our concept of belief, it still makes sense to hold that at least some animals are sensitively attuned to the passing show without having propositional attitudes like belief. Yet Aristotle misconstrues not only this conceptual relation but also the nature of belief in part because he (sometimes, not consistently) regards the state of an organism characteristic of conscious perception as a sufficient condition of the perceptual belief that here is such and such an item. It is probable that he thinks the sort of differential response to sensory stimuli of which lower animals are capable without prior training or experience constitutes awareness of the stimulus as being of a certain sort; and there is, as I have argued, some evidence from passages in which Aristotle is not discussing perception primarily that he is committed to the notion that to perceive is to judge.

The pertinent problem about the relation between per-

[4] Properly understood, the statement means something like this: having sensations that, considered *in propria persona*, are not distinguishable from sensations that are normally taken by perceivers as evidence for the presence of something white is a causally necessary condition of having the concept white. And even that carefully hedged statement is wrong if blind people can have the concept white.

[5] *De An.* III 3 428a18ff. I shall discuss this view further in Section IV.

ceiving and judging is this: perceiving is a relation between a person and a thing, and judging is a relation between a person and a proposition; but at the same time, it is at least possible (if materialism is true, it is the case) that someone's being in a state of judging is nothing more than someone's being in a certain physical state in certain circumstances. That is, what is by definition a relation between a person and a proposition may be contingently identical with a certain physical state, though one that is normally characterized in highly complex terms. Now I do not think Aristotle realizes the importance of characterizing judgments or beliefs in propositional terms; in particular, he does not see how even at a very elementary level the object of a judgment must be a proposition rather than a thing. This is at least partly because he sometimes entertains a wrongheaded theory of truth.

The difficulty with truth is well illustrated in the last chapter of *Metaphysics* Θ, where Aristotle maneuvers himself into saying (1051b23ff.) that in the case of incomposite things truth is a matter of contact and assertion, so that one cannot err concerning what a substance essentially is nor make any mistake about a non-composite substance. Conspicuously, he does not deny that one can be right, for identifying them or successfully referring to them is a sufficient condition of saying something true about them. This view is not a momentary aberration: at the end of *De An.* III 6 (430b27ff.) Aristotle says that when one thinks of an essence without predicating anything of it, the thought is true. Most importantly for present purposes, Aristotle extends the point to perception. In the next chapter (431a8) he says that sensing is similar to simple assertion and thinking; and it must follow that sensing a particular as being what it is (for example, a man) is like *saying the particular*: "this man" functions as a kind of assertion, and one that cannot be false but only true. Now between those last two passages Aristotle repeats his familiar doctrine that while seeing the special object of sight is infallibly true, judging that this white object is a man is not. What is it, then, precisely, that cannot but be true when one senses a man? Not, surely, "The white thing is a man." Apparently just the successful identification of the substance as a man is true. What Aristotle suggests is that if one really perceives a man, then one can successfully and therefore truly identify him as a man.[6]

How much one knows when one perceives a thing or event in fact depends on what one has learned. It is easy to forget that this includes items on which we can give credible non-inferential reports. The following question then arises: just what is the least that we know when we are having the sort of sensation normally connected with perception? One plausible answer is that we know for certain at least something about our sensations, that we must make some sort of inference in order to know something about physical objects and other items "outside the mind." There is something to be said for this, but as an answer to the present problem it involves a confusion: I am talking, not about what is the least we have adequate evidence for, but about what is the least that is implied about what we believe (justifiably or not) by the mere fact that we are having sensations of the sort mentioned above. And the answer is: nothing. But if one believes that to have sensations is *ipso facto* to have some beliefs, then it is more plausible to take these beliefs to be about things in the world rather than sensations; for to many people who have such sensations it seldom occurs that they are having the sensations, and it cannot occur to anybody who has not first learned how to talk about things. This is in itself only a small piece of an answer to the problem of skepticism, which in any case Aristotle does not even

---

[6] If Aristotle could show that one perceives only if one knows what one is perceiving, then this claim would make good sense; but I do not think he has a carefully worked out position on the point. Elsewhere he says that in perceiving a particular one apprehends a universal: see *An. Post.* II 19 100a16ff., to which I shall return later in this section. See also note 14 below.

discuss; and that physical objects do have this sort of conceptual primacy does not justify Aristotle in saying that
when we perceive an object or event we thereby know
something about it. For even where knowing does not require inferring, it does require at least command of certain
concepts; so while having a sensation caused by something
does not require having any concepts, believing something
to be the case about either the sensation or its cause does.

But there is more to the matter than this. By the time we
reach maturity we have become so good at recognizing
both substances and sensations that we have quite forgotten
that we bring to experience, even to immediate experience,
certain organizing categories drawn from successful deal-
ings with intersubjectively available objects. That our sensations are the items about which we can have the most certain
knowledge does not imply either that we had knowledge of
them before we had knowledge of anything else (for we
did not) or that the terms in which we describe them are
the most complete and most accurate terms that could ever
be available. A quantity of experienced items can be arranged in various ways more or less adequately, perhaps
depending on the purposes of the descriptions. This is no
less true of entities we have traditionally called mental than
of physical entities; but Aristotle does not deal fully with
mental entities of the sort that interest us, and so does not
face the possibility that what is credibly reportable might
be described far differently and better than we describe it
now.

It is all too easy to believe that our knowledge of mental
entities precedes and justifies our knowledge of middle-
sized material objects in our surroundings, and that this
knowledge in turn forms the basis for our knowledge of the
laws of nature. It is true that mental entities are a causally
necessary condition of our knowledge of nearby substances
and events, true that grownups can report certain mental
entities in a way they cannot report physical ones and can
make justifiable inferences from the former to the latter,

but false that knowledge of mental entities precedes that of physical ones, and false that mental entities (or entities of any sort) comprise an ultimate and infallible court of appeal on which all knowledge rests. It is most importantly false that one acquires concepts by first knowing or believing that something, a substance or a mental entity, is of a certain sort and then coming to grasp the concept of the sort. Quite aside from the evident logical impossibility of believing anything about anything without having the concept that gets used in the proposition one believes, any individual in the world is one of literally an infinite number of sorts of thing, and any group of things has an infinite number of features in common. So how is one to find the right universal uniting them all?

It is worth emphasizing that Aristotle does not face the same problems the contemporary philosopher of mind faces. As I argued in Chapter Five, our knowledge about our mental entities, and the way in which we classify them, rest on our knowledge about and classification of things in the public world. Therefore we do not worry about how we get started properly classifying sensory items: the right way is the way parasitic on the way in which we classify public things; and the right way to classify public things is the one that serves the purposes of common sense and natural science—or, to put the point differently, there is no one right way to classify and identify mental items. Aristotle does not worry about the classification of mental entities, not because he thinks one is unproblematically aware of them under their customary classification in advance of any learning, but rather because he does not think of them as the basis of knowledge. Aristotle's problem is that he thinks there is one classification scheme of things in the world and that he thinks there is a faculty that enables one to apprehend things as instances of the universals that correspond to the organization of the world. That faculty is *nous*, and it enables one to build knowledge up out of individual bits of perception. He would probably not believe

all this if he were clear enough on the relation between perception and belief to confine truth to the latter.

III. ARISTOTLE ON INDUCTION
AND ABSTRACTION

The proof that one can find the right universals, the ones
that properly divide the world at its joints, and so have
knowledge is that people do have knowledge. Aristotle's
account of how they achieve it is a two-sided approach to a
double problem: it is a combination of a causal account and
a justificatory account of our having the abstract entities
we do have in our souls, and the account tries to solve both
a problem of concept formation and the problem of induction. Plato has left Aristotle some difficult problems, which
Aristotle does not wish to solve by invoking a theory of
Ideas. On some topics on which progress remains to be
made, Aristotle instructively mixes insight and mistake.

Plato and Aristotle both deal with the question of our
knowledge of universals,[7] and though their answers are
thought to be quite different, their methods have much in
common. Very roughly, Plato believes that our experience
in the world reminds us of the eternal entities and the propositions concerning them that in a previous and disembodied
existence our souls knew and that the items we now experience dimly reflect. The examination by the Socratic ques-
tion-and-answer method will reveal our (imperfect) awareness of the Ideas and the connection of our opinion to them.
But no amount of ordinary experience will provide adequate
evidence for the truth of propositions concerning these
entities; that is available only by the use of dialectic, whose
details Plato does not describe. Nor would our experience
provide even a clue to the existence or nature of these entities but for the fact that our previous acquaintance with
them causes us to be reminded of them by our experiences.

[7] This is not to say that Platonic Ideas really are universals.

So Plato holds that our knowledge of what is *a priori* true rests on experience only in the sense that experience is the occasion of our beginning to (re)learn it. That such knowledge is somehow in us from the beginning enables us to solve the so-called eristic paradox: how can one find knowledge if one does not (already) know what one is looking for? Part of the answer is that in some sense one does already know what one is looking for.

Aristotle argues that our mastery of concepts as well as our knowledge of universals can be seen to be built up out of experience, both in much the same way. In fact, Aristotle makes it clear in the first few chapters of *Posterior Analytics* II that the search for proper definitions and the search for true first premises are the same search. *Posterior Analytics* begins with the argument that the first principles are not demonstrable; and Aristotle is particularly opposed to the notion that there is, as Plato claims in the *Republic*, a science that unites the first principles of the various departmental sciences by showing how they derive from the self-justifying first principles of dialectic. In I 18 he says that sense perception is a necessary condition of knowledge of universals, including those that cannot exist and therefore cannot be sensed in isolation and so are known in the abstract; we are acquainted with universals by virtue of what Aristotle calls induction (*epagōgē*) from sensory experience of particulars. Here Aristotle further parts company with Plato.

According to the last chapter of *Posterior Analytics*, one can come to know universals by induction from sense experience with the aid of *nous* (here usually translated "intuition"). The appearance of *nous* here is a bit surprising: Aristotle has been sounding like a hard-nosed empiricist up to this point in the chapter; so *nous* may seem rather a *deus ex machina*, and one not well explained. But it is not in all respects the *ad hoc* device it may appear to be. As James Lesher has shown, *nous* is generally the capacity for grasp-

ing a principle or a feature or, most frequently, an explanatory universal out of a string of observed phenomena.[8] (He
points for evidence to *An. Post.* I 31 88a5ff., I 33 88b33ff.,
I 34 89b10ff., and other passages.) The mere repeated experience of things or events of a certain sort does not by itself
bring about the presence of the right sort of universal in
the soul, whether we take the universal to be a definition,
a general principle, or a concept. What is required in addition is some act of the mind to pull out the correct universal
from the passing confusion. This is *nous*, the faculty that
makes experience yield our cognition of universals, which
accounts, as Aristotle says, for *technē* (skill) in the case
of doing and *epistēmē* in the case of knowing (100a8f.).

The doctrine appears in the *Metaphysics* as well. *Met.*
A 1 begins with a treatment of the progress of the individual
human soul from sensory apprehension of individuals to
knowledge and skill. Sensation leads to memory and *phantasia* in higher animals, but many memories of the same sort
of thing produce experience only (or almost only) in man.
Aristotle notices that experience is not easily distinguished
from knowledge or skill, but in fact the former leads to
the latter when one comes to have a universal opinion about
a certain sort of thing. For example, experience tells one that
a certain medicine cured Callias and Socrates and others,
and skill judges that that sort of medicine works on all
people of a certain constitution with a certain ailment.

Probably one of the reasons why experience seems to
differ little from *technē* is that in some cases it seems one can
immediately see what the causal connection is. Aristotle
gives the example of a burning-glass (*An. Post.* I 31 88a-
13ff.): if our eyesight were better, we could see exactly
how it works. But knowing that there is a causal connection
involves knowing that a certain sort of event happens every
time; so one is really drawing an inference, perhaps uncon-

---

[8] "The Meaning of *Nous* in the Posterior Analytics." Lesher finds
nous a common concept in Aristotle, but he finds no clear explanation
of exactly how it works.

sciously, on seeing the individual event. The distinction between seeing that B has followed A each time in the past and seeing that A causes B is not difficult to grasp, though in the particular case the reference to a universal rule may be ignored.[9]

One should keep this passage in mind in assessing the last chapter of *Posterior Analytics*. There the two crucial questions are these: (1) How do we arrive at the proper universal (the one that will encompass all possible cases)? and (2) How do we know when we have got it (since there are some future cases that could surprise us)? These are the questions that constitute the eristic paradox of the *Meno*, and the answer given in the *Meno* invokes a prenatal experience and recollection. Aristotle's answer to those questions is that we have the faculty of *nous*.

One can best summarize the function of *nous* thus: it enables us to know what is not, or not usually, given in experience. The most obvious way it does is to enable us to know about not only events and groups of events but also causal rules of nature; the next most obvious way is to allow us to progress from cognition of bare *phantasmata* to knowledge of true universals, especially species and genera. In effect, *nous* solves the problem of induction and a central problem about concept formation by finding the universals that govern not only the organization of the

[9] As Lesher concedes (pp. 62f., esp. n. 51), Aristotle says in *An. Post.* II 19 100b7-15 that *nous* is truer than knowledge, so that it, rather than knowledge, deals with first principles; but Lesher denies that Aristotle means that *nous* deals only with first principles. When Aristotle says *nous* is truer than knowledge, he means that it is more in possession of first principles. (Lesher refers to *Met.* A 1 982a25ff., *An. Post.* I 24 86a13ff., and some other passages.) Why is *nous* more in possession of the first principles than is knowledge? Because we can have knowledge only of that which can be demonstrated, and so only of that which can be the conclusion of a syllogism—that which therefore cannot be a first principle, since a first principle cannot follow logically from anything. So the passage does not imply that there can be *nous* only of the very first principles.

world but also the rules according to which events occur; and that the two sets of universals are related is clearly part of the point of *Metaphysics* Z (see Chapter One, Section III b). By the operation of *nous* universals are present in the soul of the knower and are there in the abstract. That is, if the universal triangle is in one's soul, one knows what a triangle is *qua* triangle, and so what is true of the triangle irrespective of whether it is scalene, equilateral, or isosceles. For example, having interior angles equal to two right angles belongs *universally*, not to isosceles triangle, but to triangle (*An. Post.* I 4 73b25ff.); and knowing that requires having the abstract concept triangle, a product of *nous*. The same goes for knowledge of what cures a certain sort of disease: the doctor does not think of the person suffering from it as having any particular height or weight or color, though each victim is just as tall or heavy or pale as he is.

Whence does our knowledge of first principles derive? It comes from a faculty that

. . . evidently belongs to all animals. They have an innate discriminative capacity, which is called perception. But while there is perception in all animals, there is a persistence of the *aisthēma* in some animals but not in others. In those cases in which there is no persistence, there is no cognition beyond perception at all, at any rate not of the things of which there is no persistence; in those creatures in which it does happen, the perception stays in the soul. Where this happens often, we get the following distinction: in some cases there arises a *logos* from the persistence of things of certain sorts, in some cases not.

Thus we claim memory comes out of perception; and from repeated memories of the same thing, experience: many memories constitute a single experience. From experience, further, from the whole universal stabilized in the soul, the one beside the many which is as a unity in them all, the origin of skill and knowledge—skill in the case of coming to be, knowledge in the case of being. So these states are neither innate in definite form nor derivative from other higher states of knowledge, but instead from perception, as when in a battle, when there is a retreat, one man having made a stand another does and then another, until the original formation has been restored. The soul is the sort of thing that can do that.

Let us now restate what we just said unclearly. When one of the undifferentiated items has stopped, there is first in the soul a universal: for one perceives the individual, but the perception is of the universal; e.g., man, not a particular man Callias. There is more stopping among these universals, until the indivisibles and the universals stop: e.g., first a certain sort of animal, then animal. So clearly it is necessary that we recognize the first principles by induction; for perception provides the universal in this way. (*An. Post.* II 19 99b34-100b4.)

What is this universal that gets into the soul as a result of sense perception? The examples Aristotle gives in this final chapter are man and animal; and the similarity of this passage to the description in the first chapter of the *Metaphysics* of our acquiring knowledge and skill suggests that the process Aristotle describes works for a broad range of items. I shall argue that among those items are not only important propositions, including what we should call definitions, in mathematics and natural science, but also concepts.

It is not immediately clear whether at the end of *An. Post.* II 19 Aristotle is discussing acquiring knowledge or forming concepts or both. A universal is normally regarded in the *Posterior Analytics* not as a concept but as a universal principle in propositional form; in particular, the passage about the acquisition of the universal makes it a special case of grasping a first principle rather than simply a process similar to grasping a first principle. But I think the distinction between a concept and a piece of knowledge is not crucial for Aristotle. Having the concept man and having a definition of man that mentions his essential features, including pertinent causal properties, are not distinct states. Aristotle rightly holds that definitions are informative and refrains from distinguishing sharply between the sort of proposition that is true of a thing by definition and the sort a scientist can discover to be true of it.[10] If one considers having the concept man a matter of knowing what a man is, one will think of the scientist as sharpening our concept of man by discovering what is universally and necessarily true of man. So having a concept is a matter of knowing that some propositions are true; and having a concept is a matter of degree, since one need not know all the necessarily true propositions about some sort of thing in order to have the concept at all.

Experience precedes the concept of what you experience. An example would be believing truly that every A you have seen so far is a B but not knowing precisely what the relation is between A's and B's, in particular that all A's are necessarily B's. So, for example, your mother has pointed out to you a succession of substances and told you that they are all men; therefore you believe truly that everything your mother has called a man in your presence is a man. At a certain point you are able to go on from there, beyond the scope of your experience: you can make correct identifications yourself and consistently call Callias a man and Socrates a man and so forth. According to Aristotle's account, the universal man is now in your soul. Evidence for the presence of the universal is your ability consistently· to identify men; better evidence would be your ability to say what defines men. Knowing that all substances of a certain sort are men, you can now be said to know—whereas before you only truly believed—that a certain substance is a man.[11]

---

[10] On this point see further Richard Sorabji, "Aristotle and Oxford Philosophy," esp. pp. 131f.

[11] It is not entirely clear from the structure of the passage that the

Having the concept man, knowing what a man is, requires more than simply having the ability to call up a man-like *phantasma*. One must understand that the *phantasma* called up represents a certain universal; and this involves understanding among other things that, considered as a universal, man is neither short nor tall, light nor dark, young nor old, and so on, even though any man-like *phantasma* will inevitably have some of these (irrelevant) characteristics. *Nous* is the faculty that permits humans not only to have *phantasmata* but also to have attitudes towards them constitutive of what we regard as intentional states characteristic of humans. That the attitude is something over and above the state of the person such that there is a *phantasma* of some sort in the person makes the attitude a not entirely physical state and *nous* a not entirely physical faculty. (On this point, more in the next section.) The universal is in the soul when and only when one can have an attitude that is essentially characterizable as an attitude towards (for example, a thought of) man without regard to paleness or darkness, triangle without regard to equilaterality or scalenity, or anything without regard to any of the range of properties one of which an object or a *phantasma* will necessarily have.[12]

---

universal is first stabilized in the soul when one has knowledge—in fact, the usual translation suggests that experience is sufficient for a stable universal—but to understand it otherwise would make Aristotle's overall view incoherent.

[12] Aristotle permits animals memory. When he speaks of the persistence of the *aisthēma*, he means that in some circumstances the impression can be brought back before the creature's attention as a *phantasma*. But at *Mem.* 1 451a15ff. Aristotle says memory is a state of a *phantasma*—that is, a state for which a *phantasma* is responsible —and so suggests that just having a *phantasma* originally caused by some past event is not in itself memory. He speaks of memory as an intentional attitude, one that relates to time; but he holds that it is not noetic and that animals have it (450a15ff.). How can that be? Aristotle must be willing to consider under the heading of memory a situation in which the creature has a *phantasma* caused initially by a past event, brought back to consciousness by a present event, and

Having experience of B's as opposed to the concept of B involves having some concepts—no doubt this is one reason why Aristotle says in the *Met.* A 1 passage that animals have but little experience—but not the concept of B. The very ability to form a generalization about what one's mother has said requires various concepts, and clearly it requires noetic mental acts. So it looks as though having any particular concept rests on having other concepts previously. Insofar as Aristotle's theory suggests that it is possible to be aware of a particular thing as being of a certain sort without having a whole network of concepts at one's command, it is not a good account of how concepts are formed at the very start.[13] But there is nothing absurd about saying that, in some cases, having an opinion or having an imperfect grasp of a concept requires having some knowledge and some other concepts firmly in mind. Remember, *nous* is not a faculty that deals only with the highest or most im-

---

likely to cause the creature to behave in a way roughly characteristic of remembering the past event. So the passage in *An. Post.* II 19 must be referring to the recoverable presence in the soul of a *phantasma* from the past. (The passage refers to the *aisthēma* persisting in the soul; but if it persists and can be brought again to the owner's attention, it is *ipso facto* a *phantasma*.)

[13] Aristotle does seem not to believe, as I for one do, that any human cognitive state worthy of being called awareness involves the use of a network of concepts. It is by virtue of this network of concepts that one's senses can be said to be in a state isomorphic to that of the environment. *Pace* Aristotle, this isomorphism is conventional, not natural. Accordingly, Aristotle thinks abstract concepts (which are not, according to him, necessary for successful perception) can be acquired individually and in isolation from one another. At any rate, that is how I interpret the famous passage in *An Post.* II 19 in which Aristotle likens the acquisition of concepts to a military rout being stopped by one brave soldier taking a stand (100a12ff.). A rout ends because, one man having stopped, another does, then another, until the line holds. If the analogy is taken strictly, its point is that one can acquire a particular concept by itself, and subsequently and consequently others. If so, there is a brief period during which one has only one concept; and that is surely logically impossible.

portant universals. It accounts for every instance of deriving cognition of a universal from cognition of instances of it.

The equation of having a concept with having knowledge seems to rest on the assumption that a definition is a certain sort of statement of fact. It would follow that there are universals in souls corresponding only to the sorts of thing of which one can have experience: there is no definition of a unicorn. But we can indeed have a concept of a unicorn: in fact, part of the point of postulating intentional objects in the first place was that it seemed one could talk about non-existent things and non-existent sorts of thing; and I shall argue that considerations rather like this animated Aristotle as well. But he seems to have attended here only to possible universals rather than impossible ones, and especially to universals that correspond to species and genera.

Aristotle seems to believe that the laws of possible coherent thought are isomorphic to those of possible coherent language and so to those of nature: *Met.* Z 4, for example, suggests as much (see Chapter One, Section III b). If that is Aristotle's view, then perhaps he does believe that all thinkable universals are actual. Certainly he does not consider the possibility that there is any margin for rational variance in the structure of the language(s) one can use to talk usefully about the world. Aristotle does not think the world presents itself as a blooming, buzzing confusion that we may try to put into manageable order in any of various ways, perhaps provisionally. Instead, the organization of nature is written on its face, and any rational person can come to see that divisions into form and matter, species and genus, and so on are not at all arbitrary. We cannot group things any old way and expect there to be corresponding universals. *Nous* discovers universals; it does not create them.

That is to say, by the operation of *nous* one acquires not just any old concepts but precisely the right ones, in that one comes to recognize substances as exemplars of their species and not just as instances of some accidental universal.

When as a result of repeated perception of things of a certain sort (say, men) one is able to recognize a certain perceived man as a man, an undifferentiated item (*adiaphoron*) is in the soul. That is, one recognizes the perceived object as having a certain differentia, thus a certain definition. *Aisthēsis* is then of the universal (100a16ff.) in the sense that, for the possessor of the requisite concept, perceiving something involves awareness of the pertinent species. The theory seems to demand that knowing the essence of something requires the operation of *nous*, which is restricted to humans; but animals can perceive. Minimizing the inconsistency requires discovering what in the way of perception persons can do that brutes cannot. By virtue of *nous* and the consequent ability to know the essence of some things one perceives, a person knows what he perceives in the sense that he can identify and reidentify the perceived item and distinguish it from other items, even if it undergoes accidental changes. It makes some sense to say that one really perceives something only if one is aware of what one is perceiving; and that involves having the universal in one's soul—not just any universal, but the species, which permits one to identify it as a certain sort of thing and therefore as a certain thing.

Now one cannot perceive that something is a man in advance of first having acquired the concept man, which requires a stable network of concepts and therefore facility in language and the rudiments of reasoning; and all that, in turn, requires a certain amount of experience with substances in the world. But that initial experience does not itself involve awareness of those substances as being the sorts of thing they are. I am not perfectly certain that Aristotle clearly understands this point.

Aristotle's position on perceiving and essences[14] is consist-

---

[14] His position in *Posterior Analytics*, anyway. He suggests at II 19 100a16ff. and perhaps at I 31 87b29 that perception involves an awareness of the sort of thing one is perceiving; that is what I take Aristotle to mean when he says perception is of the universal. On the other

ent with his official view that things, in particular substances, have definitions. So the process of acquiring a meaningful language is a process of coming to know the definitions of things and therefore of such words as are used to stand for them. Now if the way the world is organized puts certain requirements on any possible correct talk about it, then there will be no conflict between the notion that meaningful words are signs of states of the soul and the notion that definitions attach primarily to substances, because any successful language will be stocked with words that mean by standing for items in the world. And the *phantasmata* that can be retrieved from within the soul are the *pathē* (states) that make our words meaningful by being representations of substances in the world. The simplest case of having a thought is having an image of the object of thought, much as the simplest case of perception is having an *aisthēma* of the thing perceived; and more complex thoughts are, or at least involve, combinations of images. The question of how a *phantasma* represents the actual object of the thought is not raised, for it is no problem; representation is a matter of straight imitation, as in the case of the *aisthēma*. That this is a mistake I have already suggested and shall argue further: thoughts are isomorphic to possible sentences about the world, not to the world itself; and what makes a sentence true is not that it accurately pictures the world. It follows that having a concept is like having a word in one's vocabulary.

Recall that Aristotle holds that perception is similar to simple assertion and thinking (*De An.* III 7 431a8; cf. also Chapter Five, Section VI). So having a sensation of a par-

---

hand, he maintains in *De Anima* (e.g., at II 5 417b23f.) and elsewhere that perception is of the individual, not the universal. Perhaps part of what he is getting at in the *Posterior Analytics* and in some passages in *De Anima* (e.g., III 7 431a8) is the point discussed in *Met.* M 10 (see Chapter One, Section II): the actualization of the knowledge of a universal is in the perception of an instance of it. See note 6 above.

ticular thing when the appropriate universal is in the soul (for example, of a man when one knows what a man is) or having a thought of the universal is like a successful naming that is at the same time a true statement. The unit of thought is the apprehension of a universal; the unit of perception is the apprehension of a substance as being the sort of thing it is. And these apprehensions are units of truth. Although Aristotle does not hold that every perception is a piece of knowledge, he does believe that every *nous*-accompanied perception is: once one has the concept of man, if one perceives Callias one knows that here is a man. Now it would be wrong to accuse Aristotle of utterly mistaking the propositional character of items that can be true or false: the fact is that Aristotle thinks truth and falsity are normally features of combinations of elements. But he allows some cases in which simples can be true, and these cases include some thoughts and some perceptions. The effect of this mistake on his theory of concept formation is great, and damaging. In particular, it fits all too well with the notion that an *aisthēma* or a *phantasma* can have meaning just by virtue of its resemblance to what it signifies.

Aristotle makes the acquisition of concepts too easy. One keeps perceiving things of a certain sort, one's *aisthēmata* are reproduced as *phantasmata*, and then one finds oneself able to abstract from the *phantasmata* and so have the concept of that sort of thing—or, as Aristotle puts it, have a *logos*, a state of the soul that has some meaning and presumably imparts that meaning to the word in the language that is a symbol of the universal it stands for. Now that is not the way it is at all. Contrary to what the analogy of the brave soldier stopping the rout implies, we do not acquire our concepts one at a time as though we were born with a full understanding of what reference is and could match up each word with some entity or *phantasma* of it. Aristotle's own words suggest, as I have noted, that acquiring certain concepts requires having others. To be sure, Aristotle is aware that in order for a person to have a concept of something he must not only be able to call up *phantasmata* but also be able to have attitudes towards them. A meaningful state of the soul, or a universal in the soul, is possible only when abstraction is possible; this is no doubt what Aristotle has in mind when he says that in some cases but not others the persistence of some sort of thing in the soul generates a *logos*. But Aristotle does not take this complication as a sign that his whole notion of what meaning is is seriously wrong.

Aristotle's use of the letter A as an analogy to our cognition of particulars and universals (*Met.* M 10 1087a5-25; see Chapter One, Section II) might have instructed him better if he had carried it further. Acquaintance with a letter-type involves not only being able to recognize tokens as tokens of that type but also knowing how letters fit with other letters to form words. Having established that point, Aristotle ought also to have understood that knowing the meaning of a word involves not only knowing what, if anything, it stands for but also how it fits into the language of which it is a part.

The primary point of the letter analogy is that knowing the universal can be analyzed into knowing one or more particulars of the appropriate sort; and this presumably means that one knows the type A if and only if one can recognize tokens of A as A's. It follows that the knowledge is not, or not only, a matter of a cognitive relation between a person and a universal entity. At least Aristotle does not make the mistake of suggesting that one first knows or even believes that a particular token represents a certain sound and then comes to know or believe the same of the type.

One may be tempted to object that correctly identifying a particular as ϕ is not a very good example of knowledge from Aristotle's point of view. It is too easy for a mistake to be made and for a true opinion to become false with the passage of time. A particular identification is a better example of the exercise of a concept: opinion, true or false, requires concepts, and it makes sense to define a concept as the capacity to make judgments of a certain sort. When Aristotle is talking about knowledge being analyzable into particular events of knowing, he must be thinking of knowing in the sense of knowing, for example, what a man is: it is plausible to say that that is analyzable into instances of correctly identifying men as men (though perhaps that is not saying enough: an instance of knowledge must involve acting rationally, and not only in some discernible pattern). If one really knows what a man is, then one's mistakes will be due only to failing to notice the qualifying or disqualifying features of a particular, and not to being unsure whether a particular whose pertinent features are noticeable can be said on the basis of those features to be a man. This amounts to another indication that Aristotle regards having a concept as a form of having knowledge—indeed, apparently a central form.

The relation of the particular to the universal is a problem Aristotle never handles quite satisfactorily. As I argued in the first chapter, he is pulled in two directions at least. The strain is perhaps most evident where Aristotle defends the primacy of the individual by making knowledge only potentially of the universal, actually of the individual. If having a concept is having a capacity for making judgments of a certain sort—not just making the right noises, but meaningfully speaking (cf. *De An.* II 8 420b26ff.)—then perhaps knowing is having a capacity for making correct judgments of a certain sort. But the further condition is that, if called upon, one must be able to justify one's judgment, and that requires reference again to universals.

There is some unclarity over the particular-universal relation in the sphere of causal and logical relations as well. Aristotle argues in *An. Post.* I that knowledge and demonstration of both sorts of relation involve primarily universals rather than particulars, but he does not say that the relations themselves are primarily relations among universals; in fact, the example of the burning-glass (I 31 88a12ff., cited early in Section III) suggests just the opposite. The potencies or powers of a substance, including those it has by virtue of being a member of a certain species (or, to put it another way, those which qualify it for membership in a certain species), are features of that substance primarily: from the *Categories* on, Aristotle is committed to individual properties, individual potencies, and individual forms. It does not follow, and it is not true, that one can know the properties or powers of an individual just by perceiving the individual: the apprehension of universals must enter somewhere, even if in certain cases the logical or causal connection is clear as soon as one sees the particular things or event. Nor, *a fortiori*, is it true that one comes to know universals by first knowing individuals. But the very fact that Aristotle attributes causal and logical properties directly to individuals makes it easy for him to go wrong in two important ways: first, to assume that our organization of the world into essences and accidents is not at all arbitrary but reflects the way the inhabitants of the world are; second, to believe that one can always come to know a universal just by repeated exposure to the properties of instances of that universal. And the two problems are related. Attributing a property to an item involves already having a taxonomy, a conceptual scheme for organizing one's experiences. But how can one know from the first that it is the right taxonomy, if any such thing there be?

IV. THOUGHT: ARISTOTLE'S IMMATERIALISM

It is clear by now that the acquisition of knowledge involves getting into one's soul a universal that is abstract. It is Aristotle's view that one can neither think nor know without abstract concepts—mere *phantasmata* will not do. Now the distinction between those animals which are capable of acquiring abstract universals and those which are not divides animals into those for which materialism is false and those for which it is true. This is because the abstract nature of the concepts required for thought makes it false that thinking is identical—even accidentally identical—with any bodily event. As I shall argue, the conclusion is not warranted; but Aristotle's argument for it is an interesting one, even cogent if properly restricted.

A thought that something or other is the case is a state of a person that typically causes him to assert sincerely that something or other is the case, given that it is appropriate for him to say anything. A thought has the additional feature that it is usually credibly reportable without inference by a sophisticated thinker. Roughly, the relation between uttered sentences and thought is that between the evidence for a theory and the theoretical entities. I can see no reason why these thoughts should not finally be found to be identical with certain states of the brain and central nervous system. Aristotle would disagree.

I have said (in Section II) that by virtue of the perceiver's having concepts the sensory states of the organism are isomorphic to the perceptible landscape. Aristotle sometimes says the former cause an image of the latter. Thoughts are not in that way isomorphic to the world around them. They are isomorphic in a different way—one might say synonymous—to possible *sentences about* the world, sentences that it is possible for the thinker to utter. So the sensation is isomorphic to the environment, while the belief is isomorphic to a sentence, which may state a fact about that environment but does not directly picture it. As with sense, the isomorphism is causal: as a sensation is of-white in that it is of the sort that is typically caused by something white, and typically taken as evidence of whiteness nearby, a belief is that-p in that it is of the sort typically causing one to assert that-p. All too often throughout the history of philosophy it has been held that true propositions picture the world accurately, and Aristotle gives some signs of taking this position. His official view, explicit at the beginning of *Met.* Θ 10, taken for granted in E 4, and suggested in *De Int.* 1, is that truth is a matter of combining in thought what is combined in reality. This could be taken to mean that one combines *phantasmata* of Coriscus and white in one's heart to arrive at the truth, provided Coriscus and white are accidentally the same in reality; and it would not in itself constitute a picture theory of truth. It is as though having a thought were entertaining a proposition. But then what makes the proposition true is its isomorphism with the world: the *phantasmata*—or *noēmata*, as they are sometimes called when perception is not involved—stand to each other as the represented things do. This line of reasoning leads Aristotle to understandable puzzlement about just what arrangement of *phantasmata* or *noēmata* of Coriscus and white constitutes the thought that Coriscus is white (especially in *Met.* E 4) and forces him to confine the notions of truth and falsehood—or at least falsehood—to statements about the relations between two or more entities to the exclusion of existential statements (especially in Θ 10). The last problem shows that Aristotle is tempted towards the view that an image of thought is true just in case it correctly pictures the contemplated object.

One of the advantages of an account of thought as propositional is that it seems to account for a feature of thought that some claim makes physicalism untenable. Sentences attributing thoughts to persons are intentional—most notably, they may refer to things or states of affairs that do not exist. The further claim, usually associated with Brentano and Chisholm,[15] is that no intentional sentence can be reduced by or translated into an extensional one. Therefore no statement about what somebody believes can be analyzed into a statement about his actual or possible behavior. But the account I have just mentioned implies that thinking that something or other is the case is just as much or as little susceptible of extensional paraphrase as saying that some-

---

[15] Franz Brentano, *Psychologie vom empirischen Standpunkt*; Roderick Chisholm, "Sentences About Believing," "Notes on the Logic of Believing."

thing or other is the case, since spoken sentences are the model for thoughts.[16] There are, to be sure, genuine concerns about whether saying something, as opposed to just making certain noises, can be adequately described in extensional terms—in particular, without the use of the intentional notion of meaning. Clearly neither statements about thought nor statements about speech could be analyzed or translated, in any ordinary sense, into statements about atoms and the void. Still, it does not follow that intentional systems are not physical systems. Granted, we sometimes find it helpful to describe various pieces of the universe or explain their behavior intentionally, human behavior being the best example. But it might also be appropriate to give an intentional explanation for the migration of ducks for the winter or for the workings of a machine. The point is that questions about which events ought to be described intentionally are notoriously difficult to answer; and like questions about whether certain behavior is goal-directed, they are not amenable to evidence directly.[17] Nor is it clear

[16] Precisely how this works and what it has to do with the mind-body problem is the subject of a debate in correspondence between Roderick Chisholm and Wilfred Sellars: see the appendix of *Minnesota Studies in the Philosophy of Science*, Vol. II. Sellars takes speech and talk about speech as the model for thought and the explanation of its intentionality and generally its meaningfulness. Chisholm objects that in the order of being it is the intentionality of thought that confers intentionality on talk and not vice versa. The two finally disagree about whether it would be possible to have an adequate concept of meaning (e.g., of sentences) without having the concept of thought.

[17] How could one show that some activity is goal-directed, beyond showing that it concludes in a certain state? Aristotle does not face this question squarely: he relies on feelings he has about the appropriateness of certain bits of behavior in the light of the apparent purpose of the thing acting. When he says that it is not the natural end of wine to become vinegar (*Met.* H 5 1044b34ff.), one can sympathize without being entirely convinced.

A number of philosophers have argued for the irreducibility of teleological or purposive statements to mechanistic ones in part on

what the significance would be of definitive answers to such questions.

Aristotle's views on the relation of the psychological to the physiological in general (see Chapter Four) would lead one to expect him to hold that intentional events are accidentally identical with certain physiological events. Indeed, in *De An.* I 4 Aristotle gives *dianoeisthai* (thinking) as an example of a mental process that stands to its physiological accompaniment as form to matter; so it ought to be possible to say of thought just what was said of sensation. Notoriously, it is not possible: the faculty of thought, definitive of human life, guarantor of language and the power of reasoning, is separate from the body, though causally connected to it. The point is worth investigating in some detail.

A state of *phantasia*, a bodily state not itself abstract, is a necessary condition of thought:

> Thought, if anything, would seem to be peculiar to the soul. Yet, if thought is a sort of imagination, or not independent of imagination, it will follow that even thought cannot be independent of the body. (I 1 403a8ff.)

> Imagination, in fact, is something different from both perception and thought, and it is never found by itself apart from perception, as belief is not found apart from imagination. (III 3 427b14ff.)

> To the thinking soul images (*phantasmata*) are as sensations. (III 7 431a14f.)

---

the ground that statements involving notions like error and end, which are essential to the explanation of behavior, do not rest on observation in the way in which statements in physics do. See, e.g., Richard Taylor, *Action and Purpose*, and Charles Taylor, *The Explanation of Behavior*. It does not follow that a particular state of, say, intending or erring is not identical with any physical state. See Charles Taylor, "Mind-Body Identity, A Side Issue?" which acknowledges the point about identity but not its importance. Much of what I said about materialism in Chapter Four (esp. Section V) applies here as well.

And *phantasmata* are produced by perception: that is the point of III 8, which draws the quite correct conclusion from virtually everything Aristotle has ever said about the origin of the contents of our thought from *Posterior Analytics* on. How, then, is thought not a physical event?

In *De Anima* Aristotle gives several reasons for saying that thought is separable from the body. For one thing, though it is true that we must have sensed before we can think, we can summon up *phantasmata* for thought at will without regard to the appropriate external stimulus. (See II 5 417b23f. and III 3 427b16ff.) Again (III 4 429a18ff.), since it is possible to think of all things, thought must be unmixed with any of them; so it must have no actual nature of its own. If it did, as organs of perception do, it would not be able to think of what is of the same nature as it, since organs of perception are not able to perceive things whose nature they share and towards which nature they therefore cannot change, as they must in order to perceive. Moreover, there is no organ of thought. Finally, the power to think is not destroyed by the extremely thinkable, as senses are by too intense noises and colors. I do not find these reasons impressive, though the notion that one can think all things is attractive insofar as it suggests that one can think of what is not sensed—that is, of what is abstract and of what, in general, does not exist.[18]

Quite aside from the dubious physiology underlying Aristotle's theory of perception, there is something to be said for the notion that what one can perceive is limited by the actual contents of the world, whereas what one can think of is not. The sort of thought that is not limited by what

[18] Brentano (*Die Psychologie des Aristoteles*, pp. 120ff.) does not agree that Aristotle's arguments in III 4 are unimpressive. My own account of Aristotle's view of the non-material nature of thought owes something to Brentano's account of thought, but not much to Brentano's account of Aristotle. In fact, what I shall argue are Aristotle's best grounds for considering the thinking soul immaterial are not those on which he places the greatest emphasis.

actually exists involves, I believe, what Aristotle in *De An.* III 11 calls deliberative *phantasia*, as distinguished from perceptual *phantasia*. (The former he also calls rational *phantasia* in III 10; cf. Themistius 121, 22ff. H.) Deliberative *phantasia*, by virtue of which we can reason and decide what is the case or what is the best thing to do, depends on the immaterial element in the soul, since that is the element which makes it possible to think what is not. And it is that capacity which distinguishes the human soul from that of the brute.

A rational being can not only envisage a state of affairs that is possible but not actual, it can also calculate about the relative values of various possible future states of affairs in deciding which of them to bring about. And because animals are not able to reason by weighing both evidence and alternative possible courses of action, they cannot have certain intentional attitudes, including intention and belief, except in some weak sense. Because men have deliberative *phantasia*, they can make two moves that animals cannot make. First, they can rearrange the universals they have apprehended and remembered, so that they can have *phantasmata* not corresponding exactly to any perception: for example, a man can have the concept of a perfectly equilateral triangle or of a dodecahedron without ever having seen one, because he can form a *phantasma* of either. Thus his mind sorts out memory impressions and somehow manipulates their features. (He can make one image out of many: III 11 434a8.) Second, a human being can think of things in abstraction even from any of the sorts of feature some one of which they must actually have. As Aristotle says in *De Mem.* 1 449b31ff., abstraction entails having a thought that does not correspond to the *phantasma* that accompanies it. The thought may be indefinite, though the image cannot be.

Deliberation will involve considerations and intentions that are indefinite in that way: in deciding upon a course of action, one does not decide every detail; and if one conjures up a mental picture of the future course of action, the picture may be (though often is not) more definite than the intention is. If in forming or considering my intention to take a bus to New York I picture an orange bus, it does not follow that I intend to take an orange bus to New York. But now if Aristotle is thinking this way, then one may wonder why he should say that there are two different sorts of *phantasia* corresponding to perception and deliberation. Insofar as there are two, they are distinct because some cases of the operation of *phantasia* are the immediate result of perception while some are spontaneous, or because in some cases there is a thought corresponding to a *phantasma* and in some cases not.

Aristotle's theory seems encumbered with three incompatible distinctions. First, an *aisthēma* is somehow material and a *phantasma* is not (III 8 432a10ff.); taken by itself, this distinction suggests that the *phantasma* is characteristically indefinite whereas the *aisthēma* is not. But, second, the passage at the beginning of *De Memoria* and other passages have suggested that an *aisthēma* differs from a *phantasma* only in that the former is caused in a standard way by an item now being perceived, whereas the latter is not; and the image that accompanies a propositional attitude like belief or intention is not itself characteristically indefinite. And now, third, this distinction between perceptive and deliberative *phantasia* suggests that some *phantasmata* are definite and others not, depending on whether they accompany seeing something wrongly or having an intention. Aristotle is best advised to keep to the second course, whereby the image is definite though the thought or other intentional attitude it accompanies may not be. Perhaps the problem is that Aristotle is a bit confused about what the object of an intentional attitude is: is it the image one contemplates, or the thing that attracts one, or a shadowy entity that is itself immaterial in that it may have no definite size, shape, or other attributes not essential to the desire? Aristotle has no clear answer; nor is there a clear answer available anywhere to one who does not recognize the propositionality of intentional attitudes.

Now to the main question: what is it about this abstract character of thought that might tempt Aristotle to say that thought is not, or not entirely, a physical event? Officially, the answer is that one can think all things, presumably including what one cannot perceive. Perception is limited to what the physical organs can respond to and apprehend. So is *phantasia*: it is a physical process, and presumably limited much as perception is, though it can be manipulated within those limits. Now everything that thinks, with the possible exception of deities, must employ *phantasia*; thus thought involves a physical process. But as the passage in *De Memoria* shows, the image does not entirely determine the thought. Many different thoughts might correspond to one *phantasma*: a certain image might accompany intending to do something, intending not to do it, trying to decide whether to do it, and so on; an image of a scalene triangle might accompany a thought merely of a triangle, just as in *De An.* III 3 Aristotle suggests that a small image of the sun may accompany various thoughts of what its size is. That sort of one-many *phantasma*-thought relation is incompatible with materialism, since it is the *phantasma* that provides the physical part of thought. That is the connection between the characteristic indefiniteness of thought and non-materialism for those beings capable of abstraction. But for Aristotle what plays the role of something like the object of thought or intention, the *phantasma*, is itself physical; the thought itself, for which the *phantasma* is necessary but not sufficient, is not physical.

Simply having a *phantasma* does not by itself constitute characteristically human thinking. When he is being careful, Aristotle holds that the thought is or can be, let us say, primarily the attitude towards the *phantasma* rather than the *phantasma* itself. In perception there is no further attitude required to make a state of having an *aisthēma* in one's soul a state of perception. Aristotle might have argued that a *phantasma* that resembles something is not by itself even a thought of that thing, but perhaps he wants to grant some weak sort of thinking to animals that can have *phantasmata* but not *nous*—and not, therefore, attitudes over and above the *phantasmata*.

Because animals are not able to reason by weighing both evidence and alternative possible courses of action, they can have certain intentional attitudes (belief, for one) only in some weak sense. Whether an animal is capable of the full range even of an emotion like fear is questionable, since our concept of fear seems to encompass the capacity to fear a decline in the price of gold as well as a charging rhinoceros. But it would be most odd to deny that an animal can fear. In fact, Aristotle does not consistently deny even that animals can deliberate: he denies it in *Nic. Eth.* III 2, but in *De Mot. An.* 6 and 7 he suggests that animals employ a practical syllogism. And in some attenuated sense they do, since they can sometimes figure out the answers to problems of, for example, how to get some food. But he denies that animals have beliefs (III 3 428a16ff.), or at least that lower animals do (III 11 434a10ff.), for beliefs strictly so-called are derived from inferences (III 3 428a18ff.). In *De Mem.* 1 450a17ff. Aristotle suggests that animals have no consciousness of time, and the importance of this sense to deliberation is clear from this passage from *De An.* III 10:

> There come to be desires opposed to each other; this happens whenever reason and appetites are opposed, in those which have a sense of time: thought tells us to hold back for the sake of the future, appetite urges us on for the sake of the present; for the immediate pleasure seems pleasurable and good without qualification because we do not see the future. (433b5-10)[19]

---

[19] This passage calls to mind not only the lowest level of Plato's tripartite soul but also a famous remark of Wittgenstein's: "We say a dog is afraid his master will beat him; but not, he is afraid his

V. BELIEFS, INTENTIONS, BEHAVIORISM, AND INTENTIONALITY

At this point I want to back up a bit in order to pull together some threads from the discussion of perception and thought. Aristotle leaves us with three interlocking but distinguishable stages of cognition: the first is perception, which in the simplest case is a relation of imitation between a present thing and a sensing organism, but which in the case of adult persons in full possession of their faculties involves thought; the second is imagination, which is a relation of imitation or isomorphism between an absent or misapprehended thing and a sensing and imagining organism; the third is thought, which is a largely unexplained attitude of a person towards an image (*phantasma*). (See III 3 427-b16 and Themistius 88, 26ff. H.) Officially, all brutes are capable of the first stage, some of the second, none of the third; but in invoking each of these stages Aristotle is trying to explain behavior that he well knows extends beyond human beings. The stages overlap, and it is implausible to hold that the behavior of brutes gives no clue whatever to their possession of even the third sort of cognition. It is often tempting to invoke such third-stage capacities as deliberation to explain the behavior of animals, as Aristotle is (perhaps uncomfortably) aware.

Now I have a suggestion that may help organize Aristotle's views into a plausible position. Aristotle would agree that animals are capable of perception, imagination, and

---

master will beat him tomorrow. Why not?" (*Philosophical Investigations*, para. 650, p. 166e.)

Just as merely having a *phantasma* cannot constitute deliberation, so merely having a *phantasma* of some thing or event perceived in the past is not remembering; one must take the image to be of some past thing or event. If an animal cannot have a sense of time but only *phantasmata* stimulated by past events, then it cannot have memory in the strict sense. See note 12 above.

thought just insofar as those states can be given a straight-forward kind of physicalist analysis—indeed, partly a be-haviorist analysis. Higher animals can perceive and imagine; and perception and imagination are certain states of the physical organism. That those states seem in some way to involve having concepts and having concepts seems to in-volve having *nous*, which is non-bodily, is really no prob-lem; our attributing perception and imagination to dogs re-quires that we have the concept of belief and therefore, as Aristotle rightly says, thought, but it does not require that we attribute thought to them. But in some cases Aristotle is tempted to say that brutes do think and deliberate; and the evidence for saying it is that they sometimes act as though they do. So he can stay strictly within the evidence and say that animals have thought in the attenuated sense that they have a disposition to behave in ways we consider rational. As Chisholm and others have argued,[20] belief and thought themselves are not susceptible of straightforward analysis into dispositions to behave in certain ways. But Aristotle can give a dispositional analysis of what brutes have, namely, a weak form of thought and belief.

That brutes cannot talk is of significance here. If behav-iorist analysis of human thought and belief is possible, it must analyze their intentionality in terms of the semantic categories of human speech, which can be analyzed into ex-tensional language.[21] Such an analysis of brutish thought and belief is neither possible nor necessary. It is reasonable to attribute to them no intentional attitudes so sophisticated that they must be modeled on overt speech, of which they are not capable, because they lack *nous* and therefore in-tentional attitudes too sophisticated to be accounted for by a purely physicalist (that is, behaviorist) analysis. They cannot have (abstract) universals in their souls, but only *phantasmata.*

Note that the interlocking stages of cognition turn out

[20] See "Sentences About Believing."
[21] If Sellars is right and Chisholm wrong; see above, note 16.

to be analogous to the stages of desire. In *De An.* III 7 (431-a8ff.) Aristotle claims that perceiving is like simple assertion and that pursuit and avoidance of a sensible item are acts of the faculty of perception considered as the basic faculty of desire. Here Aristotle is making two dubious but typical moves. First, he is again making perception a matter of knowledge, or at least belief that can be true if not false: it is analogous to a special and largely unexplained kind of assertion somehow akin to a successful reference. Second, he is making some unitary acts of perception accidentally identical with unitary acts of desiring or shunning. In these cases one perceives something as desirable or to be avoided, as one might also perceive something to be a man. The object of perception must be a thing or a property of a thing such that to fail to pursue or avoid it can only be to fail to perceive it.

What can perceive, according to Aristotle at *De An.* II 2 413b21ff., can desire because it can experience pleasure and pain.[22] In the next chapter (414b1f.) he repeats that perception implies desire; but perception does not imply imagination (415a10ff.). What, then, is the relation between desire and imagination? Clearly imagination implies desire, because perception requires desire and imagination requires perception. But desire does not require imagination: all animals with a sense of touch have *orexis* but may not have *phantasia*. The ant, the bee, and the grub do not (III 3 428-a10), probably (II 3 414b16); at any rate, they seem to have only a vague sort of *phantasia*, but they do experience pleasure and pain (III 11 433b31ff.), which have been shown to imply desire. In the simplest animals a low-level sort of desire could be triggered only by the perception of some object, so that the representation of it in the soul of the animal would be an *aisthēma* rather than a *phantasma*.

Now Aristotle actually says in III 10 that a self-moving

---

[22] The word I have here translated "desire" is *epithumia*, which in *De Anima* means irrational desire. *Boulēsis* is rational desire, and *orexis* is desire in general.

animal must have *orexis* and therefore *phantasia*, either rational or perceptual; but since in the next chapter he says that the sort of *phantasia* some animals have is barely worthy of the name, and since he has established in II 3 that perception implies desire without implying imagination, it follows that the most elementary form of desire requires no more than the perception of the desired object. At any rate, Aristotle somewhat hesitantly puts forward as causes of motion *orexis*, and the desired object, and in some cases thinking. No doubt his reason for saying what he says, and for his apparent vacillation, is that each of the factors is in some cases a necessary condition of motion but none is ever by itself sufficient.

Brutes cannot make one *phantasma* out of many—that is, they cannot combine or invent images and they cannot abstract—but they can call to mind *phantasmata* corresponding to past *aisthēmata* and act on them. They can desire a present object in that they can act in a way that will contribute to their getting it, and they can desire an object not present in that they can have a *phantasma* of it and consequently act in a way likely to get it. So when an animal desires something, it is being stimulated to pursuit of it by a representation of it. The details of the representation determine what it is seeking: if it has a *phantasma* of a white rabbit, then it is pursuing not just a rabbit but a white rabbit. A human being, on the other hand, can want a rabbit of no particular color, or even something that does not exist. (In the latter case, particularly, one would like to know what Aristotle thinks the object of desire is, and how it causes movement. He would not say that the *phantasma* is the object of desire.)

Thus there are three levels of desire. The lowest is a sort of craving for what is immediately before the desirer and stimulates it to pursue (or avoid). The second kind is indicated by the pursuit of something not present but represented by a *phantasma*: this is the sort of which higher animals are capable. The third involves true intentional attitudes, with the ability to consider universals in the abstract. These three levels of desire correspond exactly to the three levels of cognition, and there is overlap in this case too.

Behaviorism cannot give a dispositional analysis of both desire and belief, because desires turn out to be dispositions to act in certain ways only given certain beliefs, while beliefs are dispositions to act in certain ways only given certain desires. There are other objections, though none so stubborn as this one, which rests on the view that all desire is mediated by thought: that is, that I want something implies that I have some opinions about it such that it is not the case that the desire would survive any change whatever of those opinions. Even desires that are barely distinguishable from physical afflictions or compulsions are thought-dependent in this way: a drug addict would not crave something he ceased to believe to be heroin; an impulse to murder would not lead me to shoot at what I thought to be only a life-like dummy of my enemy.

The thought-dependency of desires may seem to be a matter of degree.[23] On the one hand, I may experience a sudden desire for something I have just noticed and be unable to describe the thought on which the desire to have this thing is dependent. On the other hand, I may calculate and decide in great detail what I want to do, then undertake an action or a series of actions that fulfills the purpose. An example of the latter sort of desire would be one that issues from what Aristotle calls a practical syllogism: my wanting to eat this particular food rests on my having ascertained that it is dry, that dry food is good for man, that

[23] This discussion is indebted to Stuart Hampshire's *Freedom of the Individual*, particularly the second chapter. Hampshire thinks some desires are not thought-dependent at all, but he seems to mean by this that we arrive at some desires by a process of thought while others come unbidden, like impulses. He does not clearly say that one can desire an object regardless of one's thought about it; surely one cannot.

I am a man, and other pertinent information. Often, though not always, one reaches a conception of the sort of act one wants to perform or the sort of thing one wants to have and then, rather than straightway acting, must wait or search for the opportunity. This sort of desire Aristotle calls *boulēsis*, at least in *De Anima*. It requires a universal, in the sense I have discussed, in the soul:[24] what one intends to do is determined up to a point, but not every detail is set; so the *phantasma* that must accompany one's intention (III 7 431a14-17) need not fit its fulfillment in detail.

At the other end of Aristotle's spectrum is the simplest case of desire, which is bare pursuit or avoidance of something; so Aristotle suggests at III 7 431a8ff. that this bottom level of desire bears roughly the same relation to a desired object that perception bears to a perceived object. This sort of desire can be reduced to a disposition to pursue something. But does not even this case require that the desirer recognize the pursued object as what he wants? It does, but Aristotle does not discuss this issue, instead suggesting that *epithumia* is a bodily condition somewhat like hunger or thirst and that the identification of the target is unproblematical.[25]

[24] Cf. Hampshire, p. 44: "Those, and only those, who may reflect on their wants, and who may also report them, can have desires to act at determinate dates remote from the immediate present. Only through the use of concepts do I have a world of interests that is extended in time. [Cf. III 10 433b5ff.] And only language-users can follow a norm requiring consistency in their wants over a period of time, and can correct their wants by reference to a standard of consistency in their interests."

[25] One gathers from the passage that desire, pursuit, and the anticipation of pleasure are extensionally equivalent. At *Nic. Eth.* X 3 1173b7ff. Aristotle rejects the view that pain is a bodily deficiency and pleasure replenishment. But for the case of hunger he seems to admit that the proposed definition states an accidental identity. Perhaps he would go on to say that there are other cases in which desire is a bodily condition definable by reference to the sort of thing one tends to pursue in order to correct it.

In fact, all knowledge is propositional and all desire is propositional. To know something is to know that something is the case, that some proposition is true; the same for believing something. To desire something is to desire that something be the case, that some proposition be true. To have knowledge of an object is to know some crucial proposition about it, such as its definition (and that, Aristotle would say, is really knowledge of a universal); to desire an object is to desire that one have it, or that one have an object of a description this object fits. It is clear how making desire propositional eases certain problems about intentionality—for example, how it is possible to desire something that is in fact ϕ while desiring not to have anything that is ϕ—but at the same time it generates some problems that affect the accounts of both knowledge and desire. As Aristotle realizes, concepts are necessary for the sort of desire and the sort of cognition possessors of *nous* have in their most sophisticated actions and states—that is the point of the talk about universals in the soul. But surely animals do not have thoughts and thus concepts or entertain propositions? And yet they do perceive and want.

Recall that I said the concept of perception requires the concept of belief, for perception is by definition something that typically brings about belief; yet it does not follow from this connection that one believes when one perceives. Animals perceive, though on Aristotle's theory they do not believe, because they do something importantly like what we do when we perceive. So it is with desire. It is defined by reference to belief. But one can attribute desire to animals, even though they do not have concepts and therefore do not entertain propositions and hence do not have beliefs, for their behavior makes it reasonable to suppose they have states analogous to our states of belief and our states of desire. Aristotle suggests that at the lowest level of belief and desire, of which brutes are capable, there is no proper use of concepts because there are no universals in the soul since there is no capacity of *nous*. To put the point another way, desire on this level is *alogos*.[26] Again, it is significant that brutes cannot talk: brutish desire, like brutish belief, cannot and need not be analyzed in terms of human speech. Aristotle is probably right in suggesting that physicalism is adequate for analysis of animal desire for the same reason behaviorism is: and though it would be far more difficult to show that physicalism is false when it comes to beings that have intentional attitudes, Aristotle is at least right in rejecting crude behaviorism for them, as well as the notion that their states of mind can be exhaustively described by reference to just their behavioral dispositions plus the images they have in their souls. His reason is not a bad one: they have *nous*, the capacity for abstract thought.

VII. NOUS POIĒTIKOS

We can have universals in our soul because this faculty of *nous* grasps universals out of our experience. Not just any old universals, but those according to which the world is in fact organized, species and genus universals, which help us individuate substances and even explain how they behave, since their species and genus determine much of what they do always or for the most part. (In fact, Aristotle does not distinguish clearly between the laws or rules of nature and the definition of the substances that constitute nature. This is another example of how for Aristotle the world is everything that is rather than everything that is the case. See Chapter One, Section V.) Thus the faculty solves the problem of induction as well as a problem about concept formation.

Nous is not restricted to the species and genus universals, though it is capable of grasping them and it would be of far less importance if it were not. Any act of acquiring a

---

[26] At *Nic. Eth.* I 13 1106b13 Aristotle says *epithumia* is *alogos* (but in a way not, in the rather narrow sense that it can be mastered by reason).

concept is at least partly an act of *nous*. And to the question, mentioned before, of how we get the right concepts and how we know when we have them that we have them—in other words, Aristotle's version of Plato's eristic paradox—the answer is that we have the faculty of *nous*.

To be sure, if what I have said about Aristotle's conception of the universe is correct, he would have less reason to wonder about how we are able to extract the correct concepts from the stream of experience than do philosophers of the present day: he does not believe that the world as experienced presents regularities on various levels and consequent opportunities to carve experience neatly in any number of ways. The task of *nous* is easier because the regularities that are most obvious, pervasive, and reliable are those which involve classifications into species and genus. Now how does *nous* pull universals of this sort out of the bog of matter?

I believe *nous poiētikos*, which I shall call active *nous*, is supposed to answer this question.[27] It appears in *De An.* III 5, in the middle of the treatment of thought and abstractness, and not obviously anywhere else. Active *nous* is to passive *nous* as the agent is to the material on which the agent works, or as the art itself is to the material, or as light to a color it actualizes by its presence. The active *nous* is separate (or separable), unaffected, and unmixed—independent of the passive *nous*, he seems to mean; but the important thing turns out to be that it is unmixed with the body, because it is entirely an *energeia*, not at all a potency, not material at all, hence separate from what serves as its matter and superior to it as well. Actual knowledge is identical with the thing known. Potential knowledge is prior to

---

[27] This is not to say that there are no other questions *nous poiētikos* is supposed to answer. Rather than embark on a full account of this faculty, I shall deal with it primarily insofar as it answers what I consider important questions raised by Aristotle's account. I do not thereby mean to suggest that I think Aristotle is right in looking for some sort of mechanism or faculty whose function it is to implant the right universals in one's mind.

actual in the individual but not universally. Active *nous*, never potential, thinks constantly. It is what it essentially is only when separated—namely, immortal and eternal. But since it is impassive, we do not remember its action. Unlike passive *nous*, it is indestructible; without it there is no thought.

I believe active *nous* is philosophically interesting only because it is an attempt to answer a philosophically interesting question: how do we acquire concepts? One important task of active *nous* is to show how it is that we have a faculty of passive *nous* (what so far I have been calling simply *nous*), which entertains universals in the abstract: active *nous* implants concepts in the mind.

I shall treat two of the most important questions about active *nous* together—the questions of its transcendence and its non-corporeality. If it is not at all a bodily faculty, then it will be hard to see how each person can have his own active *nous*. Aristotle describes active *nous* as *chōristos* (separate or separable); but later on he says that it is immortal and eternal only when it has been separated (*chōristheis*), and that characterization suggests that active *nous* is sometimes connected with a particular body. Perhaps active *nous* is separable from the body and from its passive *nous* in life but actually separated (and immortal) only at the death of the body.

Passive *nous* itself is clearly somehow separate from the body, for although it is impossible without *phantasia*, which is a bodily faculty, its operation is not exhausted by the operation of the body; so materialism is false for organisms that have (passive) *nous*. But when I have a thought, it is my thought and nobody else's because it is connected with this body in that this body's having certain *phantasmata* is a necessary though not sufficient condition of my thinking something. When this body is no more, a particular faculty of thought is no more. If there are no human bodies at all, there are no thoughts and no concepts. Active *nous* is separable in a different way. To begin with, Aristotle quite strongly suggests that active *nous* continues even if no particular person is thinking or able to think. Now if that is true, active *nous* does not require the cooperation of a particular body or a particular *phantasma*. But then how can one distinguish between your active *nous* and mine? You and I each have a distinguishable capacity to have concepts, and presumably to acquire concepts as well; but it is not clear that each of us has a separate mechanism for acquiring concepts. Whether the active *nous* is a faculty of a particular soul or an outside agency (as *De Gen. An.* II 3 736b27 famously suggests) is not clear, in part because Aristotle gives little or no clue to how instances of active *nous* could be individuated. Perhaps this is supposed to be a vindication of Aristotle's view that matter individuates: active *nous* has no matter to it and so does not divide into individual instances.[28]

The active *nous* is always thinking. But since the connection between active *nous* and the individual person is not sufficient to make us conscious of what active *nous* is doing, because it does not stir up any *phantasmata* in our souls, we are not aware of its operation. (This seems the best possible interpretation of the statement that we do not remember because active *nous* is impassive.) What is the object of

---

[28] The possibility that active *nous* is just one thing, however many thinkers there may be, and that it is identical to the Deity as described in *Metaphysics* Λ, has been widely noticed. I should like to mention one more consideration in favor of that view. In *Physics* VIII, primarily, Aristotle seems to want to rebut the suggestion that so-called self-movers really do move themselves without any external cause, lest one begin to suspect that the cosmos as a whole might do the same, and not need God as a first cause. (On that point I am indebted to David J. Furley's "Self Movers," a paper presented to the 1975 *Symposium Aristotelicum.*) Now if what I have said about human (i.e., *nous*-impregnated) intention is correct, a person might form a desire for something that does not exist. What, then, external to the person, is the cause of the behavior? Well, *nous* is clearly responsible in some way for the behavior. Is this, then, the sort of self-movement that might threaten Aristotle's cosmology? Not if the *nous* in question is identical with the God of *Met.* Λ.

its thought? Itself, the last few lines of III 4 suggest. But what else? I think it constantly contemplates all the species and genera in nature. Aristotle does not clearly say it does; but if it does, and if as a result of its so doing we can become able to entertain universals corresponding to those species and genera, then that would be how the proper universals get into our individual souls. Aristotle gives no detailed account of how the fact that some agency with which we have a mysterious connection contemplates forms and species (and is indeed in some elusive sense identical to them) enables us to acquire the right universals. But Aristotle needs this sort of agency, for he is concerned about the question whence our concepts come. It is not enough to say that they come out of experience; experience is the occasion of them, and his statement that the soul finds universals in experience because it is the sort of thing that is able to find universals in experience is not helpful. In any case, even if we think of perceptual ability as potentially conceptual ability, it is firm Aristotelian doctrine that some prior actuality is needed to make a conceiver out of a perceiver; and that is the always actual and active *nous*.

Is it not clear that there is no explanation of philosophical importance here? We have a super-faculty with its super-objects guiding us along as we acquire concepts, putting before us at all times the objects that define our organization of the world. But there is only the vaguest explanation of the relation between active *nous* and the individual thinking person.

At this point one must think of Platonic reminiscence. Both active *nous* and reminiscence cause the mind to grasp those universals it could not by itself even set up as the objects of its search. For good Aristotelian reasons active *nous* cannot be constantly in activity if it has matter; and if it has no matter, it need never perish. Plato argues by a kind of *reductio* in the *Meno* that the source of this cognition must be prenatal, and he has no difficulty showing in the *Phaedo* that whatever is capable of such cognition can exist after death as readily as before. What the surviving soul remembers is the subject of considerable myth-making in Plato, but it is largely compatible with Aristotle's opinion that the psychic activities of life do not affect the surviving faculty of thought. Plato simply pushes the process of learning back to a point before birth when we knew the Ideas. For those who ask how we learned about them before birth, he has another tale to unfold in the *Phaedrus*; for those who want to know exactly how our having known and forgotten helps us learn again, there is no answer at all. According to Aristotle as well as Plato, once we know that a faculty somehow connected with us is constantly contemplating species and genera and indeed always has, we are supposed to need to know no more about exactly how these universals get into our souls.[29]

[29] The following are the sources I have found most helpful in arriving at my views of *nous*—views that, I confess, most of those to whom I am indebted would probably reject. Lesher, "The Meaning of *Nous*"; W. D. Ross, *Aristotle*, and Ross's Oxford edition of *Prior and Posterior Analytics*, with commentary; Jonathan Barnes's translation of and commentary on *Posterior Analytics*; Wilfrid Sellars, "Aristotelian Philosophies of Mind"; John Catan, "Recollection and Posterior Analytics II, 19"; Walter Hess, "Erfahrung und Intuition bei Aristoteles"; L. Aryeh Kosman, "Understanding, Explanation, and Insight in Aristotle's *Posterior Analytics*"; John Herman Randall, Jr., *Aristotle*. Of the ancient commentators, Zabarella seems to me to have come closest to the truth.

Select Bibliography

A. WORKS OF ARISTOTLE

Categories and De Interpretatione
Minio-Paluello, L., ed. *Aristotelis Categoriae et De Interpretatione*. Oxford: Clarendon Press, 1956.
Prior and Posterior Analytics
Ross, W. D., ed. *Aristotle's Prior and Posterior Analytics*. With a commentary. Oxford: Clarendon Press, 1949.
Topics and De Sophisticis Elenchis
Ross, W. D., ed. *Aristotelis Topica et Sophistici Elenchi*. Oxford: Clarendon Press, 1958.
Physics
Ross, W. D., ed. *Aristotle's Physics*. With a commentary. Oxford: Clarendon Press, 1936.
De Caelo
Allen, D. J., ed. *Aristotelis De Caelo*. Oxford: Clarendon Press, 1936.
De Anima
Hicks, R. D., ed. *Aristotle de Anima*. With a translation and commentary. Cambridge: Cambridge University Press, 1907.
Rodier, G., ed. *Traité de l'âme*. With a translation and commentary. Paris: Leroux, 1900.
Ross, W. D., ed. *Aristotle's De Anima*. With a translation and commentary. Oxford: Clarendon Press, 1961.
Parva Naturalia
Ross, W. D., ed. *Aristotle's Parva Naturalia*. With a commentary. Oxford: Clarendon Press, 1955.
Historia Animalium
Peck, A. L., ed. *Aristotle, Historia Animalium*. With a translation. Cambridge, Mass.: Harvard University Press, 1965.
De Partibus Animalium

Peck, A. L., ed. *Aristotle, De Partibus Animalium.* With a translation. Cambridge, Mass.: Harvard University Press, 1965.

De Motu Animalium and De Incessu Animalium

Louis, Pierre, ed. *Marche des animaux; Mouvement des animaux; Index des traités biologiques.* With translation. Paris: Guillaume Bude, 1973.

De Generatione Animalium

Drossaart-Lulofs, H. J., ed. *De Generatione Animalium.* Oxford: Clarendon Press, 1965.

Joachim, H. H., ed. *On Coming-to-Be and Passing Away: De Generatione et Corruptione.* With a commentary. Oxford: Clarendon Press, 1922.

Metaphysics

Christ, Wilhelm, ed. *Aristotelis Metaphysica.* Leipzig: Teubner, 1934.

Jaeger, W., ed. *Aristotelis Metaphysica.* Oxford: Clarendon Press, 1957.

Ross, W. D., ed. *Aristotle's Metaphysics.* With a commentary. Oxford: Clarendon Press, 1924.

Nicomachean Ethics

Bywater, I., ed. *Ethica Nicomachea.* Oxford: Clarendon Press, 1959.

Rhetoric

Ross, W. D., ed. *Aristotelis Ars Rhetorica.* Oxford: Clarendon Press, 1959.

B. TRANSLATIONS AND COMMENTARIES
(WITHOUT GREEK TEXT)

Categories

Ackrill, J. L. *Aristotle's Categories and De Interpretatione,* translated with notes. Clarendon Aristotle Series. Oxford: Clarendon Press, 1963.

Posterior Analytics

Barnes, Jonathan. *Aristotle's Posterior Analytics,* translated with notes. Clarendon Aristotle Series. Oxford: Clarendon Press, 1975.

Themistius. *Analyticorum Posteriorum Paraphrasis*. Vol. V, Part 1 of *Commentaria in Aristotelem Graeca*, ed. Maximilian Wallies. Berlin: Georg Reiner, 1900.

De Anima

Hamlyn, D. W. *Aristotle's De Anima, Books II and III*, translated with notes. Clarendon Aristotle Series. Oxford: Clarendon Press, 1968.

Philoponus, John. *In Aristotelis De Anima Libros Commentaria*. Vol. XV of *Commentaria in Aristotelem Graeca*, ed. Michael Hayduck. Berlin: Georg Reiner, 1896.

Simplicius. *In Libros Aristotelis De Anima Commentaria*. Vol. XI of *Commentaria in Aristotelem Graeca*, ed. Michael Hayduck. Berlin: Georg Reiner, 1882.

Themistius. *In Libros Aristotelis De Anima Paraphrasis*. Vol. V, Part 3 of *Commentaria in Aristotelem Graeca*, ed. Richard Heinze. Berlin: Georg Reiner, 1899.

Thomas Aquinas, Saint. *In Tres Libros De Anima Aristotelis Expositio*. Venice: Hieronymus Scotus, 1550.

Zabarella, Giacomo. *In tres Aristotelis libros de anima commentarius*. Venice: Franciscus Bolzetta, 1605.

Parva Naturalia

Alexander of Aphrodisias. *In Librum De Sensu*. Vol. III, Part 1 of *Commentaria in Aristotelem Graeca*, ed. Paul Wendland. Berlin: Georg Reiner, 1901.

Sorabji, Richard. *Aristotle on Memory*, translated with notes. London: Duckworth, 1972.

De Partibus Animalium, De Generatione Animalium

Balme, D. M. *Aristotle's De Partibus Animalium I and De Generatione Animalium I*, translated with notes. Clarendon Aristotle Series. Oxford: Clarendon Press, 1972.

Metaphysics

Alexander of Aphrodisias. *In Aristotelis Metaphysica Commentaria*. Vol. I of *Commentaria in Aristotelem Graeca*, ed. Michael Hayduck. Berlin: Georg Reiner, 1891.

Kirwan, Christopher. *Aristotle's Metaphysics Books* Γ, Δ, E, translated with notes. Clarendon Aristotle Series: Oxford: Clarendon Press, 1971.

C. SECONDARY SOURCES

Ackrill, J. L. "Aristotle's Definitions of *Psuche*," *Proceedings of the Aristotelian Society*, LXIII (1972-73), 119-133.

———. "Aristotle's Distinction between *Energeia* and *Kinēsis*," *New Essays on Plato and Aristotle*, ed. J. Renford Bambrough, pp. 121-141. New York: Humanities Press, 1965.

Albritton, Rogers. "Forms of Particular Substances in Aristotle's Metaphysics," *Journal of Philosophy*, LIV (1957), 699-708.

Allen, R. E. "Individual Properties in Aristotle's Categories," *Phronesis*, XIV (1969), 31-39.

Anscombe, G.E.M. "The Principle of Individuation," *Proceedings of the Aristotelian Society* (Supplementary Volume), XXVII (1953), 83-96.

———, and P. T. Geach. *Three Philosophers*. Oxford: Basil Blackwell, 1963.

Barnes, Jonathan. "Aristotle's Concept of Mind," *Proceedings of the Aristotelian Society*, LXXII (1971-72), 101-110.

Block, Irving. "Aristotle and the Physical Object," *Philosophy and Phenomenological Research*, XXI (1960), 93-101.

———. "The Order of Aristotle's Psychological Writings," *American Journal of Philology*, LXXXII (1961), 50-77.

———. "Truth and Error in Aristotle's Theory of Sense Perception," *Philosophical Quarterly*, XI (1961), 1-9.

Bolton, Robert. Review of Henry B. Veatch's *Aristotle: A Contemporary Appreciation*, in *Philosophical Review*, LXXXV (1976), 251-253.

Brentano, Franz. "The Distinction between Mental and

Physical Phenomena," *Realism and the Background of Phenomenology*, ed. Roderick M. Chisholm, pp. 39-61. Glencoe, Ill.: The Free Press, 1960.

———. *Die Psychologie des Aristoteles, insbesondere seine Lehre von nous poiētikos*. Mainz: Verlag von Franz Kirchheim, 1867.

———. *Psychologie vom empirischen Standpunkt*. Leipzig: Duncker, 1874.

———. *The True and the Evident*. Ed. and trans. Oskar Kraus and Roderick M. Chisholm. New York: Humanities Press, 1966.

Brody, B. A. "Towards an Aristotelian Theory of Scientific Explanation," *Philosophy of Science*, XXXIX (1972), 20-31.

Cantin, Stanislas. "La perception des sensibles communs au moyen du mouvement d'après Aristote," *Laval Théologique et Philosophique*, XVII (1961), 9-21.

Cashdollar, Stanford. "Aristotle's Account of Incidental Perception," *Phronesis*, XVIII (1973), 156-175.

Catan, John. "Recollection and *Posterior Analytics* II, 19," *Apeiron*, IV (1970), 34-57.

Chen, Chung-Hwan. "Universal Concrete: A Typical Aristotelian Duplication of Reality," *Phronesis*, IX (1964), 48-57.

Cherniss, Harold F. *Aristotle's Criticism of Plato and the Academy*. Reissued. New York: Russell & Russell, Inc. 1962.

Chisholm, Roderick M. *Perceiving: A Philosophical Study*. Ithaca, N.Y.: Cornell University Press, 1957.

———. "Sentences About Believing," *Proceedings of the Aristotelian Society*, LVI (1955-56), 125-148.

———. *Theory of Knowlege*. Englewood Cliffs, N.J.: Prentice-Hall, 1966.

———, and Wilfrid S. Sellars. "Intentionality and the Mental," an Appendix to *Minnesota Studies in the Philosophy of Science, Vol. II: Concepts, Theories, and the Mind-*

Body Problem, ed. Herbert Feigl, Michael Scriven, and Grover Maxwell, pp. 507-539. Minneapolis: University of Minnesota Press, 1958.

Cooper, John. Review of Richard Sorabji's *Aristotle on Memory*, in *Archiv für Geschichte der Philosophie*, LVII (1975), 63-69.

Dancy, Russell. "On Some of Aristotle's First Thoughts about Substances," *Philosophical Review*, LXXXIV (1975), 338-373.

————. *Sense and Contradiction: A Study in Aristotle.* Dordrecht: D. Reidel, 1975.

Davidson, Donald. "Actions, Reasons, and Causes," *Journal of Philosophy*, LX (1963), 685-700.

————. "The Individuation of Events," *Essays in Honor of Carl G. Hempel*, ed. Nicholas Rescher, pp. 216-234. Dordrecht: D. Reidel, 1969.

Dennett, D. C. *Content and Consciousness.* New York: Humanities Press, 1969.

————. "Intentional Systems," *Journal of Philosophy*, LXVIII (1971), 87-106.

Engmann, Joyce. "Imagination and Truth in Aristotle," *Journal of the History of Philosophy*, XIV (1956), 259-265.

Feigl, Herbert. "The 'Mental' and the 'Physical'," *Minnesota Studies in the Philosophy of Science, Vol. II: Concepts, Theories, and the Mind-Body Problem*, ed. Herbert Feigl, Michael Scriven, and Grover Maxwell, pp. 370-497. Minneapolis: University of Minnesota Press, 1958.

Fodor, Jerry. "Explanations in Psychology," *Philosophy in America*, ed. Max Black, pp. 161-174. Ithaca, N.Y.: Cornell University Press, 1965.

————. "Materialism," *Materialism and the Mind-Body Problem*, ed. David M. Rosenthal, pp. 128-149. Englewood Cliffs, N.J.: Prentice-Hall, 1971.

Frankfurt, Harry G. "Freedom of Will and the Concept of a Person," *Journal of Philosophy*, LXVIII (1971), 5-20.

Frede, Michael. "Some Remarks on Aristotle's Notion of a Substance." Unpublished.

Furley, David J. "Self Movers." Forthcoming in "Proceedings of the Seventh Symposium Aristotelicum," ed. G.E.R. Lloyd and G.E.L. Owen.

Geach, Peter T. *Mental Acts*. London: Routledge & Kegan Paul, 1957.

——. *Reference and Generality*. Ithaca, N.Y.: Cornell University Press, 1962.

Gunderson, Keith. *Mentality and Machines*. Anchor Books. Garden City, N.Y.: Doubleday, 1971.

Hamlyn, D. W. "Aristotle's Account of Aesthesis in the De Anima." *Classical Quarterly*, IX (1959), 6-16.

——. "Behavior." *The Philosophy of Mind*, ed. V. C. Chappell, pp. 60-73. Englewood Cliffs, N.J.: Prentice-Hall, 1962.

——. "Koine Aisthesis," *Monist*, LII (1968), 195-209.

Hampshire, Stuart. *Freedom of the Individual*. Expanded edition. Princeton: Princeton University Press, 1975.

——. Review of Gilbert Ryle's *Concept of Mind*, *Mind*, LIV (1950), 237-255.

Hardie, W.F.R. *Aristotle's Ethical Theory*. Oxford: Clarendon Press, 1968.

——. "Aristotle's Treatment of the Relation between the Soul and the Body," *Philosophical Quarterly*, XIV (1964), 53-72.

——. "Concepts of Consciousness in Aristotle," *Mind*, LXXXV (1976), 388-411.

Harman, Gilbert. *Thought*. Princeton: Princeton University Press, 1973.

Hess, Walter. "Erfahrung und Intuition bei Aristoteles," *Phronesis*, XV (1970), 48-82.

Hintikka, Jaakko. "The Once and Future Sea Fight," *Philosophical Review*, LXXIII (1964), 461-492.

——. "Time, Truth, and Knowledge in Ancient Greek Philosophy," *American Philosophical Quarterly*, IV (1967), 1-14.

Jones, Barrington. "Aristotle's Account of Aesthesis in the De Anima." Unpublished.

Jones, Barrington. "Individuals in Aristotle's *Categories*," *Phronesis*, XVII (1972), 107-123.

————. "An Introduction to Aristotle's *Metaphysics*." In preparation.

Kahn, Charles H. "Sensation and Consciousness in Aristotle's Psychology," *Archiv für Geschichte der Philosophie*, XLVIII (1966), 43-81.

Katz, Leonard. "Did the Ancients Have Feelings Without Raw Feels? Notes toward a Philosophical Prehistory of Cartesian Dualism." Unpublished.

Kenny, A.J.P. "The Argument from Illusion in Aristotle's Metaphysics (Γ 1009-10)," *Mind*, LXXVI (1967), 184-197.

Kim, Jaegwon. "Events and their Descriptions: Some Considerations," *Essays in Honor of Carl G. Hempel*, ed. Nicholas Rescher, pp. 198-215. Dordrecht: D. Reidel, 1969.

Kosman, Aryeh. "Perceiving that we Perceive: *On the Soul* III, 2." *Philosophical Review*, LXXXIV (1975), 499-519.

————. "Understanding, Explanation, and Insight in Aristotle's *Posterior Analytics*," *Exegesis and Argument: Studies in Greek Philosophy presented to Gregory Vlastos*, ed. E. N. Lee, A.P.D. Mourelatos, R. M. Rorty, pp. 374-393. New York: Humanities Press, 1973.

Kripke, Saul. "Naming and Necessity," *Semantics of Natural Language*, ed. Donald Davidson and Gilbert Harman, pp. 253-355. Dordrecht: D. Reidel, 1972.

Land, Edwin H. "Experiments in Color Vision," *Scientific American*, CC (May 1959), 84-99.

Lesher, James. "The Meaning of *Nous* in the Posterior Analytics," *Phronesis*, XVIII (1973), 44-68.

Leszl, Walter. "Knowledge of the Universal and Knowledge of the Particular in Aristotle," *Review of Metaphysics*, XXV (1971-72), 278-313.

Lewis, David K. "An Argument for the Identity Theory," *Materialism and the Mind-Body Problem*, ed. David M. Rosenthal, pp. 162-171. Englewood Cliffs, N.J.: Prentice-Hall, 1971.

Lloyd, A. C. "Aristotle's Principle of Individuation," *Mind*, LXXIX (1970), 519-529.

Lykos, K. "Aristotle and Plato on 'Appearing'." *Mind*, LXXIII (1964), 496-514.

McCann, Edwin W. "Locke's Theory of Essence." Unpublished Ph.D. thesis, University of Pennsylvania, 1975.

Matson, Wallace I. "Why Isn't the Mind-Body Problem Ancient?" *Mind, Matter, and Method: Essays in Philosophy and Science in Honor of Herbert Feigl*, ed. Paul K. Feyerabend and Grover Maxwell, pp. 93-102. Minneapolis: University of Minnesota Press, 1966.

Matthews, G. B., and S. M. Cohen. "The One and the Many," *Review of Metaphysics*, XXI (1967-68), 630-655.

Miller, Fred D., Jr. "Did Aristotle Have the Concept of Identity?" *Philosophical Review*, LXXXII (1973), 483-490.

Moravcsik, J.M.E. "Strawson and Ontological Priority," *Analytical Philosophy*, Second Series, ed. R. J. Butler, pp. 106-119. Oxford: Basil Blackwell, 1965.

Moreau, Joseph. "Aristote et la vérité antéprédicative," *Aristote et les problèmes de méthode*, ed. Suzanne Mansion, pp. 21-33. Louvain: Publications Universitaires, 1961.

Murphy, Jeffrie G. "Rationality and the Fear of Death," *Monist*, LIX (1976), 187-203.

Nagel, Thomas. "Brain Bisection and the Unity of Consciousness," *Synthese* XXII (1970-71), 396-413.

———. "Physicalism," *Philosophical Review*, LXXIV (1965), 339-356.

Nuyens, Franciscus Johannes Christiaan Jozef. *L'Évolution de la psychologie d'Aristote*, trans. Théo Schillings. Louvain: Éditions de l'Institut superieur de philosophie, 1948.

Owen, G.E.L. "Aristotle on the Snares of Ontology," *New Essays on Plato and Aristotle*, ed. J. Renford Bambrough, pp. 69-95. New York: Humanities Press, 1965.

———. "Inherence," *Phronesis*, X (1965), 97-105.

———. "Logic and Metaphysics in some Earlier Works of Aristotle," *Aristotle and Plato in the Mid-Fourth Cen-*

tury, ed. I. During and G.E.L. Owen, pp. 163-190. Göteborg: Almquist & Wiksell, 1960.

──── . "Plato and Parmenides on the Timeless Present," *Monist*, L (1966), 317-340.

──── . "The Platonism of Aristotle," *Studies in the Philosophy of Thought and Action*, ed. P. F. Strawson, pp. 147-174. New York: Oxford University Press, 1968.

──── . "Tithenai ta Phainomena," *Aristotle: A Collection of Critical Essays*, ed. J.M.E. Moravcsik, pp. 167-190. Anchor Books. Garden City, N.Y.: Doubleday, 1967.

Owens, Joseph. *The Doctrine of Being in Aristotle's Metaphysics*. 2nd edn. Toronto: Pontifical Institute of Medieval Studies, 1963.

Parfit, Derek. "Personal Identity," *Philosophical Review*, LXXX (1971), 1-27.

Penner, Terry. "Verbs and the Identity of Actions," *Ryle, A Collection of Critical Essays*, ed. George Pitcher and O. P. Wood, pp. 393-453. Anchor Books. Garden City, N.Y.: Doubleday, 1970.

Putnam, Hilary. "The Mental Life of Some Machines," *Intenionality, Minds, and Perception*, ed. Hector-Neri Castaneda, pp. 177-200. Detroit: Wayne State University Press, 1967.

──── . "Minds and Machines," *Dimensions of Mind: A Symposium*, ed. Sidney Hook, pp. 130-164. New York: New York University Press, 1960.

──── . "Robots: Machines or Artificially Created Life?" *Journal of Philosophy*, LXI (1964), 668-691.

──── . "The Nature of Mental States," *Materialism and the Mind-Body Problem*, ed. David M. Rosenthal, pp. 150-161. Englewood Cliffs, N.J.: Prentice-Hall, 1971.

Quine, W.V.O. "Natural Kinds," *Essays in Honor of Carl G. Hempel*, ed. Nicholas Rescher, pp. 5-23. Dordrecht: D. Reidel, 1969.

Randall, John Herman, Jr. *Aristotle*. New York: Columbia University Press, 1960.

Rist, John M. "Notes on Aristotle 'De Anima' 3.5," *Classical Philology*, LXI (1966), 8-20.

Rorty, Richard. "Functionalism, Machines, and Incorrigibility," *Journal of Philosophy*, LXVIII (1972), 203-220.

———. "Genus as Matter: A Reading of Metaphysics Z-H," *Exegesis and Argument: Studies in Greek Philosophy presented to Gregory Vlastos*, ed. E. N. Lee, A.P.D. Mourelatos, and R. M. Rorty, pp. 393-420. New York: Humanities Press, 1973.

Ross, W. D. *Aristotle*. 2nd edn. Oxford: Clarendon Press, 1930.

Ryle, Gilbert. *The Concept of Mind*. New York: Barnes and Noble, 1949.

Schneider, Rudolf. *Seele und Sein: Ontologie bei Augustin und Aristoteles*. Stuttgart: Kohlhammer, 1957.

Sellars, Wilfrid. "Aristotelian Philosophies of Mind," *Philosophy for the Future*, ed. Roy Wood Sellars, V. J. McGill, and Marvin Farber, pp. 544-572. New York: Macmillan, 1949.

———. *Philosophical Perspectives*. Springfield, Ill.: Charles C. Thomas, 1967.

———. *Science, Perception and Reality*. New York: Humanities Press, 1963.

Shoemaker, Sydney. *Self-Knowledge and Self-Identity*. Ithaca, N.Y.: Cornell University Press, 1963.

Slakey, Thomas J. "Aristotle on Perception," *Philosophical Review*, LXX (1961), 470-484.

Sorabji, Richard. "Aristotle and Oxford Philosophy," *American Philosophical Quarterly*, VI (1969), 127-135.

———. "Aristotle on Demarcating the Five Senses," *Philosophical Review*, LXXX (1971), 55-79.

———. "Body and Soul in Aristotle," *Philosophy*, XLIX (1974), 63-89.

———. *Aristotle on Memory*, translated with notes. Providence: Brown University Press, 1972.

Stich, Stephen P. "Grammars, Psychological Theories

and Turing Machines." Unpublished Ph.D. thesis, Princeton University, 1968.

Strawson, P. F. *Individuals*. London: Methuen, 1959.

Taylor, Charles. *The Explanation of Behavior*. New York: Humanities Press, 1964.

———. "Mind-Body Identity, A Side Issue?" *Philosophical Review*, LLXXVI (1967), 201-213.

Taylor, Richard. *Action and Purpose*. Englewood Cliffs, N.J.: Prentice-Hall, 1966.

Tracy, Theodore. "Heart and Soul in Aristotle." Unpublished.

Veatch, Henry B. *Aristotle: A Contemporary Appreciaton*. Bloomington: Indiana University Press, 1974.

Vision, Gerald. "Essentialism and the Senses of Proper Names," *American Philosophical Quarterly*, VII (1970), 321-330.

de Vogel, C. J. "La méthode d'Aristote en métaphysique d'après *Métaphysique* A 1-2," *Aristote et les problèmes de méthode*, ed. Suzanne Mansion, pp. 147-170. Louvain: Publications Universitaires, 1961.

Weinberg, Julius R. *Abstraction, Relation, and Induction*. Madison: University of Wisconsin Press, 1965.

White, Nicholas. "Aristotle on Sameness and Oneness," *Philosophical Review*, LXXX (1971), 177-197.

———. "Origins of Aristotle's Essentialism," *Review of Metaphysics*, XXVI (1972-73), 57-85.

Wieland, W. "The Problem of Teleology," *Articles on Aristotle: 1. Science*, ed. Jonathan Barnes, Malcolm Schofield, and Richard Sorabji, pp. 141-160. London: Duckworth, 1975.

Wiggins, David. *Identity and Spatio-Temporal Continuity*. Oxford: Basil Blackwell, 1967.

———. "Identity-Statements," *Analytical Philosophy*, Second Series, ed. R. J. Butler, pp. 40-71. Oxford: Basil Blackwell, 1965.

Williams, Bernard. "Are Persons Bodies?" *The Philos-*

ophy of the Body, ed. Stuart F. Spicker, pp. 137-155. Chicago: Quadrangle Books, 1970.

————. "The Self and the Future," *Philosophical Review*, LXXXIX (1970), 161-180.

Wittgenstein, Ludwig. *Philosophical Investigations.* 2nd edn. Trans. G.E.M. Anscombe. New York: Macmillan, 1968.

Woods, Michael J. "Identity and Individuation," *Analytical Philosophy*, Second Series, ed. R. J. Butler, pp. 120-130. Oxford: Basil Blackwell, 1965.

Index

Index of Passages
in the Works of Aristotle

LIBRARY OF CONGRESS CATALOGING IN PUBLICATION DATA

Hartman, Edwin, 1941-
Substance, body, and soul.

Bibliography: p.
Includes index.
1. Aristoteles.   2. Substance (Philosophy).
3. Mind and body.   4. Soul.   I. Title.
B491.S8H37   185   77-71984
ISBN 0-691-07223-X